take off in

Russian

Dr Nick Ukiah

OXFORD
UNIVERSITY PRESS

OXFORD
UNIVERSITY PRESS

Great Clarendon Street, Oxford OX2 6DP

Oxford University Press is a department of the University of Oxford.
It furthers the University's objective of excellence in research, scholarship,
and education by publishing worldwide in

Oxford New York

Auckland Cape Town Dar es Salaam Hong Kong Karachi
Kuala Lumpur Madrid Melbourne Mexico City Nairobi
New Delhi Shanghai Taipei Toronto

With offices in
Argentina Austria Brazil Chile Czech Republic France Greece
Guatemala Hungary Italy Japan Poland Portugal Singapore
South Korea Switzerland Thailand Turkey Ukraine Vietnam

Oxford is a registered trade mark of Oxford University Press
in the UK and in certain other countries

Published in the United States
by Oxford University Press Inc., New York

British Library Cataloguing in Publication Data
Data available

Library of Congress Cataloging in Publication Data
Data available

ISBN 978-0-19-953429-6 (Book and CDs)
ISBN 978-0-19-860312-2 (Coursebook)

This coursebook is only available as a component of Take Off In Russian

1

Commissioning and editorial development: Tracy Miller
Project management: Natalie Pomier
Audio production: Daniel Pageon, Actors World Production Ltd
Music: David Stoll
Design and typesetting: Gecko Ltd

Every effort has been made to contact the copyright holders of the
illustrative material in this title. If notified, the publisher will be
pleased to amend the acknowledgement in any future edition.

Printed in China through Phoenix Offset

I would like to extend my particular thanks to two individuals, Olga
Deszko and Elena Khorishko, without whom this book could not
have been written. I am also most grateful to Tracy Miller, Albina
Ozieva, Natasha Kurashova, Lucy Baranenkova, Nora Mikeladze,
and Tom Birchenough and Kostya Fyodorov in Moscow, who made
helpful suggestions regarding different parts of the text.

This book is dedicated to Karl Tettey Mason

Contents

Introduction

Oxford Take Off In Russian is designed to help the beginner develop the basic language skills necessary to communicate in Russian in most everyday situations. It is intended for learners working by themselves, providing all the information and support necessary for successful language learning. There are 14 units dealing with everyday situations such as shopping, ordering in a restaurant or café, buying tickets, and travelling. Each unit consists of 14 pages of text (an introduction, 6 learning spreads, and a summary) and approximately 17 minutes of recorded material. You'll find the following sections in each unit:

Opening page (book): *unit objectives* : what you will be able to do by the end of the unit *learning hints*: suggestions to help you improve your learning

Learning spreads 1, 2, 3 (recording/book): introduction and practice of the language through dialogues – the recording contains dialogues, pronunciation practice, listening and speaking activities; the book contains transcripts of the recording dialogues, translations of new vocabulary, explanations of grammar and usage (the *Language Building* section), and written activities

Learning spread 4 – Culture (book): reading comprehension activities based on an aspect of Russian culture related to the theme of the unit

Learning spread 5 – The Story (recording/book): an ongoing story to listen to, with related activities in the book

Test (book): 2 pages of exercises covering the language introduced in the learning spreads

Summary (recording/book): review of the main language points of the unit revision suggestions before moving on to the next unit

How to use the course
The book and the recording are closely integrated, as the emphasis is on speaking and listening. The course is led by the recording, which contains step-by-step instructions on how to work through the units. The presenters on the recording will tell you when to use the recording on its own, when to use the book, and when and how to use the two together. The book provides support in the form of transcriptions of the recording material, translations of new vocabulary, and grammar explanations. You'll find this icon in the book when you need to listen to the recording.

1 (recording/book) Read the unit objectives on the first page telling you what you will learn in the unit, and then begin by listening to the **dialogue** on the recording. You may not understand everything the first time you hear it, but try to resist the temptation to look at the transcript in the book. The first activity on the recording will help you develop your listening skills by suggesting things to concentrate on and listen out for. You'll be given the opportunity to repeat some of the key sentences and phrases from the dialogue before you hear it a second time. You may need to refer to the vocabulary list (book) before completing the second activity (book). Listen to the dialogue as many times as you like, but as far as possible try not to refer to the dialogue transcript (book).

2 (book) Once you have listened to all the new language, take some time to work through the **Vocabulary, Language Building,** and **Activities** in the book to help you understand how it works.

3 (recording) Then it's time to practise speaking. First you'll find **Pronunciation practice** on the recording, focusing on an aspect of pronunciation that occurs in the dialogue. Next is the **Your turn** activity. You will be given all the instructions and cues you need by the presenter on the recording. The first few times you do this you may need to refer back to the vocabulary and language building sections in the book, but aim to do it without the book after that.

4 (book) The fourth learning section, **Culture**, concentrates on reading practice. Try reading it first without referring to the vocabulary list to see how much you can already understand, making guesses about any words or phrases you are not sure of. The activities which accompany the text will help you develop reading comprehension skills.

5 (recording/book) For the final learning section, return to the recording to listen to the **Story**. This section gives you the opportunity to have some fun with the language and hear the characters in the story use the language you have just learnt in different situations. The aim is to give you the confidence to cope with authentic Russian. There are activities in the book to help you.

6 (book) Return to the book, and work through the activities in the **Test** section to see how well you can remember and use the language you have covered in the unit. This is best done as a written exercise. Add up the final score and, if it is not as high as you had hoped, try going back and reviewing some of the sections.

7 (recording/book) As a final review, turn to the **Summary** on the last page of the unit. This will test your understanding of the new situations, vocabulary, and grammar introduced in the unit. Use the book to prepare your answers, either by writing them down or speaking aloud, then return to the recording to test yourself. You will be given prompts in English on the recording, so you can do this test without the book.

8 (book) At the very end of each unit you will find some suggestions for **revision** and ideas for extending your practice with the language of the unit.

Each unit builds on the work of the preceding units, so it's very important to learn the vocabulary and structures from each unit before you move on. There are review sections after units 3, 7, 10, and 14 for you to test yourself on the material learnt so far.

Other support features
If you want a more detailed grammar explanation than those given in the *Language Building* sections, you will find a *Grammar Summary* at the end of the book. For a definition of the grammar terms used in the course, see the *Glossary of Grammatical Terms* on page 242.

The *Answers* section at the end of the book has the answers to all the activities in the book. Some activities require you to give information about yourself, so you may also need to check some vocabulary in a dictionary.

At the end of the book you'll find a comprehensive Russian–English *Vocabulary*.

Hints on learning a language
Learning a language takes time, but learning strategies are given throughout the course to help you expand your knowledge quickly and easily. Here are a few of the most important to help you on your way.

Go at your own pace Don't try to do too much at one time. You will probably learn more effectively if you study little and often, rather than attempting to cover large amounts of material in one session.

Review often Don't expect to understand everything the first time. Listen to the recording as many times as you need to before moving on to the next section. Go back periodically and listen to sections from previous units and have another go at activities you have already tried once.

Learn with someone else If you have another person to learn with, you can test each other, speak in Russian to each other, and support each other.

Speak out If you do not have opportunities to speak Russian to anyone else, then talk to yourself. Speaking aloud is very different from speaking inside your head! Try recording your voice, too.

Learn vocabulary Test yourself with the vocabulary lists in the book by covering one of the columns. Keep your own notebook with a record of useful vocabulary - try dividing it into sections (food, family, transport, etc.) to help organize the words and phrases. Expand your vocabulary beyond the course by buying a dictionary.

Keep going You will probably need to work through the material in a unit several times before you feel ready to move on to the next, but don't let yourself get stuck. If you have particular difficulties with one section, then leave it for a while and move on to the next. You may find that things fall into place at a later stage.

The Russian Language
Russian is the world's fifth most popular language, in terms of numbers of speakers. It is the mother-tongue of more than 150 million people and a further 60 million people speak it as their second language. Despite the wide geographical area over which Russian is spoken, you will encounter very little variation in terms of dialects, since the language and pronunciation introduced in this course – more or less the language as spoken in Moscow – is considered the standard version throughout the Russian-speaking area.

Russian and English are only distantly related, but you will be able sometimes to spot similarities between Russian and English words: 'brother' is **брат** (brat), 'cat' is **кот** (kot). Less basic words will often present less difficulty, their forms in English and Russian being very similar: 'Australia' is **Австра́лия** (Avstraliya), 'excursion' is **экску́рсия** (ekskursiya), 'yoga' is **йо́га** (ioga). You will also find that if you have studied any other European languages, many more words will be familiar: 'ticket' is **биле́т** (bilet), 'lawyer' is **адвока́т** (advokat), 'potato' is **карто́фель** (kartofel'), 'beach' is **пляж** (plyazh), 'hall' is **зал** (zal), 'novel' is **рома́н** (roman). In addition, there are many specifically Russian words which you may recognise immediately, such as **борщ** (borshch) 'bortsch', **рубль** (rubl') 'rouble', **во́дка** (vodka) 'vodka', **коммуни́ст** (kommunist) 'Communist'.

The grammar of Russian can seem complex for the English-speaking learner. Russian is a highly inflected language: that is, the forms of nouns, pronouns, adjectives, and so on, change according to gender (masculine, feminine, neuter), number (singular or plural), and case (Russian has six cases: nominative, accusative, genitive, dative, instrumental, and prepositional). Because this puts quite a strain on the memory of most learners, these different forms are introduced gradually in this course, with patterns and regularities pointed out wherever possible. However, many learners like to see the overall picture as well, and so full tables of the different forms are given at the end of the book (*Grammar Summary*).

Learning to communicate in another language may be challenging, but it is also a very rewarding and enriching experience. Since rather few English speakers attempt to learn their language, the Russians you come across will be greatly impressed by your attempts and very encouraging. It can be fun too! We have made this course as varied and entertaining as possible, and we hope you enjoy it.

The Russian Alphabet

The Russian or *Cyrillic* alphabet was developed around the 9th century and is based on the Greek alphabet. Some of the letters look and sound the same as those used in English; others look the same as English letters but have a different pronunciation; still others look unfamiliar, but in fact represent sounds which also occur in English. One major advantage of Russian spelling is that it is more or less 'phonetic', with each sound in the language generally being written using a single letter. This makes it far more straightforward than English, and means that you have a good chance of reading aloud a written word correctly first time, even if you have not met it before (bearing in mind the difference in pronunciation between stressed and unstressed vowels – see Unit 1).

As well as learning to read the printed alphabet, we also suggest that you learn to write. Russian handwritten forms, which are a little different from printed letters, are also given in the alphabet summary chart below. Although learning handwritten as well as printed letters means a little extra work at the beginning of the course, you will immediately find it necessary to begin writing down the new words you meet, in order to help you remember them. You also need the handwritten forms to complete many of the exercises in this book.

Alphabet

Printed forms lower-case	capital	Letter name	Approx. pron.	Translit-eration	Handwritten forms lower-case	capital
а	А	'ah'	a	a	*а*	*А*
б	Б	'beh'	b	b	*б*	*Б*
в	В	'veh'	v	v	*в*	*В*
г	Г	'geh'	g	g	*г*	*Г*
д	Д	'deh'	d	d	*д*	*Д*
е	Е	'yeh'	ye	e	*е*	*Е*
ё	Ё	'yoh'	yo	yo	*ё*	*Ё*
ж	Ж	'zheh'	*French 'j'*	zh	*ж*	*Ж*
з	З	'zeh'	z	z	*з*	*З*
и	И	'ee'	ee	i	*и*	*И*
й	Й	*short i*	*y in diphthong*	i	*й*	*Й*
к	К	'kah'	k	k	*к*	*К*
л	Л	'el'	l	l	*л*	*Л*
м	М	'em'	m	m	*м*	*М*
н	Н	'en'	n	n	*н*	*Н*
о	О	'oh'	o	o	*о*	*О*
п	П	'peh'	p	p	*п*	*П*
р	Р	'err'	*rolled 'r'*	r	*р*	*Р*
с	С	'es'	s	s	*с*	*С*
т	Т	'teh'	t	t	*т*	*Т*
у	У	'oo'	u	u	*у*	*У*
ф	Ф	'ef'	f	f	*ф*	*Ф*
х	Х	'hah'	h	kh	*х*	*Х*
ц	Ц	'tseh'	ts	ts	*ц*	*Ц*
ч	Ч	'cheh'	ch	ch	*ч*	*Ч*
ш	Ш	'shah'	*hard 'sh'*	sh	*ш*	*Ш*
щ	Щ	'ssshah'	*soft 'sssh'*	shch	*щ*	*Щ*
ъ	Ъ	*hard sign*	–	"	*ъ*	*Ъ*
ы	Ы	'uy'	uy	y	*ы*	*Ы*
ь	Ь	*soft sign*	–	'	*ь*	*Ь*
э	Э	*backwards e*	e	e	*э*	*Э*
ю	Ю	'yoo'	yoo	yu	*ю*	*Ю*
я	Я	'yah'	ya	ya	*я*	*Я*

Vowels

There are ten vowels in the Russian alphabet. Five are the so-called 'hard vowels' and five are the so-called 'soft vowels'. When pronounced on their own, or at the beginning of a word, the first four 'soft' vowels have a *y-* sound at the beginning.

'Hard' vowels	а	э	о	у	ы
'Soft' vowels	я	е	ё	ю	и

Consonants

Most consonants in Russian can be either 'soft' or 'hard'. A consonant is hard when it is followed by a so-called 'hard' vowel, or if it comes at the end of a word and does not have a soft sign (**-ь**) after it. Here are the hard variants of consonants followed by some so-called 'hard' vowels.

Hard variants of	бу	во	да	гу	за	ко	лы	
consonants	ма	нэ	по	ра	со	ты	фы	хы

A consonant is soft when it is followed by a so-called 'soft' vowel or has a soft sign (**-ь**) after it. When pronouncing a soft consonant, the main part of the tongue is pushed up against the roof of the mouth, giving the sound a 'y'-like quality. Here are the soft variants of consonants followed by some so-called 'soft' vowels.

Soft variants of	бю	вё	дя	ги	зя	ки	ли	
consonants	мя	не	пё	ря	сё	ти	фю	хи

And here are some examples of soft consonants followed by a soft sign (**-ь**). The vowel **а** has been added before the consonant: **аль, ань, ать**. Without the soft sign these would be hard: **ал, ан, ат**.

Not all consonants have hard and soft variants. There are three inherently hard consonants, which are hard no matter what sort of vowel follows them, and there are two inherently soft consonants.

Inherently hard consonants	ж	ц	ш
Inherently soft consonants	ч	щ	

Stress has an important effect on the pronunciation of some vowels. In this book the stressed syllable in words of more than one syllable is marked with an acute accent – **онó, емý, говори́ть**. In normal written Russian however – books, newspapers, signs, letters, etc. – stress is not marked, since Russians' knowledge of their own language tells them where it falls.

Starting out
Поéхали!

▷ ▷ ▷ ▷ ▷ ▷ ▷ ▷ ▷ ▷ ▷ ▷ ▷ ▷

OBJECTIVES

In this unit you'll learn how to:

- ✓ pronounce Russian words
- ✓ greet people
- ✓ ask simple questions
- ✓ make simple statements

And cover the following grammar and language:

- ✓ э́то 'this is', 'that is'
- ✓ gender of nouns
- ✓ pronouns

LEARNING RUSSIAN 1

The first challenge in learning Russian is familiarizing yourself with the script. Although it may look daunting to begin with, you will soon find that you can recognize the words you hear on the recordings quickly and that there are few surprises in Russian spelling. To start with, however, you will need to practise reading as much as possible. Reading exercises are included in this unit.

Although this course concentrates on listening and speaking, one of the best ways of learning new words is by writing them down, and then writing them out several times if possible. For this you will need to know Russian handwritten forms, which are a little different from printed letters (see page ix). Learning them now may seem like an extra burden to begin with, but your efforts will be repaid when you find you are reading and writing with ease!

 Now start the recording for Unit 1.

1.1 The alphabet
Алфавит

 If you haven't already, listen now to the Pronunciation Guide and look at the alphabet chart on page ix. When you feel you are familiar with the alphabet, come back to the book and try the activity below.

ACTIVITY 1

Russian uses many words borrowed from English and many 'international' terms. Try to work out the meanings of the following words.

1	борщ	9	циклóн
2	фóрум	10	я́нки
3	э́ра	11	хóбби
4	гара́ж	12	Лóндон
5	ви́за	13	Чика́го
6	майонéз	14	Нью-Йóрк
7	шофёр	15	Амéрика
8	интерьéр	16	Санкт-Петербу́рг

LANGUAGE BUILDING

✓ **Stress and vowels**

You now know all you need to know to read Russian words of one syllable correctly, and read out longer words in a slow and deliberate style.

In this book the stressed syllable in words of more than one syllable is marked with an acute accent (**Москва́, хорошó**). (In books for Russian native speakers stress is not marked, since Russians' knowledge of their own language tells them where it falls.)

Stress has an important effect on the pronunciation of some vowels. The following points are vital to your understanding and speaking of Russian:

- an unstressed **o** sounds something like 'ah' or 'uh'

- an unstressed **e** sounds something like 'i' or 'yi'

- an unstressed **я** before the stressed syllable sounds like 'i' or 'yi'

Thus the word **онó**, meaning 'it', will sound something like 'uh-**no**', and the word **емý**, meaning 'to him', sounds something like 'yi-**moo**'.

ACTIVITY 2

Read the following words out loud. Remember, words of one syllable have no stress mark, and their vowels are pronounced as normal. Try to learn the meanings of the words as you go.

Words of one syllable:

да	yes
нет	no
кто?	who?
где?	where?
я	I
ты	you [*familiar, singular*]
он	he / it
мы	we
вы	you [*plural; also polite singular*]

Words of two syllables:

она́	she / it
оно́	it
они́	they
вокза́л	main railway station
Москва́	Moscow
тётя	aunt [*no stress marked as* ё *is always stressed*]
сло́во	word
язы́к	language
окно́	window

Words of three syllables:

рабо́та	work
у́лица	street
хорошо́	OK; well

 Now do activities 3, 4, and 5 on the recording.

Здра́вствуйте!

ACTIVITY 6 is on the recording.

ACTIVITY 7

A Listen to the recording. Which of the following words and phrases do you hear?

1 Пока́!
2 Прия́тного аппети́та!
3 Пожа́луйста!

B Which of the phrases above would you use:

a when offering somebody something?
b on starting a meal?
c when saying goodbye to a close friend?

DIALOGUE 1

○ Пожа́луйста, ваш борщ.
■ Спаси́бо. А смета́на?
○ Вот, пожа́луйста, смета́на.
■ Спаси́бо.
○ Пожа́луйста, ва́ши щи.
▲ Мммм! Спаси́бо!
○ И хлеб, пожа́луйста. Прия́тного аппети́та!
■ Спаси́бо!

VOCABULARY

здра́вствуйте!	hello
до свида́ния!	goodbye
приве́т!	hi! [*informal*]
пока́!	bye! [*informal*]
пожа́луйста	please; you're welcome
спаси́бо	thank you
ваш, ва́ши	your
а	and [*with slight contrast*]; but
смета́на	sour cream
вот	here is [*said whilst pointing or indicating in some way*]
щи	cabbage soup
и	and
хлеб	bread
прия́тного аппети́та!	enjoy your meal!

Rather than giving you any new grammar in this section, here is some more reading practice. For both activities, read the words out loud, repeating them several times. You will probably need to check back to the alphabet summary chart on page ix. Also, bear in mind how stress affects the vowels **o**, **e**, and **я** (see page 2).

ACTIVITY 8

Read the following words out loud carefully. Try to learn the meanings as you go.

Words of one syllable:

наш	our
но	but [*strong contrast*]
там	there
здесь	here

Words of two syllables:

когда́ ?	when?
о́чень	very
то́же	also
го́род	town, city
ма́ма	mum

Phrases:

я могу́	I can
я хочу́	I want
я люблю́	I like, I love

Words of four syllables:

извини́те!	sorry!
свида́ние	meeting, rendezvous

ACTIVITY 9

Try to work out the meanings of the following words.

1	бар	8	анора́к	15	эмба́рго
2	факс	9	хулига́н	16	фемини́зм
3	са́ммит	10	парла́мент	17	авока́до
4	при́нтер	11	пи́цца	18	гимна́стика
5	ви́ски	12	йо́га	19	литерату́ра
6	футбо́л	13	оптими́ст	20	револю́ция
7	нейло́н	14	культу́ра	21	организа́ция

Now do activities 10 and 11 on the recording.

1.3 Are you a student?
Вы – студе́нтка?

🎧 **ACTIVITY 12** is on the recording.

ACTIVITY 13

What three things do Gleb and Svetlana have in common?

DIALOGUE 2

○ Светла́на, вы – студе́нтка?
■ Да, я – студе́нтка. А вы – студе́нт?
○ Да, я то́же студе́нт. А Све́та, вы – москви́чка?
■ Да, москви́чка. А вы?
○ Я то́же москви́ч. Но я люблю́ Санкт-Петербу́рг.
■ Я то́же люблю́ Санкт-Петербу́рг. О́чень люблю́.

VOCABULARY

студе́нтка	student [*female*]
студе́нт	student [*male*]
Све́та	*familiar form of the name* Светла́на
москви́чка	Muscovite [*female*]
москви́ч	Muscovite [*male*]

LANGUAGE BUILDING

✓ **э́то 'this is', 'that is'**

The word **э́то** means 'this is' or 'that is'. (Notice that the word **что** is spelled with **ч**, not **ш** as you might expect.)

Кто э́то? Who is that?
Э́то Ива́н. That is Ivan.
Что э́то? What is that?
Э́то борщ. It's bortsch.

✓ **Simple statements**

There is no verb 'to be' in the present tense. In writing it is sometimes indicated by a dash.

Я – Ни́на. I am Nina.
Ты – москви́чка. You're a Muscovite.
Она́ – врач. She's a doctor.
Ива́н – оптими́ст. Ivan's an optimist.

✓ Questions

Simple questions are made by keeping the same word order as the statement, but using a question intonation.

Ни́на – **врач.** Nina is a doctor.
Ни́на – **врач?** Is Nina a doctor?

✓ Gender of nouns

It is easy to tell the gender of a Russian noun from the ending on the form in which it appears in the dictionary. This form is called the nominative singular. Nouns ending in a consonant in the nominative singular are *masculine*. Here are some examples you know already:

борщ, хлеб, язы́к, вокза́л, го́род, Санкт-Петербу́рг, врач, студе́нт, москви́ч, футбо́л, хулига́н

Most nouns ending in the letter **-a**, its 'soft' equivalent **-я**, or **-ия** are *feminine*:

ма́м<u>а</u>, смета́н<u>а</u>, Москв<u>а́</u>, рабо́т<u>а</u>, у́лиц<u>а</u>, пи́цц<u>а</u>, студе́нтк<u>а</u>, москви́чк<u>а</u>, тёт<u>я</u>, ви́з<u>а</u>, револю́ц<u>ия</u>

Nouns ending in the letters **-o** or **-ие** are *neuter*.

сло́в<u>о</u>, окн<u>о́</u>, авока́д<u>о</u>, свида́н<u>ие</u>

✓ Pronouns

singular		plural	
I	**я**	we	**мы**
you [*familiar*]	**ты**	you [*plural; also polite singular*]	**вы**
he/masculine nouns	**он**	they/nouns of any gender	**они́**
she/feminine nouns	**она́**		
neuter nouns	**оно́**		

ACTIVITY 14

In A and B below, match the questions with the appropriate answer.

A 1 Где хлеб?   a Оно́ здесь.
   2 Где смета́на?   b Он там.
   3 Где авока́до?   c Вот она́.

B 1 Где борщ?   a Они́ здесь.
   2 Где ма́ма?   b Вот он. Пожа́луйста!
   3 Где Глеб и Ива́н? c Она́ здесь.

🎧 Now do activities 15, 16, and 17 on the recording.

1.4 Who is that?

Кто э́то?

Below are some short biographies to introduce the main characters in our story 'The Larin Family'. The first episode follows in 1.5.

Э́то Евге́ния
Па́вловна Ла́рина.
Она́ – ба́бушка.

А э́то Ива́н
Григо́рьевич Ла́рин.
Он – де́душка.
Он лю́бит борщ.

Э́то тётя Та́ня.
Она́ – врач.
Она́ то́же лю́бит
борщ.

Э́то Мари́я Ива́новна
Жа́рова.
Она́ – мать.
Она́ – журнали́стка.

А вот Ле́на.
Она́ – дочь.

Э́то Оле́г Ива́нович
Ла́рин.
Он – преподава́тель.

А э́то Мо́йра.
Она́ – шотла́ндка.
Она́ студе́нтка.

Э́то Пётр Ива́нович
Ла́рин.
Он – худо́жник.

А вот Руста́м.
Он тата́рин.

8

бáбушка	grandmother [*used colloquially of any old woman*]
дéдушка	grandfather [*used colloquially of any old man*]
лю́бит	loves
врач	doctor
мать	mother
журналúстка	journalist [*female*]
журналúст	journalist [*male*]
дочь (*f*)	daughter
преподавáтель	teacher
худóжник	artist
шотлáндка	Scottish woman
татáрин	Tartar

ACTIVITY 18

Read the biographies aloud several times, checking back in your book if you have forgotten any letters. Translate the text as you go, using the pictures to help you, and learn the new words.

ACTIVITY 19

You're at a business reception and you think you see Aleksei Semyonovich Gagarin, a Russian businessman who has done some work for your company. Check with your Russian host that it is indeed Aleksei Semyonovich, and then go over and say hello.

Don't be discouraged if at this stage you're still finding the alphabet hard going. It will take quite a while before you feel really confident in reading and writing. If you keep practising, however, one day you'll suddenly realize you're reading or writing something in Cyrillic without even thinking about it, and all the hard work will have been worthwhile.

In the meantime, keep checking back over the alphabet chart on page ix and revising the early parts of the book. The more reading and writing practice you do, the easier it will be to learn new words and absorb grammar points.

Ла́рины – The Larin Family

Прогу́лка по Тверско́му бульва́ру
A stroll along the Tverskoi Boulevard

The scene takes place on Moscow's Tverskoi Boulevard, where Evgeniya Pavlovna Larina, her daughter Mariya Ivanovna Zharova, and her granddaughter Lena are taking an afternoon stroll. By chance, they meet someone Mariya Ivanovna knows.

VOCABULARY

моя́ my [*with feminine nouns*]
Ле́ночка *diminutive form of Lena – 'little Lena'*

ACTIVITY 20

Listen to the story and write in the missing words below.

1 Мари́я Ива́новна, _____ _____?
2 Бори́с Миха́йлович, э́то моя́ _____, Евге́ния Па́вловна.
3 _____, Евге́ния Па́вловна.
4 А _____ э́то?
5 _____ моя́ дочь, Ле́на.
6 _____, Ле́ночка.

ACTIVITY 21

Listen to the story again and answer the questions.

1 What is the name of the man they meet?
2 Who does Mariya introduce him to first?
3 What does the man ask Mariya next?
4 How does Mariya answer?
5 What is the man's profession?

STORY TRANSCRIPT

Boris Mikhailovich	Мари́я Ива́новна, э́то вы? Здра́вствуйте!
Mariya Ivanovna	Здра́вствуйте, Бори́с Миха́йлович! Бори́с Миха́йлович, э́то моя́ ма́ма, Евге́ния Па́вловна.
Boris Mikhailovich	Здра́вствуйте, Евге́ния Па́вловна!
Evgeniya Pavlovna	Здра́вствуйте!
Boris Mikhailovich	А кто э́то?
Mariya Ivanovna	Э́то моя́ дочь, Ле́на. Ле́на, э́то Бори́с Миха́йлович. Он то́же журнали́ст.
Boris Mikhailovich	Приве́т, Ле́ночка!

Test

Now it's time to test your progress in Unit 1.

1 Match 1–8 with the English equivalents from a–h.

1	пожа́луйста!	a	hi!
2	здра́вствуйте!	b	OK!
3	до свида́ния!	c	hello
4	кто э́то?	d	you're welcome
5	прия́тного аппети́та!	e	thank you
6	приве́т!	f	who is that?
7	хорошо́!	g	goodbye
8	спаси́бо!	h	enjoy your meal

| 8 |

2 Pair up the sentences 1–6 with the correct response from a–f to make six mini-dialogues.

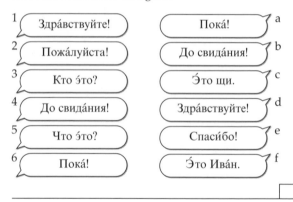

1 Здра́вствуйте!   Пока́! a

2 Пожа́луйста!   До свида́ния! b

3 Кто э́то?   Э́то щи. c

4 До свида́ния!   Здра́вствуйте! d

5 Что э́то?   Спаси́бо! e

6 Пока́!   Э́то Ива́н. f

| 6 |

3 Complete the replies by adding the correct pronoun: **он** (masculine), **она́** (feminine), **оно́** (neuter), or **они́** (plural).

1 Где хлеб? Вот ____ .
2 Где окно́? Вот ____ .
3 Где студе́нт? ____ здесь.
4 Где у́лица? ____ здесь.
5 Где Ива́н и Бори́с? ____ там.
6 Где ма́ма? ___ там.

| 6 |

4 Complete each sentence with the appropriate word from the box below.

он	что	люблю́
она́	кто	аппети́та
они́	то́же	свида́ния

1 Глеб студе́нт, и Светла́на _____ студе́нтка.
2 До _____, Пётр Ива́нович!
3 ____ э́то? Э́то Бори́с.
4 Где борщ? ___ здесь.
5 Прия́тного _____!
6 Я _____ Санкт-Петербу́рг.
7 Э́то Ни́на. ____ – врач.
8 ____ э́то? Э́то щи.
9 Где де́душка и ба́бушка? Вот ____ .

9

5 How would you say the following things in Russian?
   (2 points for each correct answer, 1 point if you make only one error)

1 Thank the hotel receptionist for giving you your key.
2 Say you're a student.
3 Ask your tour-guide if she's a Muscovite.
4 Say you love beetroot soup!
5 Say 'hello' to some business colleagues.
6 Ask where Ivan Alekseyevich is.
7 Say 'goodbye' to a close Russian friend.
8 Apologize for stepping on someone's toe in a crowded bus.

16

TOTAL SCORE **45**

If you scored less than 35, go through the dialogues and the Language Building sections again before completing the Summary on page 14.

Summary 1

 Now try this final test summarizing the main points covered in this unit. You can check your answers on the recording.

How would you:
1 greet a business colleague? a close friend?
2 say goodbye to a business colleague? to a close friend?
3 say 'enjoy your meal'?
4 ask 'who is that?'
5 say 'it's Ivan'?
6 ask where Nina is?
7 say 'she's here'?
8 ask a man you've just met if he's a doctor?
9 say you love St Petersburg?

REVISION

Before moving on to Unit 2, play Unit 1 through again and compare what you can say and understand now with what you knew when you started. Go over any vocabulary you still feel unsure of.

Don't be discouraged if you find you're still having difficulties with the Russian alphabet. We've included plenty of reading practice in the next few units to help drive it home. In the meantime, keep testing yourself on the alphabet, remembering to write things down as often as you can; practising handwritten forms will also help you remember the alphabet. For further practice look at other Language Building sections later in this book – you could try the names of the countries on page 91 (Unit 7) and page 115 (Unit 8), the days of the week on page 65 (Unit 5), or the months on page 113 (Unit 8). At this stage you will probably still need to refer back to the alphabet summary chart in the Introduction to this book a good deal. Don't worry – in time it will stick!

Once you have worked through the next few units, review Unit 1 again. This will help to consolidate everything you have learned so far.

2

First steps
Пе́рвые шаги́

> ### OBJECTIVES
>
> In this unit you'll learn how to:
>
> ⊘ express likes and dislikes
>
> ⊘ correct mistakes
>
> ⊘ request things
>
> And cover the following grammar and language:
>
> ⊘ the present tense of Ia, Ib, and II verbs
>
> ⊘ the accusative singular of nouns
>
> ⊘ nouns ending in a soft sign
>
> ⊘ the accusative of pronouns
>
> ⊘ imperatives 1
>
> ⊘ the plural of nouns

LEARNING RUSSIAN 2

Russian is a highly inflected language, which means that many words in the sentence alter their endings to express elements of grammatical meaning – for example, to show which word is the subject, which is the object, and so on.

For many people, remembering the correct inflectional endings to put on words is one of the most difficult aspects of learning Russian. There are different ways of approaching this task. In this course the different inflectional endings are introduced progressively, with examples and explanations in the Language Building sections. However, many people find it useful to look at all the inflectional endings together, presented in the form of a table: the information is presented in this way in the Grammar Summary at the end of this book.

🎧 Now start the recording for Unit 2.

2.1 I play football
Я игра́ю в футбо́л

🔊 **ACTIVITY 1** is on the recording.

ACTIVITY 2

1 Does Svetlana like football?
2 Does Gleb play football well?
3 Does Gleb's brother play football well?

DIALOGUE 1

○ Светла́на, вы лю́бите футбо́л?
■ Да, я люблю́ футбо́л. А вы игра́ете в футбо́л?
○ Да, я игра́ю в футбо́л ка́ждый день. Но я пло́хо игра́ю.
   Мой брат то́же игра́ет в футбо́л.
■ Ой, как интере́сно! А он хорошо́ игра́ет?
○ Нет, пло́хо. Мы пло́хо игра́ем, но о́чень лю́бим игра́ть.

VOCABULARY

игра́ть в футбо́л	to play football
ка́ждый	every, each
день (*m*)	day
пло́хо	badly
брат	brother
как интере́сно!	how interesting!

LANGUAGE BUILDING

✓ The present tense

There are two main types of verbs in Russian: type I and type II, differing in their endings in the present tense. Infinitives end in **-ть** (apart from a few forms in **-ти** and **-чь**). Verbs with an **-а-** before the infinitive ending are often type I, and verbs with an **-и-** are often type II. However, there are exceptions and it is better to learn which type a verb is when you learn the verb itself.

Type I is further divided into type Ia and Ib, depending on the type of stem. With type Ia verbs, the stem ends in a vowel. When you meet a new verb, note the first person singular form (listed in the vocabulary glossary), as this will give you the present tense stem.

Type Ia verbs (stem ending in a vowel)

рабо́тать – to work (stem: **рабо́та-**)

я **рабо́таю**	I work (or I am working, etc.)
ты **рабо́таешь**	you work [*familiar singular*]
он, она́, оно́ **рабо́тает**	he, she, it works
мы **рабо́таем**	we work
вы **рабо́таете**	you work [*polite singular, plural*]
они́ **рабо́тают**	they work

Other type Ia verbs: **игра́ть** 'to play' (я игра́ю), **чита́ть** 'to read' (я чита́ю), **отдыха́ть** 'to relax' (я отдыха́ю), **де́лать** 'to do', 'to make' (я де́лаю), **понима́ть** 'to understand' (я понима́ю), **изуча́ть** 'to learn' (я изуча́ю), **слу́шать** 'to listen' (я слу́шаю), **знать** 'to know'.

With type Ib verbs, the stem ends in a consonant.

Type Ib verbs (stem ending in a consonant)

ждать – to wait (stem: **жд-**)		**е́хать** – to go (by transport) (stem: **е́д-**)	
я **жду**	I wait	я **е́ду**	I go
ты **ждёшь**	you wait	ты **е́дешь**	you go
он **ждёт**	he waits	он **е́дет**	he goes
мы **ждём**	we wait	мы **е́дем**	we go
вы **ждёте**	you wait	вы **е́дете**	you go
они́ **ждут**	they wait	они́ **е́дут**	they go

If the verb is stressed on the ending, it has **-ё-** instead of **-e-**.

Other type Ib verbs: **идти́** 'to go (on foot)' (я иду́), **жить** 'to live' (я живу́).

Type II verbs

говори́ть - to speak, talk (stem: **говор-**)		**люби́ть** – to love (stem: **любл-, люб-**)	
я **говорю́**	I speak	я **люблю́**	I love
ты **говори́шь**	you speak	ты **лю́бишь**	you love
он **говори́т**	he speaks	он **лю́бит**	he loves
мы **говори́м**	we speak	мы **лю́бим**	we love
вы **говори́те**	you speak	вы **лю́бите**	you love
они́ **говоря́т**	they speak	они́ **лю́бят**	they love

Some verbs, such as **люби́ть** above, have a slightly different stem from the second person singular onwards; for such verbs, the first and the second person singular forms are listed in the vocabulary glossary.

Other type II verbs: **смотре́ть** 'to look, watch' (я смотрю́, ты смо́тришь), **ви́деть** 'to see' (я ви́жу, ты ви́дишь).

 Now do activities 3 and 4 on the recording.

(2.2) I don't like coffee

Я не люблю́ ко́фе

ACTIVITY 5 is on the recording.

ACTIVITY 6

Correct the statements which are false.

1 Kolya's mother doesn't like coffee.	T / F
2 She sometimes drinks tea.	T / F
3 She orders milk and a bun.	T / F
4 She sends the bun back.	T / F

DIALOGUE 2

○ Ма́ма, ты хо́чешь ко́фе?

■ Нет, не хочу́. Ко́ля, ты зна́ешь, что я не люблю́ ко́фе.

○ А, мо́жет быть, чай?

■ Нет, я вообще́ не пью чай.

○ Ма́ма, а что ты хо́чешь?

■ Я хочу́ молоко́ и бу́лочку.

○ Принеси́те, пожа́луйста, молоко́ и бу́лочку.

...

▲ Вот, пожа́луйста, молоко́ и бу́лочка. Прия́тного аппети́та!

■ Спаси́бо, Ко́ленька, но бу́лочку я не хочу́.

○ Ма́ма, я не понима́ю. Ты хо́чешь бу́лочку и́ли не хо́чешь?

■ Я её не хочу́, Ко́ленька, дорого́й. Она́ для тебя́. Ку́шай, ку́шай на здоро́вье!

VOCABULARY

ко́фе (*m*)	coffee
ты хо́чешь	you want
что	that [*conjunction*]
не	not
мо́жет быть	maybe
чай (*m*)	tea
вообще́ не	not at all
я пью, ты пьёшь	I drink, you drink
молоко́	milk
бу́лочка	bun
и́ли	or
её	it, her [*accusative of* **она́**]
дорого́й	dear, my dear
для тебя́	for you
ку́шай на здоро́вье!	eat! enjoy it!

✓ The accusative singular of nouns

The grammar of a Russian sentence requires that nouns (and adjectives, etc.) should be in a particular form or *case*. There are six cases in Russian. You have already met the *nominative*, which is the case used when a noun is the subject of a verb and also in dictionary entries.

The accusative is the case used for the direct object of verbs. For masculine nouns (except for those referring to people and animals – see Unit 3) and for all neuter nouns, the accusative singular is the same as the nominative singular.

Я изучáю **рýсский язы́к.** I am studying Russian.
Принеси́те, пожáлуйста, **молокó.** Could I have some milk, please?

Feminine nouns change their endings from **-а** to **-у** or **-ия** to **-ию.**

Я хочý **бýлочку.** I want a bun.
Вы ви́дите **у́лицу?** Can you see the street?

✓ Nouns ending in a soft sign (-ь)

Nouns ending in a soft sign may be either masculine or feminine. The nominative and the accusative forms are identical (except for masculine nouns referring to people or animals – see Unit 3). Here are some examples:

m: **рубль** ('rouble'), **гость** ('guest'), **день** ('day'), **Кремль** ('Kremlin')
f: **плóщадь** ('square'), **дверь** ('door'), **цéрковь** ('church')

✓ The accusative of pronouns

Pronouns have a different form when used in the accusative.

	nom.	accusative		nom.	accusative
I	**я**	**меня́**	we	**мы**	**нас**
you (*sing.*)	**ты**	**тебя́**	you (*pl., formal*)	**вы**	**вас**
he	**он**	**егó**	they	**они́**	**их**
she	**онá**	**её**			
it	**онó**	**егó**			

Он лю́бит **меня́.** He loves me.
Они́ знáют **тебя́?** Do they know you?

ACTIVITY 7

Put the words into the accusative.

1 сметáна	2 Лóндон	3 цéрковь
4 у́лица	5 молокó	6 день

Now do activities 8 and 9 on the recording.

Could I have ... ?

Да́йте, пожа́луйста, ...

ACTIVITY 10 is on the recording.

ACTIVITY 11

1 What newspaper is Valerii Borisovich given first of all?
2 What is wrong with the copy of *Pravda*?
3 What does the postcard turn out to be?
4 What three items does Valerii Borisovich buy in the end?

DIALOGUE 3

○ Да́йте, пожа́луйста, «Пра́вду» и спи́чки.

■ Вот пожа́луйста.

○ Э́то не «Пра́вда», а «Незави́симая Газе́та».

■ О, извини́те, пожа́луйста. Вот «Пра́вда».

○ Но э́то ста́рая, со вто́рника.

■ А что? Сего́дня не вто́рник?

○ Нет, сего́дня не вто́рник, а среда́.

■ Ах, да! Пра́вильно! Извини́те, пожа́луйста. Вот но́вая «Пра́вда». Ещё что-нибу́дь?

○ Да́йте, пожа́луйста, ещё э́ту откры́тку.

■ Э́то не откры́тка, а календа́рик.

○ Ну хорошо́, я возьму́ календа́рик, «Пра́вду» и спи́чки.

■ Пожа́луйста.

VOCABULARY	
да́йте	could I have ... ? [*literally:* give]
«Пра́вда»	*Pravda*
«Незави́симая газе́та»	*Nezavisimaya Gazeta*
спи́чки	matches
ста́рая	old
с, со	from
вто́рник	Tuesday
сего́дня	today
среда́	Wednesday
пра́вильно	that's right
но́вая	new
ещё	still, else, further
что́-нибудь	anything, something
ещё что́-ниудь?	anything else?
откры́тка	postcard
календа́рик	little calendar
возьму́	will take [*from the verb* взять *Ib*]

✓ Imperatives 1

You've already met the following examples of the formal or plural imperative (for situations where you would use **вы**): **слу́шайте** 'listen', **извини́те** 'excuse me, sorry', **здра́вствуйте** 'hello', **принеси́те** 'bring'.

Here are some more examples:

Да́йте, пожа́луйста, хлеб. Please give me some bread.
Смотри́те! Look!
Входи́те! Come in!
Скажи́те, пожа́луйста, где метро́? Can you tell me, please, where the metro is?

For the informal singular imperative (for situations where you would use **ты**), the final **-те** is dropped: **извини́! дай! смотри́! скажи́!**

✓ The plural of nouns in the nominative and accusative

With the exception of nouns referring to animals and people (see Unit 4), the accusative plural is the same as the nominative plural.

Masculine nouns ending in

| consonant | add **-ы** | вокза́л<u>ы</u>, студе́нт<u>ы</u> |
| **-ь** | replace with **-и** | рубл<u>и́</u>, го́ст<u>и</u> |

Feminine nouns ending in

-a	replace with **-ы**	ви́з<u>ы</u>, у́лиц<u>ы</u>
-ь	replace with **-и**	пло́щад<u>и</u>, две́р<u>и</u>
-ия	replace with **-ии**	револю́ц<u>ии</u>

Neuter nouns ending in

| **-o** | replace with **-a** | слов<u>а́</u>, о́кн<u>а</u> |
| **-ие** | replace with **-ия** | свида́н<u>ия</u> |

Following Spelling Rule 1 (see Grammar Summary page 221 for details) the letter **ы** must be replaced by **и** after **к, г, х, ж, ч, ш,** or **щ**. This affects many plurals, such as: **спи́чк<u>и</u>** ('matches'), **откры́тк<u>и</u>** ('postcards'), **язык<u>и́</u>** ('languages'), **врач<u>и́</u>** ('doctors').

ACTIVITY 12

Match the situations 1–4 with the expressions from a–d.

1 Asking directions.   a Да́йте, пожа́луйста, «Пра́вду».
2 Ordering a drink.   b Скажи́те, пожа́луйста, где метро́?
3 Buying a paper.   c Входи́те!
4 Knock on door.   d Принеси́те, пожа́луйста, чай.

🎧 Now do activities 13 and 14 on the recording.

Вы́вески

ACTIVITY 15

Here are some common words you will see around you on signs, shops and other buildings. They are all in capital letters – you may need check back to the alphabet summary chart on page ix to remind yourself of the forms. See if you can work out the meanings. Complete the activity and then check the vocabulary list which follows.

1	**ПОЧТА**	2	МОРОЖЕНОЕ
3	ВХОД	4	**ТРОЛЛЕЙБУС**
5	**АВТОБУС**	6	ТУАЛЕТЫ
7	КНИГИ	8	**ВОКЗАЛ**
9	КИОСК	10	КИНО
11	РЕСТОРАН	12	**КВАС**
13	**МЕТРО**	14	ПИВО
15	**КАССА**	16	ТАКСИ
17	АПТЕКА	18	**ТЕЛЕФОН**

авто́бус	bus
апте́ка	chemist's
вход	entrance
ка́сса	ticket-office, box-office, cash-desk
квас	kvass [*a Russian drink made from black bread*]
кино́	cinema, movies
кни́га	book
моро́женое	ice-cream
пи́во	beer
по́чта	post office

ACTIVITY 16

Now here are some names of streets, museums, cafés, and so on. Identify the places with the help of the vocabulary list below.

1
КАФЕ
«КОПАКАБАНА»

2
**МУЗЕЙ
КЕРАМИКИ**

3
ТВЕРСКОЙ
БУЛЬВАР

4
ДОМ-МУЗЕЙ К. С.
СТАНИСЛАВСКОГО

5
НОВАЯ
ПЛОЩАДЬ

6
ДОМ-МУЗЕЙ
А. П. ЧЕХОВА

7
УНИВЕРСИТЕТ

8
**ПЛОЩАДЬ
РЕВОЛЮЦИИ**

9
РЕСТОРАН
«У БАБУШКИ»

10
КРЕМЛЬ

11
**МУЗЕЙ
РЕВОЛЮЦИИ**

12
КРАСНАЯ
ПЛОЩАДЬ

кера́мика	ceramics
у (+ *gen.*)	at someone's house, at, by
дом	house
кра́сная	red

2.5 Ла́рины

Ле́на покупа́ет моро́женое
Lena buys an ice-cream

Evgeniya Pavlovna, Mariya Ivanovna, and little Lena are continuing their afternoon stroll along the Tverskoi Boulevard.

VOCABULARY	
коне́чно	of course
како́е	what sort of ... ?
эскимо́	choc-ice
пломби́р	'plombières' [*ice-cream with candied fruit*]
купи́ть II (куплю́, ку́пишь)	to buy [*here* we should buy]
наве́рное	probably
ну и ну!	well, I never!
про́сто	simply
э́то чу́до!	it's wonderful!

ACTIVITY 17

Who's speaking: Mariya Ivanovna, Lena, or the ice-cream man?

1 Ты хо́чешь моро́женое?
2 Я люблю́ моро́женое!
3 Я хочу́ эскимо́.
4 Да́йте, пожа́луйста, эскимо́.
5 Ещё что́-нибудь?
6 Вы не лю́бите, а я люблю́.

ACTIVITY 18

Listen to the story and decide whether the following statements are true or false. Correct the statements which are false.

1 Lena doesn't feel like an ice-cream.
2 Mariya Ivanovna asks the ice-cream man for a choc-ice.
3 The ice-cream man gives Lena the wrong ice-cream by mistake.
4 They buy an ice-cream for Evgeniya Pavlovna too.
5 Mariya Ivanovna doesn't like ice-cream.

ACTIVITY 19

Now listen to the story again and note all the imperative forms you hear in the dialogue: there are four in total. Write them out below, giving their meanings.

1 _____ *meaning:* _____
2 _____ *meaning:* _____
3 _____ *meaning:* _____
4 _____ *meaning:* _____

STORY TRANSCRIPT

Mariya Ivanovna	Лёночка, смотри! Видишь морóженое? Ты хóчешь морóженое?
Lena	Урá! Морóженое! Конéчно, хочý! Я люблю́ морóженое!
Mariya Ivanovna	Лёночка, скажи, какóе ты хóчешь морóженое?
Lena	Мммм, мóжет быть эскимó? Нет... да, эскимó. Я хочý эскимó.
Mariya Ivanovna	Дáйте, пожáлуйста, эскимó.
Ice-cream man	Вот, пожáлуйста.
Lena	Но э́то не эскимó, а пломби́р.
Ice-cream man	О, прáвильно! Извини́, пожáлуйста. Вот эскимó.
Lena	Спаси́бо.
Ice-cream man	Ещё чтó-нибудь?
Lena	Мáма, мóжет быть, купи́ть для бáбушки? Онá, навéрное, тóже хóчет морóженое.
Mariya Ivanovna	Нет, Лёночка, бáбушка не лю́бит морóженое.
Lena	А ты, мáма, не хóчешь морóженое?
Mariya Ivanovna	Нет, спаси́бо, Лёночка, я тóже не люблю́ морóженое.
Lena	Ну и ну! Вы не лю́бите, а я люблю́. Морóженое – э́то прóсто чýдо!

Test

Now it's time to test your progress in Unit 2.

1 Match the following phrases with their English equivalents.

1	я зна́ю её	a he is playing
2	он игра́ет	b I am waiting
3	принеси́те, пожа́луйста, пи́во	c where is the church?
4	где це́рковь?	d I know her
5	молоко́ и бу́лочка	e I'd like a beer, please
6	тётя, э́то ты?	f do you like Moscow?
7	вы лю́бите Москву́?	g is that you, Auntie?
8	я жду	h milk and a bun

8

2 Pair up 1–6 with the correct response a–f to make up six mini-dialogues.

1 Что вы де́лаете?
2 Э́то не ко́фе, а ча́й.
3 Ты ви́дишь тётю?
4 Я не могу́.
5 Здра́вствуйте, Ива́н Григо́рьевич!
6 Да́йте, пожа́луйста, откры́тку.

a Ах, извини́те, пожа́луйста!
b А я то́же не могу́!
c Вот, пожа́луйста.
d О, входи́те, входи́те!
e Мы отдыха́ем.
f Нет, я её не ви́жу.

6

3 Put the verb in brackets into the correct form.

1 Я _____ (ждать, Ib)
2 Мы _____ (рабо́тать, Ia)
3 Она́ _____ (говори́ть, II)
4 Они́ _____ (люби́ть, II)
5 Вы _____ (понима́ть, Ia)
6 Ты _____ (е́хать, Ib)

6

4 Give the gender of the words, then make them plural.

1	студе́нт	m/f/n	_____
2	у́лица	m/f/n	_____
3	окно́	m/f/n	_____
4	гость	m/f/n	_____
5	москви́чка	m/f/n	_____

10

5 Complete each sentence with an appropriate noun or pronoun in the accusative taken from the box below.

язы́к	пи́во	их
меня́	Москву́	рестора́н
его́	тебя́	«Пра́вду»

1 Где Оле́г? Я _____ не ви́жу.
2 Я вообще́ не пью _____ .
3 Она́ ка́ждый день чита́ет _____ .
4 Ты её лю́бишь, а она́ _____ не лю́бит.
5 Я зна́ю _____ «У ба́бушки».
6 Я говорю́, а вы не слу́шаете _____!
7 Мы изуча́ем ру́сский _____ .
8 Ма́ма лю́бит Санкт-Петербу́рг, а па́па лю́бит _____ .
9 Где Глеб и Светла́на? Вы ви́дите _____?

9

6 How would you do the following in Russian?
(2 points if correct, 1 point if only one error)
1 Tell someone you love football.
2 Ask where the telephone is.
3 Say sorry, you don't understand.
4 Ask the hotel receptionist if he understands you.
5 Order some ice-cream in a restaurant.
6 Ask for a post-card in a kiosk.
7 Say 'come in!'
8 Say you don't like beer.

16

TOTAL SCORE **55**

If you scored less than 45, go through the dialogues and the Language Building sections again before completing the Summary on page 28.

Summary 2

 Now try this final test summarizing the main points covered in this unit. You can check your answers on the recording.

How would you:
1 say you understand?
2 say you don't understand?
3 say you don't know?
4 say you love Moscow?
5 ask a business colleague if he likes beer?
6 say it's not tea, it's coffee?
7 say it's not Ivan, it's Oleg?
8 ask the waiter to bring some milk?
9 ask for a postcard at a kiosk?

REVISION

Before moving on, play Unit 2 through again and see how much you have already learnt. Go over any points of grammar you still feel unsure of, and check that you know the new vocabulary introduced in the unit.

If you have not already done so, have look at the tables in the Grammar Summary at the end of the book. See how the cases you have learned – the nominative and the accusative – fit into the information given in the tables. If you find it useful, you may like to write out these tables a few times – it may help the different forms stick in your mind. Don't worry, however, if you're finding all these different forms bewildering at the moment. As you continue through the course you'll see that, although the system is complex, the patterns are generally regular and there are very few exceptions.

Practise the new grammar from this unit by imagining real-life situations. For example, how would you order different things in a restaurant or buy things from a kiosk? How would you say whether you like or don't like them? Imagining real situations such as these will help the different endings for verbs and nouns stay at the front of your mind.

Finding your way
Как туда́ пройти́

In this unit you'll learn how to:

✓ ask where places are

✓ find your way around

✓ ask and understand directions

And cover the following grammar and language:

✓ the genitive singular of nouns, pronouns

✓ prepositions taking the genitive

✓ **у** + genitive meaning 'to have'

✓ masculine animate nouns in the singular

✓ imperatives 2

✓ adverbs

LEARNING RUSSIAN 3

One good way of learning vocabulary is to use a vocabulary book, jotting down every new word you meet, its meaning, and perhaps the phrase in which it first appeared. You might also want to include some basic grammatical information – what gender it is, its endings, and so on. The simple process of *writing words down* will help you to remember them.

There are various ways to organize new vocabulary: you can do it alphabetically or grammatically (according to whether the words are nouns, verbs, adjectives, and so on). It can also be useful to group words according to topic. These methods will all give you a context in which to learn the words, which can make memorizing vocabulary much easier.

Now start the recording for Unit 3.

(3.1) Where is it?

Где э́то?

(1A) **ACTIVITY 1** is on the recording.

ACTIVITY 2

1 What does Gleb like reading?
2 Which two writers does Svetlana like most of all?
3 Where does Svetlana think the second-hand bookshop is?
4 Where is it in fact located?

DIALOGUE 1

○ Глеб, вы лю́бите чита́ть?

■ Да, коне́чно, я люблю́ чита́ть. О́чень люблю́.

○ А что и́менно вы лю́бите чита́ть?

■ Да всё. Я всё люблю́. А вы что лю́бите?

○ Бо́льше всего́ я люблю́ рома́ны Турге́нева и, коне́чно, стихи́ Пу́шкина. Без Пу́шкина я жить не могу́! Я его́ про́сто обожа́ю! Для меня́, Пу́шкин …

■ Слу́шайте, Све́та, я зна́ю о́чень хоро́ший букинисти́ческий магази́н.

○ А где э́то? Э́то ма́ленький магази́н о́коло ста́нции метро́ «Пло́щадь Револю́ции»?

■ Нет, он нахо́дится далеко́ от це́нтра, бли́зко от метро́ «Университе́т». Вы са́ми не найдёте – я вас провожу́!

○ Спаси́бо!

VOCABULARY

и́менно	namely, exactly
всё	everything
бо́льше всего́	above all
рома́н	novel
стихи́	poetry, poems
обожа́ть Ia	to adore, to worship
хоро́ший	good
букинисти́ческий	second-hand book [*adjective*]
магази́н	shop, store
ма́ленький	small
ста́нция	station [*metro station*]
находи́ться II	to be located
центр	centre
са́ми	yourself
вы не найдёте	you won't find
проводи́ть II (**провожу́**)	to accompany

✅ Nouns in the genitive (singular)

The genitive case has a number of uses. The most common are:
- to express possession (the equivalent of the English 's)
- to translate 'of' in expressions of quantity
- after the following: **мно́го** 'a lot of', **немно́го** 'a little', **ско́лько** 'how much?'
- after certain prepositions

The genitive singular is formed as follows:

Masculine nouns ending in

| consonant | add **-а** | вокза́л<u>а</u>, го́род<u>а</u>, бра́т<u>а</u> |
| **-ь** | replace with **-я** | рубл<u>я́</u>, го́ст<u>я</u>, Кремл<u>я́</u> |

Feminine nouns ending in

-а	replace with **-ы**	ви́з<u>ы</u>, у́лиц<u>ы</u>
-ь	replace with **-и**	пло́щад<u>и</u>, две́р<u>и</u>
-ия	replace with **-ии**	револю́ц<u>ии</u>

Note the effect of Spelling Rule 1 (**ы** replaced by **и**): апте́к<u>и</u>, ба́бушк<u>и</u>, кни́г<u>и</u>.

Neuter nouns ending in

| **-о** | replace with **-а** | слов<u>а́</u>, вин<u>а́</u>, молок<u>а́</u> |
| **-ие** | replace with **-ия** | свида́н<u>ия</u> |

Note that some neuter nouns (marked *) never change their form:
for example, **авока́до** ('avocado'), **метро́** ('metro'), **кино́** ('cinema').

дом **ба́бушки** Grandma's house
буты́лка **вина́** и немно́го **хле́ба** a bottle of wine [**вино́** 'wine'] and a little bit of bread
Ско́лько **во́дки?** How much vodka? [**во́дка** 'vodka']

Examples of prepositions taking the genitive

без	without	**по́сле**	after
для	for	**у**	by
до	up to, as far as, until	**напро́тив**	opposite
из	from, out of	**бли́зко от**	near
о́коло	near, by	**далеко́ от**	far away from
от	from	**недалеко́ от**	not far from

ко́фе без **молока́** – coffee without milk
Я живу́ далеко́ от **Ло́ндона.** I live a long way from London.

 Now do activities 3 and 4 on the recording.

Have you got ... ?

У вас есть ... ?

🎧 **ACTIVITY 5** is on the recording.

ACTIVITY 6

Which map corresponds to the directions given in the dialogue?

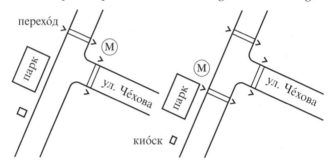

DIALOGUE 2

○ У вас есть план го́рода?

■ Нет, у нас есть то́лько газе́ты, журна́лы и сигаре́ты.

○ А вы не ска́жете, где нахо́дится у́лица Че́хова?

■ Э́то о́чень бли́зко, мо́жно пешко́м дойти́. Вот здесь, вы ви́дите ма́ленький парк? О́коло па́рка нахо́дится ста́нция метро́. А у́лица Че́хова – напро́тив ста́нции метро́. Там есть перехо́д. Вы без труда́ её найдёте.

○ Большо́е спаси́бо.

■ Не́ за что.

VOCABULARY	
у вас есть ... ?	have you got ... ?
то́лько	only
журна́л	magazine
сигаре́та	cigarette
вы не ска́жете ... ?	could you tell me ... ?
мо́жно	it is possible, one can
пешко́м	on foot
дойти́ Ib **(я дойду́)**	to get there, to go there
перехо́д	crossing
труд	difficulty
большо́е спаси́бо	thanks a lot
большо́й	big
не́ за что	don't mention it

✓ y + genitive 'to have'

The verb 'to have' is translated in Russian by the following expression:

y + noun/pronoun in the genitive + **есть** + noun in nominative
[*literally* 'by someone there is something']

The item possessed is in the nominative, since grammatically it is the subject. The word **есть** 'there is' is often omitted.

У Ива́на есть откры́тка. Ivan has a postcard.
У Ни́ны есть кни́га. Nina has a book.

The genitive of pronouns is the same as the accusative: **меня́, тебя́, его́, её, его́, нас, вас, их** (see page 19). However, after most prepositions – including **y** in the 'to have' construction – the pronouns **его́, её,** and **их** gain an initial **н-**, becoming **него́, неё, них.**

У **него́** есть план го́рода. He has a city plan.
У **них** есть дом в Чика́го. They have a house in Chicago.
Без **неё** я жить не могу́. I can't live without her.

✓ Masculine animate nouns in the singular

Nouns referring to people and animals are called animate nouns. Masculine animate nouns differ from other masculine nouns in the accusative singular: instead of having the same endings as the nominative singular, they have the same endings as the genitive singular: **-a** or **-я**.

Я зна́ю **Ива́на.** I know Ivan.
Ты чита́ешь **Че́хова?** Are you reading Chekhov?
Я не люблю́ **Пу́шкина.** I don't like Pushkin.
Вы зна́ете **го́стя?** Do you know the guest?

ACTIVITY 7

Complete each sentence by putting the word in brackets into the genitive.

1 У _____ есть дом. (ма́ма)
2 У _____ есть буты́лка вина́. (Оле́г)
3 У _____ есть хоро́ший преподава́тель. (Ни́на)
4 У _____ есть брат. (я)
5 У _____ есть мно́го хле́ба. (она́)
6 У _____ есть всё. (он)

🔊 Now do activities 8 and 9 on the recording.

I'm looking for the ...

Я ищу́ ...

ACTIVITY 10 is on the recording.

ACTIVITY 11

Fill in the missing directions.

Go (1) _____ , to the (2) _____ , then
turn (3) _____ , then (4) _____ , then
(5) _____ . There there is a (6) _____ ,
and the hotel is situated (7) _____ .

DIALOGUE 3

○ Прости́те, пожа́луйста, я ищу́ гости́ницу «Ко́смос». Вы не
   ска́жете, как туда́ пройти́?

■ Иди́те пря́мо, до конца́ у́лицы, пото́м поверни́те нале́во,
   пото́м напра́во, пото́м опя́ть нале́во. Там нахо́дится парк,
   а гости́ница нахо́дится о́коло па́рка.

○ А э́то далеко́?

■ Далеко́. Два́дцать мину́т пешко́м.

○ Бо́же мой, а у меня́ там встре́ча че́рез пять мину́т! Где тут
   побли́зости телефо́н-автома́т?

■ Иди́те пря́мо, пото́м нале́во, до конца́ у́лицы. Там
   найдёте автома́т.

VOCABULARY	
прости́те	excuse me [*imperative*]
я ищу́ (+ *acc.*)	I'm looking for
гости́ница	hotel
как туда́ пройти́	how to get there (on foot)
туда́	to there
иди́те (*from* идти́)	go (on foot) [*imperative*]
коне́ц (*gen.* конца́)	end
пото́м	then
поверни́те	turn [imperative]
опя́ть	again
два́дцать	twenty
Бо́же мой!	good grief!
встре́ча	meeting
че́рез (+ *acc.*)	in [*with time expressions*]; across
тут	here
побли́зости	near here
телефо́н-автома́т	pay-phone

✓ Imperatives 2

In the dialogue you met some useful imperatives: **прости́те, иди́те, поверни́те**. Here are two more forms you should know: **повтори́те** ('repeat'), **говори́те** ('speak').

And here are some which you might need in an emergency: **спеши́те!** ('hurry!'), **прекрати́те!** ('stop it!'), **вы́зовите врача́!** ('call a doctor!'), **помоги́те!** ('help!'), **держи́ во́ра!** ('stop, thief!').

✓ Adverbs

Many adverbs end in **-о**: you have already met **хорошо́** ('well'), **пло́хо** ('badly'), **бли́зко** ('near'), **далеко́** ('far'), **недалеко́** ('not far'), **напра́во** ('right'), **нале́во** ('left'), **пря́мо** ('straight on'), **про́сто** ('simply'). Below are some more examples.

Он говори́т **бы́стро** и **ти́хо**. He speaks quickly and quietly.
Я чита́ю о́чень **ме́дленно** по-ру́сски. I read Russian very slowly.
Она́ о́чень **гро́мко** говори́т. She speaks loudly.
Вы **хорошо́** говори́те по-ру́сски. You speak Russian well.

ACTIVITY 12

Find the phrase which fits each of the following situations.

1 Telling someone what you're looking for.
2 Telling someone to turn left.
3 Telling someone to go straight on.
4 Asking someone where there is one nearby.
5 Asking someone how to get there.
6 Asking someone if it's far.

a Как туда́ пройти́?
b Поверни́те нале́во.
c Э́то далеко́?
d Где тут побли́зости …?
e Иди́те пря́мо.
f Я ищу́ …

ACTIVITY 13

Supply the missing adverb.

1 Оле́г говори́т о́чень _____ . (quickly)
2 Ма́ма о́чень _____ говори́т. (loudly)
3 Поверни́те _____ . (right)
4 Я _____ чита́ю по-ру́сски. (slowly)
5 Вы _____ говори́те по-ру́сски. (well)

🎧 Now do activities 14 and 15 on the recording.

(3.4) Our office

Наш óфис

ACTIVITY 16

You've arrived in Moscow on a business trip and found this note waiting for you at your hotel. It's from your Russian colleague, giving instructions on how to get to his office from your hotel. Read the note and plot your route on the map.

CULTURE

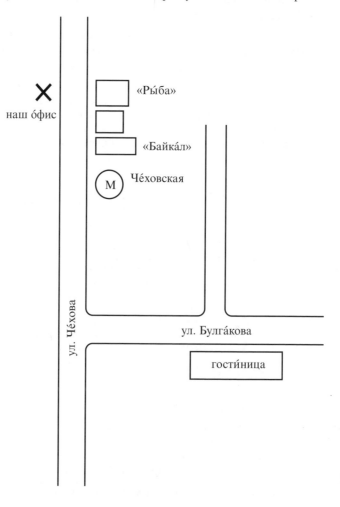

Как дойти до нашего офиса

Выйдите из гостиницы и поверните налево. Это улица Булгакова. Идите прямо до конца улицы, потом поверните направо. Там будет улица Чехова. Идите прямо. Через 500 метров вы увидите станцию метро «Чеховская». Около станции метро находится ресторан «Байкал». Недалеко от ресторана вы увидите магазин «Рыба». Наш офис находится напротив магазина, на другой стороне улицы. Наш адрес – улица Чехова, дом 26. Если вы не сможете нас найти, то позвоните нам (наш телефон – 213 65 02) или возьмите такси.

До встречи!

Семён Пирогов

VOCABULARY

дойти до Ib	to get to [*on foot*]
нашего, наш	our
офис	office
выйдите	go out
будет	will be
метр	metre
вы увидите	you will see
рыба	fish
на другой стороне	on the other side
другой	other
сторона	side
адрес	address
если	if
сможете	will be able to
позвоните	telephone [*imperative*]
позвонить II	to telephone
нам	us
возьмите	take
до встречи!	see you!

ACTIVITY 17

One of Semyon's colleagues is going to bring some files over to your hotel. Using the map on page 36, write a short note giving instructions on how to get from his office to your hotel.

(3.5) Ла́рины

Мари́я Ива́новна и́щет магази́н
(◄)) Mariya Ivanovna looks for the shop

Mariya Ivanovna is searching for a present for Evgeniya
Pavlovna's forthcoming 65th birthday. However, she's having
difficulty finding the particular shop she wants.

VOCABULARY	
сувени́р	souvenir
э́ту	this, that [f acc. form]
ника́к … не	in no way
ника́к не найду́ его́	I just can't find it

ACTIVITY 18

Listen to the story and decide whether the following
statements are true or false. Correct the statements which
are false.

1 The first passer-by doesn't know where the shop is.
2 The second passer-by says the shop is far away.
3 The second passer-by tells Mariya Ivanovna to turn left,
   then go straight on.
4 The third passer-by says the shop is near a restaurant.
5 The fourth passer-by says she's looking for the same shop!
6 The fourth passer-by offers to show Mariya Ivanovna the
   way.

ACTIVITY 19

Mariya Ivanovna uses different expressions each time to ask
for directions to the shop. Listen to the story again and fill in
the missing words and phrases.

1 Извини́те, пожа́луйста, _____ _____ _____,
   где магази́н «Сувени́ры»?
2 Прости́те, пожа́луйста, магази́н «Сувени́ры» – э́то
   _____ ?
3 А вы не ска́жете, _____ _____ _____ ?
4 _____, пожа́луйста, где _____ магази́н
   «Сувени́ры»?
5 Прости́те, пожа́луйста, я _____ магази́н «Сувени́ры».

STORY TRANSCRIPT

Mariya Ivanovna	Извини́те, пожа́луйста, вы не ска́жете, где магази́н «Сувени́ры»?
Passer-by #1	Я не зна́ю.
	…
Mariya Ivanovna	Прости́те, пожа́луйста, магази́н «Сувени́ры» – э́то далеко́?
Passer-by #2	Нет, бли́зко.
Mariya Ivanovna	А вы не ска́жете, как туда́ пройти́?
Passer-by #2	Вот здесь поверни́те нале́во, пото́м иди́те пря́мо.
Mariya Ivanovna	Большо́е спаси́бо.
	…
Mariya Ivanovna	Скажи́те, пожа́луйста, где нахо́дится магази́н «Сувени́ры»?
Passer-by #3	Это не здесь. Вот вы ви́дите э́ту у́лицу? Поверни́те напра́во, пото́м опя́ть напра́во. Там нахо́дится рестора́н «Ара́гви», а недалеко́ от рестора́на вы уви́дите магази́н «Сувени́ры».
Mariya Ivanovna	Спаси́бо.
	…
Mariya Ivanovna	Прости́те, пожа́луйста, я ищу́ магази́н «Сувени́ры». Ника́к не найду́ его́.
Passer-by #4	Магази́н «Сувени́ры»? А я то́же туда́ иду́! Я вас провожу́.
Mariya Ivanovna	Большо́е спаси́бо!

Before completing the test on pages 40–41 revise the genitive forms with the activity below.

ACTIVITY 20

Complete each sentence by putting the word in brackets into the genitive. Not all the words will change.

1 Он живёт далеко́ от _____ (Москва́)
2 Я не о́чень люблю́ стихи́ _____ (Пу́шкин)
3 Вы пьёте чай без _____? (молоко́)
4 Ста́нция метро́ недалеко́ от _____ (Кремль)
5 Дом нахо́дится о́коло _____ (кино́)

Test

Now it's time to test your progress in Unit 3.

1 Match the phrases 1–8 with a–h.

1	вот дом Ива́на	a	turn left
2	до конца́ у́лицы	b	a little bit of bread
3	она́ говори́т ти́хо	c	a long way from the station
4	ты зна́ешь го́стя	d	here is Ivan's house
5	у меня́ есть брат	e	to the end of the street
6	немно́го хле́ба	f	you know the guest
7	далеко́ от вокза́ла	g	I have a brother
8	поверни́те нале́во	h	she speaks quietly

8

2 Match each of the sentences 1–6 with a response from a–f.

1 Да́йте, пожа́луйста, план го́рода.

2 Э́то далеко́?

3 Напра́во и́ли нале́во?

4 Вы не ска́жете, где нахо́дится по́чта?

5 Где тут побли́зости телефо́н-автома́т?

6 Я вас провожу́.

a Большо́е спаси́бо.

b Нале́во.

c У нас есть то́лько газе́ты и журна́лы.

d Она́ нахо́дится недалеко́ от вокза́ла.

e Два́дцать мину́т пешко́м.

f Там, о́коло по́чты.

6

3 Match the sentences 1–4 with a response from a–d.

1	Где нахо́дится кио́ск?	a	Бо́льше всего́ – стихи́ Ле́рмонтова.
2	Где вы живёте?	b	Спаси́бо!
3	Что вы лю́бите чита́ть?	c	Он нахо́дится недалеко́ от вокза́ла.
4	Я вас провожу́!	d	Я живу́ далеко́ от це́нтра го́рода.

4

4 Put the noun in brackets into genitive singular.

1 Я люблю́ стихи́ _____ . (Ле́рмонтов)
2 Он пьёт ко́фе без _____ . (молоко́)
3 Я живу́ недалеко́ от _____ . (по́чта)
4 Э́то для _____ . (гость)
5 По́сле _____ . (револю́ция)
6 Буты́лка _____ . (вино́)

6

5 Complete each sentence with a word from the box.

иди́те	нахо́дится	ищу́
есть	пешко́м	побли́зости
до	туда́	поверни́те

1 У меня́ _____ кни́га.
2 Вы не ска́жете, как _____ пройти́?
3 Э́то бли́зко. Пять мину́т _____ .
4 _____ пря́мо.
5 _____ нале́во.
6 Дом _____ напро́тив магази́на.
7 Я _____ гости́ницу «Метропо́ль».
8 Где тут _____ телефо́н-автома́т?
9 _____ встре́чи!

9

6 How would you say the following things in Russian?
(2 points if correct, 1 point if only one error)

1 Ask where the hotel is located.
2 Ask if it's far.
3 Ask how to get there.
4 Ask where there is a post-office nearby.
5 Ask the hotel reception if they have a city map.
6 Say you're looking for the restaurant 'Aragvi'.
7 Say 'thanks a lot'.
8 Say you love Pushkin.

16

TOTAL SCORE **49**

If you scored less than 39, re-read the Language Building
sections before completing the Summary on page 42.

Summary 3

 Now try this final test summarizing the main points covered in this unit. You can check your answers on the recording.

How would you:
1 ask a passer-by where the metro station is?
2 say you're looking for the kiosk?
3 ask where there is a toilet nearby?
4 say it's a long way from the railway station?
5 tell a business colleague you'll show her the way?
6 ask at a kiosk if they have *Pravda*?
7 tell your tour guide that she speaks very quickly?
8 say you know Boris?

REVISION

Before moving on to the next unit, play Unit 3 through again and check your progress. If you are unsure of any of the grammar, re-read the relevant Language Building section and redo the exercises. Remember that there is also a glossary of grammatical terms at the end of this book, which you may find helpful.

If you are keeping a vocabulary book, go over the new words you have written down from this unit now. Take time to review the endings you've learnt so far in the Grammar Summary at the back of the book.

In particular, practise the genitive of nouns by forming sentences relating to what you see around you in your home – 'I have a book', 'I have a map', 'you have a postcard'. You could also practise the genitive of nouns with what you see outside – 'the house is near the park', 'the shop is not far from the post-office', and so on.

To practise asking for and giving directions, use a town map showing local facilities as well as roads and streets.

Review 1

There are four Review sections in the course. These consist of activities which will test you on the language introduced up to that point. Answers to the activities can be found in the Answer section, pp 213–220.

VOCABULARY

1 Which is the odd one out in each group?

1 чай / молоко́ / хлеб / вино́
2 приве́т / пока́ / до свида́ния / до встре́чи
3 о́фис / дом / магази́н / ры́ба
4 пря́мо / нале́во / то́лько / напра́во
5 спи́чки / врачи́ / ба́бушки / худо́жники

2 Match each English sentence 1–5 with the correct Russian version from a–e.

1 Он не лю́бит гости́ницу.	a The hotel is far away.
2 Я ищу́ гости́ницу.	b That's not a hotel, it's a station.
3 Гости́ница далеко́.	c I'm looking for the hotel.
4 Гости́ница нахо́дится о́коло вокза́ла.	d He doesn't like the hotel.
5 Э́то не гости́ница, а вокза́л.	e The hotel is near the station.

GRAMMAR AND USAGE

3 Complete the sentences with the appropriate pronoun: **он, она́, оно́,** or **они́**.

1 Где Глеб и Светла́на? Вот _____ .
2 Гость отдыха́ет? Нет, _____ игра́ет в футбо́л.
3 Где по́чта? _____ напро́тив магази́на.
4 Ма́ма чита́ет? Нет, _____ пьёт ко́фе.
5 Где вокза́л? _____ здесь.

4 Complete the sentences with the correct present tense form of the verb.

   1 Ты _____ Чика́го? (люби́ть)
   2 На́стя и О́льга _____ . (идти́)
   3 Сего́дня мы _____ . (рабо́тать)
   4 Вы _____ по-ру́сски? (говори́ть)
   5 Я не _____ . (понима́ть)

5 Complete the sentences with the accusative singular forms of the nouns.

   1 Да́йте, пожа́луйста, _____ . (газе́та)
   2 Он лю́бит _____ . (тётя)
   3 Я изуча́ю ру́сский _____ . (язы́к)
   4 Принеси́те, пожа́луйста, _____ . (молоко́)
   5 Они́ не лю́бят _____ . (Ива́н)

6 Complete the sentences with the accusative / genitive form of the pronouns, as appropriate.

   1 Мы слу́шаем _____ . (она́)
   2 У _____ есть дом. (мы)
   3 Я иду́ туда́ без _____ . (вы)
   4 Я зна́ю _____ . (ты)
   5 У _____ есть журна́л. (я)

7 Complete the sentences with the nominative / accusative plural forms of the nouns.

   1 Я не люблю́ _____ . (сигаре́та)
   2 Вы ви́дите _____ ? (окно́)
   3 У них есть _____ . (откры́тка)
   4 _____ игра́ют в футбо́л. (студе́нт)
   5 Она́ лю́бит _____ . (язы́к)

8 Complete the sentences with the genitive forms of the nouns.

   1 буты́лка _____   (вино́)
   2 мно́го _____   (хлеб)
   3 без _____   (смета́на)
   4 стихи́ _____   (Пу́шкин)
   5 о́коло _____   (ста́нция метро́)

9 Svetlana has accepted an invitation to dinner from Gleb, but is having problems finding the restaurant. Here she is, asking a passer-by for directions. Listen to the recording and fill in the blanks in the directions she receives.

1 It's close, you can get there _____ .
2 Go _____
3 to the _____
4 and then _____ .
5 There _____ a small park
6 and _____ the park is a post-office.
7 The restaurant is _____ the post-office.

10 Nina from Kazan has stopped at a kiosk. Listen to the recording and answer the questions.

1 What does Nina ask for first of all?
2 What newspapers does the kiosk have?
3 Which newspaper does Nina decide on?
4 What else would she like to buy?
5 Why can't she buy this?
6 What street is she looking for?
7 Why can't the man in the kiosk help her?

🔊 **SPEAKING**

11 How you would ask the following questions? First of all write down the Russian, then try to do the activity using only the recording, without looking at your notes. Use polite forms (**вы**) wherever possible.

1 Are you a (female) student?
2 Where is the hotel located?
3 Is that Nina or Mariya?
4 Do you like Moscow?
5 Are you working today?
6 What is he doing?
7 Could you tell me where the post office is?
8 Is it far?
9 Have you got a city map?
10 Where is there a telephone near here?

12 Now it's time for you to answer some questions. Listen to the questions on the recording and give an appropriate answer – the answers don't have to be true, but they should be correct Russian! You'll be asked about the following, but not necessarily in this order: who you are, whether you speak Russian, whether you understand, and whether you like certain things and particular activities.

4

Shopping
Поку́пки

OBJECTIVES

In this unit you'll learn how to:

- ✓ get by when shopping
- ✓ get by at the post office
- ✓ count
- ✓ ask prices
- ✓ attract attention

And cover the following grammar and language:

- ✓ the genitive plural of nouns
- ✓ animate nouns in the accusative plural
- ✓ нет + the genitive
- ✓ numbers
- ✓ the case of nouns after numbers
- ✓ the irregular verb хоте́ть ('to want')
- ✓ the prepositions в ('into') and на ('onto')

LEARNING RUSSIAN 4

Before attempting the dialogue activities, always try listening to the recordings several times and only then look at the transcript in your book. This will give you a feel for the language and train you to listen to detail.

Now start the recording for Unit 4.

В магази́не

🎧 **ACTIVITY 1** is on the recording.

ACTIVITY 2

1 Why is Svetlana not interested in Nabokov?
2 Does the shop have Lermontov's letters?
3 How much does the complete works of Lermontov cost?
4 What is different about the second set?

DIALOGUE 1

○ Светла́на, у вас, наве́рное, мно́го книг.

■ Да, о́чень мно́го. Но здесь мно́го интере́сных ре́дких книг.

○ Све́та, смотри́те, Набо́ков. У вас есть рома́ны Набо́кова?

■ Нет, у меня́ нет рома́нов Набо́кова. Я не о́чень люблю́ писа́телей двадца́того ве́ка. Де́вушка, у вас есть пи́сьма Ле́рмонтова?

▲ Нет, отде́льно пи́сем Ле́рмонтова нет, но есть по́лное собра́ние сочине́ний.

■ Покажи́те его́, пожа́луйста. Ско́лько оно́ сто́ит?

▲ Три́ста рубле́й.

■ А есть подеше́вле?

▲ Есть ещё вот э́то собра́ние, но оно́ непо́лное.

■ А ско́лько э́то сто́ит?

▲ Сто во́семьдесят рубле́й.

■ Хорошо́, я его́ возьму́.

VOCABULARY	
ре́дкий	rare
писа́тель (*m*)	writer
двадца́тый век	twentieth century
де́вушка	*way of addressing a young woman*
письмо́	letter
отде́льно	separately
по́лный	complete, full
собра́ние	collection
по́лное собра́ние сочине́ний	complete works
покажи́те	show me
ско́лько сто́ит ...?	how much is the ...?
три́ста	300
подеше́вле	(something) cheaper
сто во́семьдсят	180

✓ The genitive plural of nouns

Masculine nouns ending in

consonant	add -ов	вокза́лов, городо́в, домо́в
-ь	replace with -ей	рубле́й, гост**е́й**, писа́тел**ей**

Feminine nouns ending in

-a	drop the -a	виз, у́лиц, гости́ниц
-ь	replace with -ей	площад**е́й**, двер**е́й**
-ия	replace with -ий	револю́ц**ий**, ста́нц**ий**

Neuter nouns ending in

-o	drop the -o	слов, вин, пив
-ие	replace with -ий	свида́н**ий**

An extra vowel (-o- or -e-) may appear in forms which lose their ending:

окно́ – о́к<u>о</u>н, письмо́ – пи́с<u>е</u>м, буты́лка – буты́л<u>о</u>к

✓ Animate nouns in the accusative plural

The accusative plural of animate nouns of all genders is the same as the genitive plural.

Я не люблю́ **писа́телей** двадца́того ве́ка. I don't like twentieth-century writers.

✓ нет + the genitive ('there is no …', 'there are no …')

The negative of **есть** ('there is') is **нет**, followed by the genitive.

Нет молока́. There is no milk.
У меня́ **нет рома́нов** Набо́кова. I don't have Nabokov's novels.
Есть Глеб? **Его́ нет.** Is Gleb in? No, he isn't in.

ACTIVITY 3

Supply the genitive plural (or animate accusative plural) as appropriate.

1 У нас нет _____ . (кни́га)
2 О́коло метро́ нет _____ . (кио́ск)
3 Нет _____ . (гости́ница)
4 У меня́ нет _____ Че́хова. (письмо́)
5 Мы не лю́бим _____ . (гость)

🎧 Now do activities 4 and 5 on the recording.

Числа

🎧 **ACTIVITY 6** is on the recording.

ACTIVITY 7

Complete the following price list with the information from the dialogue.

bananas: _____ roubles per kilogram
apples: _____ roubles per kilogram
oranges: _____ roubles per kilogram
red cherries: _____ roubles per kilogram

DIALOGUE 2

○ Де́вушка, скажи́те, пожа́луйста, ско́лько сто́ят гре́йпфруты?

■ Гре́йпфруты сто́ят три́дцать рубле́й за килогра́мм.

○ А бана́ны?

■ Бана́ны по два́дцать два рубля́.

○ Ой, э́то о́чень до́рого. А почём я́блоки?

■ По три́дцать пять.

○ А апельси́ны ско́лько сто́ят?

■ Апельси́ны сто́ят два́дцать оди́н рубль за кило́. О́чень дёшево.

○ А ви́шня?

■ Э́то не ви́шня, а чере́шня, по два́дцать во́семь рубле́й.

○ Ну, да́йте, пожа́луйста, оди́н гре́йпфрут, два апельси́на и пять я́блок.

VOCABULARY	
гре́йпфрут	grapefruit
килогра́мм	kilogram
кило́ [n*]	kilogram
бана́н	banana
до́рого	expensive
почём	how much? [informal]
я́блоко (pl. я́блоки)	apple
по (+ acc.)	at ('a certain price')
апельси́н	orange
дёшево	cheap
ви́шня	black cherry
чере́шня	red cherry

✓ Numbers

1 оди́н	11 оди́ннадцать	21 два́дцать оди́н	100	сто
2 два	12 двена́дцать	22 два́дцать два	200	две́сти
3 три	13 трина́дцать	23 два́дцать три	300	три́ста
4 четы́ре	14 четы́рнадцать	30 три́дцать	400	четы́реста
5 пять	15 пятна́дцать	40 со́рок	500	пятьсо́т
6 шесть	16 шестна́дцать	50 пятьдеся́т	600	шестьсо́т
7 семь	17 семна́дцать	60 шестьдеся́т	700	семьсо́т
8 во́семь	18 восемна́дцать	70 се́мьдесят	800	восемьсо́т
9 де́вять	19 девятна́дцать	80 во́семьдесят	900	девятьсо́т
10 де́сять	20 два́дцать	90 девяно́сто	1,000	ты́сяча

'zero' is **ноль.**

оди́н ('one') has different forms according to the gender of the following noun: **оди́н магази́н** (*m*), **одна́ газе́та** (*f*), **одно́ окно́** (*n*).
два ('two') has two different forms: **два** (*m/n*), **две** (*f*).
ты́сяча ('thousand') is a regular feminine noun.

✓ The case of nouns after numbers

After **оди́н/одна́/одно́** and compound numbers ending in
оди́н/одна́/одно́ (e.g. 21, 31, 101), nouns are in the *singular*:
    два́дцать одна́ **копе́йка** ('21 kopecks [hundredth part of a rouble]'),
    три́дцать одна́ **откры́тка** ('31 postcards')

After the numbers **два/две, три,** and **четы́ре** ('two', 'three', and 'four'),
nouns go into the *genitive singular*:
    два магази́на ('2 shops'), **четы́ре копе́йки** ('4 kopeks')

After compound numbers ending in **два/две, три,** and **четы́ре**
(e.g. 22–24, 32–34, 102–104), nouns also go into the *genitive singular*:
    два́дцать два магази́на ('22 shops'), **сто четы́ре рубля́** ('104 roubles')

After all other numbers, nouns go into the *genitive plural*:
    пять магази́нов ('5 shops'), **оди́ннадцать копе́ек** ('11 kopeks'),
    сто пять рубле́й ('105 roubles')

ACTIVITY 8

Match the following words and numbers.

6	пять	16	шестьсо́т шесть
40	шесть	15	четы́рнадцать
76	шестьдеся́т семь	606	шестна́дцать
4	пятна́дцать	14	со́рок
5	четы́ре	67	се́мьдесят шесть

🎧 Now do activities 9 and 10 on the recording.

At the post office

На по́чте

ACTIVITY 11 is on the recording.

ACTIVITY 12

Listen to the dialogue and fill in the prices in the table below.

Airmail letter to England:
Postcard to America:
Postcard to Canada:
Postcard to Armenia:

DIALOGUE 3

○ Молодо́й челове́к, где мо́жно купи́ть ма́рки?

■ Пе́рвое и второ́е окно́.

...

○ Скажи́те, пожа́луйста, ско́лько сто́ит ма́рка на письмо́ в А́нглию?

▲ Авиапо́чтой – во́семь рубле́й.

○ Да́йте, пожа́луйста, одну́ ма́рку по во́семь рубле́й и пять ма́рок на э́ти откры́тки.

▲ А куда́ откры́тки?

○ Две откры́тки в Аме́рику, две в Кана́ду, а одна́ в Арме́нию.

▲ В Аме́рику и в Кана́ду – семь рубле́й пятьдеся́т копе́ек, а в Арме́нию – пять рубле́й пятьдеся́т копе́ек. Всего́ – со́рок три рубля́ пятьдеся́т копе́ек.

○ Вот, пожа́луйста, пятьдеся́т рубле́й.

VOCABULARY

молодо́й челове́к	*way of addressing a young man*
купи́ть II	to buy
ма́рка (*gen. pl.* **ма́рок**)	stamp
пе́рвый	first
второ́й	second
А́нглия	England
авиапо́чтой	by airmail
куда́?	where (to)?
Аме́рика	America
Кана́да	Canada
Арме́ния	Armenia
всего́	altogether, that makes

LANGUAGE BUILDING

✓ хотéть ('to want') – irregular verb

The verb **хотéть** is irregular.

я **хочý**	мы **хоти́м**
ты **хо́чешь**	вы **хоти́те**
он, она́, оно́ **хо́чет**	они́ **хотя́т**

Ма́ма **хо́чет** стака́н молока́. Mummy wants a glass of milk.
Мы **хоти́м** бана́ны. We want bananas.
Они́ **хотя́т** жить в Чика́го. They want to live in Chicago.

✓ The prepositions в and на + the accusative

The prepositions **в** 'in', 'into' and **на** 'on', 'onto' are used with a noun in the accusative to express movement, in answer to the question **куда́** 'where to?'. Note that some nouns idiomatically take **на**, rather than **в**.

Куда́ ты идёшь? **В** апте́ку. Where are you going? To the chemist's.
Куда́ он е́дет? **В** Кана́ду. Where is he going? To Canada.
За́втра я е́ду **в** Москву́. I'm going to Moscow tomorrow.
Он идёт **на** вокза́л. He's walking to the station.
Я иду́ **на** по́чту. I'm going to the post-office.
Письмо́ **в** А́нглию. A letter to England.

ACTIVITY 13

Complete the sentences with the correct form of the irregular verb **хотéть**.

1 Ле́ночка _____ моро́женое.
2 Ма́ма и ба́бушка не _____ моро́женое.
3 Ты _____ ко́фе?
4 Вы _____ идти́ пешко́м?
5 Мы _____ чита́ть сти́хи Пу́шкина.
6 Я _____ чита́ть Турге́нева.

ACTIVITY 14

Complete 1–5 with the accusative case of the nouns.

1 Две откры́тки в _____ . (Кана́да)
2 Письмо́ в _____ . (Аме́рика)
3 За́втра он е́дет в _____ . (А́нглия)
4 Я е́ду в _____ . (Москва́)
5 Мы идём на _____ . (вокза́л)

Now do activities 15 and 16 on the recording.

(4.4) Exchange rates

Ку́рсы обме́на

ACTIVITY 17

Using the exchange rates below, find the currencies which have the following purchase rate.

Currency   *Purchase rate*

_____ пятьдеся́т три рубля́ пятьдеся́т шесть копе́ек

_____ со́рок два рубля́ шестьдеся́т де́вять копе́ек

_____ два́дцать пять рубле́й три́дцать пять копе́ек

_____ девятна́дцать рубле́й девяно́сто три копе́йки

_____ три́дцать шесть рубле́й девяно́сто одна́ копе́йка

_____ четы́рнадцать рубле́й шестна́дцать копе́ек

Обме́нный пункт «Золото́й петушо́к»
Ку́рсы обме́на нали́чной валю́ты

	Валю́та	Поку́пка	Прода́жа
Австрали́йский до́ллар		16,74	17,01
Австри́йский ши́ллинг	(за 10)	19,93	20,25
Англи́йский фунт		42,69	43,36
Белору́сский рубль	(за 1.000)	29,39	29,86
Бельги́йский франк	(за 100)	67,97	69,04
Голла́ндский гу́льден		12,44	12,64
Гре́ческая дра́хма	(за 1.000)	83,12	84,43
Да́тская кро́на	(за 10)	36,91	37,49
До́ллар США		25,35	25,75
Е́вро		27,42	27,85
Испа́нская песе́та	(за 100)	16,48	16,74
Италья́нская ли́ра	(за 1.000)	14,16	14,38
Каза́хский те́нге	(за 100)	18,27	18,56
Кана́дский до́ллар		17,44	17,72
Неме́цкая ма́рка		14,02	14,24
Норве́жская кро́на	(за 10)	33,16	33,68
Португа́льское эску́до	(за 100)	13,68	13,89
Туре́цкая ли́ра	(за 1.000.000)	53,94	54,79
Украи́нская гри́вна	(за 10)	53,56	54,41
Фи́нская ма́рка	(за 10)	46,11	46,84
Францу́зский франк	(за 10)	41,80	42,46
Шве́дская кро́на	(за 10)	31,56	32,06
Швейца́рский франк		17,18	17,45
Япо́нская ие́на	(за 100)	24,43	24,82

обмéнный пункт	exchange office
золотóй	golden
петушóк	cockerel
курс	(exchange) rate
обмéн	exchange
налúчный	cash [*adjective*]
валю́та	(hard) currency
покýпка	purchase ['we buy at']
продáжа	sale ['we sell at']
США	USA
éвро	Euro

Note that in Russian numbers a decimal point is used
(1.000.000) where English uses a comma (1,000,000), and a
comma is used (19,93) where English uses a decimal point
(19.93).

Country adjectives

австралúйский	Australian	немéцкий	German
англúйский	English	норвéжский	Norwegian
белорýсский	Belorussian	португáльский	Portuguese
бельгúйский	Belgian	турéцкий	Turkish
голлáндский	Dutch	украúнский	Ukrainian
грéческий	Greek	фúнский	Finnish
дáтский	Danish	францýзский	French
испáнский	Spanish	швéдский	Swedish
италья́нский	Italian	швейцáрский	Swiss
казáхский	Kazakh	япóнский	Japanese
канáдский	Canadian		

The feminine and neuter forms of adjectives are described in
Unit 6, page 79.

ACTIVITY 18

Look at the exchange rates above again and read the sale rates
(**продáжа**) aloud, adding the correct forms of the words **рубль**
(genitive singular **рубля́**, genitive plural **рублéй**) and **копéйка**
(genitive singular **копéйки**, genitive plural **копéек**).

Example: Австралúйскии дóллар – семнáдцать рублéй однá
копéйка

🔊 Мари́я Ива́новна выбира́ет пода́рок
Mariya Ivanovna chooses a present

At last Mariya Ivanovna has found the shop «Сувени́ры».
Now she's trying to choose a present which Evgeniya
Pavlovna will like and which is within her budget.

VOCABULARY

ча́йник	tea-pot
сли́шком	too
тако́й	this sort of
вот тако́й	one like this
краси́вый	beautiful
выбира́ть Ia	to choose
пода́рок	present
ей испо́лнится	
шестьдеся́т пять лет	she is turning sixty-five
посу́да	crockery
поня́тно	I understand
тогда́	then
ча́шка	cup
фарфо́р	china
с блю́дцем/-цами	with saucer(s)
ча́йный серви́з	tea-set
ла́дно	all right, very well
вам заверну́ть?	shall I wrap it for you?

ACTIVITY 19

Listen to the story and fill in the prices of the various items
Mariya Ivanovna asks about.

first teapot	_____
second teapot	_____
third teapot	_____
china cup and saucer	_____
tea-service	_____

ACTIVITY 20

Listen to the story again and decide who's speaking: Mariya Ivanovna or the shop assistant?

1 Ско́лько он сто́ит?
2 Вам заверну́ть?
3 Тогда́, мо́жет быть, э́ти ча́шки из фарфо́ра?
4 Я выбира́ю пода́рок для ма́мы.
5 Он сто́ит две́сти пятьдеся́т четы́ре рубля́.
6 У вас есть подеше́вле?

STORY TRANSCRIPT

Mariya Ivanovna	Де́вушка, покажи́те, пожа́луйста, э́тот ча́йник.
Shop assistant	Пожа́луйста.
Mariya Ivanovna	Ско́лько он сто́ит?
Shop assistant	Три́ста три́дцать оди́н рубль.
Mariya Ivanovna	За ча́йник? Э́то сли́шком до́рого. У вас есть подеше́вле?
Shop assistant	Есть вот тако́й ча́йник за сто два́дцать три рубля́, а есть ещё за шестьдеся́т пять рубле́й.
Mariya Ivanovna	Нет, они́ не о́чень краси́вые. Я выбира́ю пода́рок для ма́мы. Ей испо́лнится шестьдеся́т пять лет. Она́ о́чень лю́бит посу́ду.
Shop assistant	А, поня́тно. Тогда́, мо́жет быть, э́ти ча́шки из фарфо́ра?
Mariya Ivanovna	Да, они́ о́чень краси́вые! Ско́лько они́ сто́ят?
Shop assistant	Одна́ ча́шка с блю́дцем сто́ит два́дцать пять рубле́й. Ещё есть вот тако́й ча́йный серви́з – ча́йник и шесть ча́шек с блю́дцами. Он сто́ит две́сти пятьдеся́т четы́ре рубля́.
Mariya Ivanovna	Э́то о́чень до́рого, но о́чень краси́во. Ла́дно, я возьму́ э́тот серви́з.
Shop assistant	Вам заверну́ть?
Mariya Ivanovna	Да, пожа́луйста.

Test

Now it's time to test your progress in Unit 4.

1 Match 1–8 with the correct English version from a–h.

1	у меня́ нет молока́	a	would you like me to wrap it for you?
2	вам заверну́ть?	b	22 roubles a kilo
3	её нет	c	have you got anything cheaper?
4	у вас есть подеше́вле?	d	show me the cup, please
5	два́дцать два рубля́ за кило́	e	she's not in
6	где мо́жно купи́ть ма́рки?	f	he's going to the station
7	он идёт на вокза́л	g	where can I buy stamps?
8	покажи́те, пожа́луйста, ча́шку	h	I have no milk

8

2 Match the following words and numbers.

1	две́сти три	a	93
2	девяно́сто три	b	39
3	ты́сяча девятна́дцать	c	1.019
4	три́дцать де́вять	d	930
5	ты́сяча девяно́сто де́вять	e	203
6	девятьсо́т три́дцать	f	1.099

6

3 Complete the sentences with the genitive plural (or animate accusative plural) of the nouns in brackets, as appropriate.

1 Я не люблю́ _____ . (гость)
2 У них нет _____ . (ви́за)
3 Пять _____ . (апте́ка)
4 Шесть _____ вина́. (буты́лка)
5 Нет _____ Че́хова. (письмо́)
6 Во́семь _____ . (дом)

6

4 Match the sentences 1–4 with responses a–d.

1 Ско́лько э́то сто́ит? a Есть ещё вот э́то собра́ние.
2 Есть Оле́г? b 180 рубле́й.
3 А есть подеше́вле? c Нет, вообще́ нет гости́ниц.
4 Есть гости́ница? d Нет, его́ нет.

4

5 Supply the appropriate form of the verb **хоте́ть**.

1 Светла́на _____ купи́ть пи́сьма Пу́шкина.
2 Я _____ де́сять ма́рок по во́семь рубле́й.
3 Вы _____ ма́рки на откры́тки и́ли на пи́сьма?
4 Она́ не _____ ча́йник за три́ста три́дцать оди́н рубль.
5 Мы _____ бана́ны.
6 Ты _____ сто рубле́й?
7 Глеб не _____ жить у бра́та.
8 Ба́бушки не _____ слу́шать Шостако́вича.
9 Они́ _____ игра́ть в волейбо́л.

9

6 Complete the sentences with the correct form of the nouns, stating what case, and singular or plural.

1 Оди́н _____ (рубль). Case: _____
2 Три́дцать одна́ _____ (копе́йка). Case: _____
3 Три _____ (апельси́н). Case: _____
4 Со́рок два _____ (рубль). Case: _____
5 Пять _____ (магази́н). Case: _____
6 Два́дцать семь _____ (рубль). Case: _____

6

7 How would you do the following in Russian?
   (2 points if correct, 1 point if only one error)

1 Ask to be shown the teapot.
2 Ask how much it costs.
3 Say it's very expensive.
4 Ask where you can buy post-cards.
5 Ask how much a stamp for a letter to America costs.
6 Ask for one ten-rouble stamp.

12

TOTAL SCORE **51**

If you scored less than 41, re-read the Language Building sections before completing the Summary on page 60.

Summary 4

 Now try this final test summarizing the main points covered in this unit. You can check your answers on the recording.

How would you:

1 attract the attention of a female shop-assistant? of a young man?
2 ask to be shown a teapot? a book?
3 ask how much something costs?
4 ask if there's anything cheaper?
5 say one shop? two shops? five shops?
6 say twenty-one roubles? twenty-two roubles? twenty-five roubles?
7 ask how much a stamp costs for a letter to England?
8 ask for a stamp for a postcard to America?

REVISION

Apart from listening to the numbers and writing them down, there are many other ways in which you can increase your familiarity with them. Count out loud in time with your steps as you walk around the house, climb the stairs, or exercise. Read out prices, telephone numbers, house numbers, and page numbers in Russian. Think of your age in Russian and the ages of your family. Count your money in Russian. Count sheep in Russian to help you fall asleep at night.

There are also different ways of counting. Count in two's, count the tens, count the hundreds. Count down from ten, from fifty, from a hundred. Exercises of this sort — and you can probably think of many more — will soon result in you being able to understand and produce Russian numbers without effort.

Time
Врéмя

OBJECTIVES

In this unit you'll learn how to:

✓ ask and tell the time

✓ ask about train times

✓ talk about opening and closing times

✓ refer to the days of the week

And cover the following grammar and language:

✓ the ordinal numbers 1st to 12th

✓ the genitive of ordinal numbers

✓ **в** in time expressions

✓ reflexive verbs

✓ **с ... до ...** in time expressions

LEARNING RUSSIAN 5

Increase your exposure to the Russian language as much as you can. This can be done in various ways – by watching subtitled Russian films, listening to Russian radio broadcasts, reading dual-language texts, listening to Russian opera. It is not so important at this stage that you understand everything you hear or read – simply increasing the number of different contexts in which you hear Russian or see it written down will improve your familiarity with the language.

Listen repeatedly to the recordings that accompany this book. This is worth doing even when you are not able to give them your full attention – as you travel to work, do the housework, have breakfast, or even fall asleep at night. This will reinforce your knowledge of the words and grammar you have studied, and attune you to the sounds of the language.

Now start the recording for Unit 5.

Кото́рый час?

🔊 **ACTIVITY 1** is on the recording.

ACTIVITY 2

Write down the time given by Kolya in each of the locations mentioned.

1 In the hotel foyer   _____
2 In the café   _____
3 On the street   _____
4 In the shop   _____
5 In the theatre bar   _____
6 On the street again   _____

DIALOGUE 1

○ Ко́ля, кото́рый час?
■ Де́вять часо́в.
…
○ Ко́ленька, кото́рый час?
■ Де́сять мину́т двена́дцатого.
…
○ Ко́ля, дорого́й, ско́лько вре́мени?
■ Почти́ два часа́.
…
○ Ко́ленька, ми́лый, кото́рый час?
■ Два́дцать мину́т пя́того.
…
○ Ко́ля, дорого́й, ско́лько сейча́с вре́мени?
■ Сейча́с полови́на восьмо́го.
…
○ Ма́ма, уже́ оди́ннадцатый час – пойдём домо́й!
■ Но Ко́ля, ми́ленький, ещё ра́но! Пойдём в рестора́н!

VOCABULARY	
ми́лый	dear
ми́ленький	dear, darling [*diminutive of* ми́лый]
почти́	almost
сейча́с	now
пойдём	let's go
домо́й	home [*adverb*]
ра́но	early

✅ Asking the time

There are two ways of asking the time. Both are in common use.

Кото́рый час? What's the time?
Ско́лько (сейча́с) вре́мени? What's the time?

✅ On the hour

час means 'hour' or 'one o'clock'. After a number, it goes into the genitive, singular or plural as appropriate (see page 51).

Час. One o'clock.
Два часа́, три часа́, четы́ре часа́. Two, three, four o'clock.
Пять часо́в, шесть часо́в … двена́дцать часо́в. Five, six … twelve o'clock.

✅ The ordinal numbers 1st to 12th

The hour from twelve to one is referred to as 'the first hour', the hour from one to two as 'the second hour', and so on.

	nom.	*gen.*	*Indicates hour*
first	пе́рвый	пе́рвого	from 12 to 1
second	второ́й	второ́го	from 1 to 2
third	тре́тий	тре́тьего	from 2 to 3
fourth	четвёртый	четвёртого	from 3 to 4
fifth	пя́тый	пя́того	from 4 to 5
sixth	шесто́й	шесто́го	from 5 to 6
seventh	седьмо́й	седьмо́го	from 6 to 7
eighth	восьмо́й	восьмо́го	from 7 to 8
ninth	девя́тый	девя́того	from 8 to 9
tenth	деся́тый	деся́того	from 9 to 10
eleventh	оди́ннадцатый	оди́ннадцатого	from 10 to 11
twelth	двена́дцатый	двена́дцатого	from 11 to 12

✅ From the hour to half past

'Five past twelve' is translated as 'five minutes of the first'; 'ten past twelve' as 'ten minutes of the first'; and so on up to half past the hour. Note **мину́та** ('minute') (genitive singular **мину́ты**, genitive plural **мину́т**), **че́тверть**; (f) ('a quarter') (genitive singular **че́тверти**), and **полови́на** ('half'), often replaced colloquially by **пол-**.

Пять мину́т пе́рвого. Five past twelve
Де́сять мину́т тре́тьего. Ten past two
Пятна́дцать мину́т пя́того or **че́тверть пя́того.** A quarter past four.
Два́дцать мину́т шесто́го. Twenty past five.
Два́дцать пять мину́т седьмо́го. Twenty-five past six.
Полови́на седьмо́го or **пол-седьмо́го.** Half past six.

🔊 Now do activities 3 and 4 on the recording.

5.2 At the station

На вокза́ле

🎧 **ACTIVITY 5** is on the recording.

ACTIVITY 6

Fill in the gaps in the following notes.

Trains to Kazan

day-train: departs _____ arrives _____
night-train: departs _____ arrives _____
price: _____

DIALOGUE 2

○ Скажи́те, пожа́луйста, во ско́лько отхо́дит по́езд в Каза́нь?

■ Есть по́езд в де́вять часо́в два́дцать мину́т. Он прибыва́ет в Каза́нь в семна́дцать часо́в три мину́ты. А есть вече́рний – отхо́дит в два́дцать два часа́ со́рок пять мину́т. Он прибыва́ет в Каза́нь в оди́ннадцать часо́в со́рок пять мину́т.

○ Да́йте, пожа́луйста, оди́н биле́т на два́дцать мину́т деся́того.

■ А когда́ вы е́дете? Сего́дня?

○ Нет, во вто́рник. Ско́лько сто́ит биле́т?

■ Сто шестьдеся́т два рубля́.

○ Пожа́луйста, две́сти рубле́й.

■ Вот ваш биле́т и сда́ча – три́дцать во́семь рубле́й.

○ Спаси́бо.

■ Пожа́луйста.

VOCABULARY	
во ско́лько	at what time?
отходи́ть II	to leave [*of trains*]
по́езд	train
прибыва́ть (Ia) **в** (+ *acc.*)	to arrive in
вече́рний	evening, night [*adjective*]
биле́т	ticket
биле́т на (+ *acc.*)	a ticket for
сда́ча	change

⊘ More on time: Between half past and the hour

Between half past and the hour, Russian 'looks back' from the approaching hour. 'Five to one' is translated as 'without five, one'; 'twenty to two' as 'without twenty, two', and so on. Note that the number after the preposition **без** is in the genitive.

Без пяти́ час. Five to one.
Без десяти́ семь. Ten to seven.
Без пятна́дцати or **без че́тверти де́сять.** A quarter to ten.
Без двадцати́ во́семь. Twenty to eight.
Без двадцати́ пяти́ двена́дцать. Twenty-five to twelve.

⊘ в in time expressions

The preposition **в** + the accusative (same form as the nominative) is used to say 'at' a certain time. **в** is omitted, however, in times beginning with **без**, i.e. between half past and the hour. Exceptionally, 'on the half-hour' is **в полови́не.**

Когда́ вы позвони́те? **В три часа́.** When will you ring? At 3 o'clock.
По́езд отхо́дит **в де́вять три́дцать.** The train leaves at 9.30.
В полови́не девя́того. At half past eight.
Мы бу́дем у вас **без десяти́ четы́ре.** We will be at your place at ten to four.

⊘ The twenty-four hour clock

The twenty-four hour clock is in common use in Russia, especially – but not exclusively – in official contexts. The words **час** and **мину́та** may be used.

двена́дцать (часо́в) три́дцать (мину́т)	12.30
пятна́дцать со́рок пять	15.45
девятна́дцать часо́в	19.00

⊘ The days of the week

The days of the week do not take a capital letter in Russian. **в** + the accusative is used to say 'on' a particular day.

понеде́льник	Monday	в понеде́льник	on Monday
вто́рник	Tuesday	во вто́рник	on Tuesday
среда́	Wednesday	в сре́ду	on Wednesday
четве́рг	Thursday	в четве́рг	on Thursday
пя́тница	Friday	в пя́тницу	on Friday
суббо́та	Saturday	в суббо́ту	on Saturday
воскресе́нье	Sunday	в воскресе́нье	on Sunday

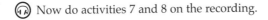 Now do activities 7 and 8 on the recording.

У кассы

🎧 **ACTIVITY 9** is on the recording.

ACTIVITY 10

1 What are the box-office opening hours?
2 What is the price of a stalls ticket?
3 What time does the performance start?

DIALOGUE 3

○ Алло́. Слу́шаю.

■ Здра́вствуйте. Скажи́те, пожа́луйста, во ско́лько открыва́ется ка́сса?

○ Ка́сса рабо́тает со вто́рника до суббо́ты с десяти́ утра́ до восемна́дцати, а в воскресе́нье – с двена́дцати до восемна́дцати.

■ А в понеде́льник?

○ В понеде́льник ка́сса закры́та.

■ Спаси́бо.

    …

■ Скажи́те, пожа́луйста, есть биле́ты на «Пи́ковую да́му»?

○ Есть.

■ Да́йте, пожа́луйста, два биле́та в парте́р. А ско́лько сто́ят биле́ты?

○ Две́сти рубле́й за оди́н биле́т.

■ Ну ла́дно. Да́йте, пожа́луйста, два биле́та. Во ско́лько начина́ется спекта́кль?

○ В девятна́дцать часо́в.

■ Спаси́бо. Я о́чень люблю́ бале́т.

○ Э́то не бале́т, а о́пера.

■ Зна́ю-зна́ю. О́перу я то́же люблю́.

VOCABULARY

слу́шаю	said when answering the telephone
теа́тр	theatre
закры́та	shut, closed
«Пи́ковая да́ма»	The Queen of Spades [an opera]
в парте́р	in the stalls
спекта́кль (m)	performance, show

✓ Reflexive verbs

Reflexive verbs have the normal endings for verbs, but have an additional 'reflexive' ending: **-ся** after a final consonant, and **-сь** after a final vowel. Here are **надеяться** Ia ('to hope'), stem **наде-** and **волноваться** Ia ('to worry'), stem **волну-**.

я **надеюсь**	I hope	я **волнуюсь**	I worry
ты **надеешься**	you hope	ты **волнуешься**	you worry
он **надеется**	he hopes	он **волнуется**	he worries
мы **надеемся**	we hope	мы **волнуемся**	we worry
вы **надеетесь**	you hope	вы **волнуетесь**	you worry
они **надеются**	they hope	они **волнуются**	they worry

Other useful reflexive verbs: **начинаться** ('to begin'), **заканчиваться** ('to end'), **длиться** ('to last, continue'), **открываться** ('to open'), **закрываться** ('to close').

Я **надеюсь**, что это не Вагнер. I hope it's not Wagner.
Не **волнуйтесь**! Don't worry!
Во сколько **открывается** касса? What time does the box-office open?
Когда **начинается** спектакль? What time does the show begin?
Сколько времени **длится** фильм? How long does the film last?

✓ с ... до ... + the genitive to express times 'from ... to ...'

с десяти до семнадцати	from 10 to 5
с понедельника до пятницы	from Monday to Friday

✓ a.m. and p.m.

To indicate a.m. or p.m., the genitive of the words for 'morning', 'day', 'evening', and 'night' are added to the time as appropriate.

утра – from 4 a.m. to 11 a.m.	**вечера** – from 6 p.m. to 10 p.m.
дня – from 12 noon to 5 p.m.	**ночи** – from 10 midnight to 3 a.m.

десять утра	10 a.m	**двенадцать часов ночи** 12 midnight

ACTIVITY 11

Match the following phrases with possible responses.

1 Во сколько открывается касса?
2 Когда он работает?
3 Сколько времени длится фильм?
4 Когда касса закрыта?
5 Я надеюсь, что это не Бах.

a Она закрыта в понедельник.
b Фильм длится два часа.
c Не волнуйтесь, это Моцарт.
d Она открывается в десять утра.
e С понедельника до пятницы.

🎧 Now do activities 12 and 13 on the recording.

Досу́г

ACTIVITY 14

During your trip to Moscow you're particularly keen to go to an opera or a ballet at the Bolshoi, and to visit the Kremlin. The following cultural listings are taken from a free newspaper aimed at visitors to Moscow. Read the information and note down the days and times when this will be possible.

Bolshoi: _____

Kremlin: _____

КУЛЬТУ́РА

Конце́рты

V Моско́вский фестива́ль «Джаз-Ра́лли». Моско́вская консервато́рия, Большо́й зал. Четве́рг – воскресе́нье, в девятна́дцать часо́в. Ка́сса откры́та с десяти́ до шестна́дцати с понеде́льника до суббо́ты.

О́пера

«Пи́ковая да́ма». Большо́й теа́тр. Вто́рник и четве́рг в девятна́дцать часо́в три́дцать мину́т. «Русла́н и Людми́ла». Среда́, в девятна́дцать часо́в. «Князь И́горь». Суббо́та, в девятна́дцать часо́в. Ка́сса откры́та со вто́рника до суббо́ты с десяти́ утра́ до восемна́дцати, в воскресе́нье с двена́дцати до восемна́дцати.

Бале́т

«Спарта́к». Гости́ница «Ко́смос», Конце́ртный зал. Среда́, в девятна́дцать часо́в три́дцать мину́т. «Лебеди́ное о́зеро». Дворе́ц съе́здов. Воскресе́нье, в пятна́дцать часо́в.

Мю́зиклы

«Метро́». Теа́тр опере́тты. Среда́ – воскресе́нье, в два́дцать часо́в.

Ку́кольный теа́тр

«Петру́шка». Центра́льный ку́кольный теа́тр. Среда́ – воскресе́нье, в трина́дцать и девятна́дцать часо́в.

Музе́и

Кремль. С десяти́ до семна́дцати. В четве́рг Кремль закры́т. Музе́й древнеру́сской культу́ры и́мени Андре́я Рублёва. С четверга́ до воскресе́нья с оди́ннадцати до семна́дцати часо́в.

Галере́и

Центра́льный дом худо́жника. Галере́я откры́та со вто́рника до воскресе́нья с оди́ннадцати до двадцати́ часо́в. Третьяко́вская галере́я – закры́та.

Цирк

Но́вый цирк. Понеде́льник, вто́рник, среда́ и пя́тница – в девятна́дцать часо́в. Суббо́та – в пятна́дцать часо́в. Воскресе́нье – в оди́ннадцать часо́в три́дцать мину́т и в пятна́дцать часо́в.

концéрт	concert
московский	Moscow [adjective]
консерватóрия	conservatoire, musical academy
зал	hall
откры́та	is open
«Князь Игорь»	Prince Igor [an opera]
«Руслáн и Людми́ла»	Ruslan and Ludmilla [an opera]
«Спартáк»	Spartacus [a ballet]
концéртный	concert [adjective]
«Лебеди́ное óзеро»	Swan Lake [a ballet]
Дворéц съéздов	The Palace of Congresses
мю́зикл	musical
оперéтта	operetta
ку́кольный	puppet [adjective]
«Петру́шка»	Petrushka [Russian Punch and Judy show]
центрáльный	central
древнеру́сский	ancient Russian [adjective]
и́мени	named after
галерéя	gallery, balcony
цирк	circus

ACTIVITY 15

Looking at your business schedule, you see that in fact you will probably only have Sunday evening and Monday morning free, until about lunch-time. Make a list of your entertainment and sightseeing possibilities.

Sunday evening:
Monday morning:

5.5 Ла́рины

Пётр и Руста́м выбира́ют пода́рок
Pyotr and Rustam choose a present

Pyotr – Evgeniya and Ivan's younger son – and his flat-mate
Rustam have decided to buy Evgeniya tickets to an opera or a
ballet for her birthday. They are looking through a cultural
listings paper, trying to choose a show they think she will like.

VOCABULARY

петь Ia (пою́)	to sing
ты с ума́ сошёл?	are you crazy?
«Ле́ди Макбе́т	*Lady Macbeth of the Mtsensk*
Мце́нского уе́зда»	*District* [*an opera by Shostakovich*]
компози́тор	composer
«Евге́ний Оне́гин»	*Eugene Onegin* [*an opera*]
замеча́тельный	wonderful
идеа́льно	ideal
бу́дут	there will be
уже́	already
пробле́ма	problem
по́мнить II	to remember

ACTIVITY 16

Listen to the story and decide whether the following
statements are true or false.

1 *The Queen of Spades* is rejected because it is too long.
2 *The Queen of Spades* starts at 7 p.m. and finishes at midnight.
3 Evgeniya Pavlovna likes twentieth-century composers.
4 *Eugene Onegin* starts at 7 p.m. and finishes at 10 p.m.
5 Evgeniya doesn't like opera very much.
6 Rustam thinks they will be able to get tickets for *Swan Lake*
   through a friend.

ACTIVITY 17

What days are the following operas and ballets on?

1 *The Queen of Spades*   _____
2 *Lady Macbeth of the Mtsensk District*   _____
3 *Eugene Onegin*   _____
4 *Spartacus*   _____
5 *Swan Lake*   _____

STORY TRANSCRIPT

Rustam	Пётр, смотри́! В сре́ду бу́дет «Пи́ковая да́ма». Поёт Гали́на Горчако́ва. Я обожа́ю Гали́ну Горчако́ву.
Pyotr	Руста́м, ты с ума́ сошёл? «Пи́ковая да́ма» дли́тся почти́ четы́ре часа́. О́пера начина́ется в семь часо́в, а зака́нчивается о́коло оди́ннадцати ве́чера.
Rustam	А вот в четве́рг бу́дет «Ле́ди Макбе́т Мце́нского уе́зда». Евге́ния Па́вловна лю́бит Шостако́вича?
Pyotr	Нет, не лю́бит. Она́ вообще́ не лю́бит компози́торов двадца́того ве́ка.
Rustam	Тогда́, мо́жет быть, «Евге́ний Оне́гин» в пя́тницу? Поёт Хворосто́вский – замеча́тельный барито́н. Спекта́кль начина́ется в девятна́дцать часо́в, а зака́нчивается в два́дцать два часа́.
Pyotr	Ты зна́ешь, Руста́м, ма́ма не о́чень лю́бит о́перу. Каки́е там бале́ты?
Rustam	«Спарта́к» в четве́рг и «Лебеди́ное о́зеро» в воскресе́нье.
Pyotr	«Лебеди́ное о́зеро» – идеа́льно. Я наде́юсь, что ещё бу́дут биле́ты.
Rustam	Наве́рное, уже́ нет биле́тов. Но э́то не пробле́ма. Ты по́мнишь Арту́ра? Он найдёт для нас биле́ты.

Before completing the test on pages 72–73 revise time expressions and days of the week with the activities below.

ACTIVITY 18

Match the following times.

3.00	два́дцать пять мину́т деся́того
3.05	три часа́
4.15	полови́на девя́того
6.45	без пятна́дцати семь
8.30	че́тверть пя́того
9.25	пять мину́т четвёртого

ACTIVITY 19

Complete each sentence by adding the day of the week in the correct case.

1 В _____ я игра́ю в те́ннис. (Monday)

2 Во _____ я чита́ю Пу́шкина. (Tuesday)

3 В _____ я отдыха́ю. (Wednesday)

4 В _____ я игра́ю в бри́дж. (Thursday)

5 В _____ я чита́ю Турге́нева. (Friday)

6 В _____ я слу́шаю о́перу. (Saturday)

7 В _____ я пью ко́фе и отдыха́ю. (Sunday)

Test

Now it's time to test your progress in Unit 5.

1 Match 1–7 with the correct English version.

1	сколько сейчас времени?	a	here's your change
2	поезд прибывает в три часа	b	the train leaves at three o'clock
3	поезд отходит в три часа	c	the train arrives at three o'clock
4	когда вы едете?	d	the box-office is shut
5	вот ваша сдача	e	what's the time?
6	касса закрыта	f	it starts at three o'clock
7	он начинается в три часа	g	when are you going?

7

2 Match each of the sentences 1–6 with a response from a–f.

1 Который час?
2 Пойдём домой!
3 Во сколько поезд прибывает в Москву?
4 Сколько времени длится фильм?
5 Алло, это Третьяковская галерея?
6 Дайте, пожалуйста, один билет.

a В пятнадцать тридцать.
b Да. Слушаю вас.
c Ещё рано! Пойдём в ресторан!
d Половина десятого.
e На какой день?
f Фильм длится почти три часа.

6

3 Give the following times in figures.
1 двадцать минут седьмого _____
2 четверть четвёртого _____
3 десять часов _____
4 без двадцати пяти два _____
5 девятнадцать тридцать _____
6 пятнадцать часов сорок минут _____

6

4 Complete the sentences with a word from the box.

пя́тницы	утра́	до
наде́юсь	дли́тся	понеде́льник
без	волну́йтесь	зака́нчивается

1 Ка́сса откры́та с десяти́ _____ шестна́дцати.
2 Фильм _____ в полови́не деся́того.
3 В _____ ма́ма игра́ет в бадминто́н.
4 Галере́я откры́та с вто́рника до _____ .
5 Я _____, что э́то недалеко́.
6 Спекта́кль начина́ется в де́сять _____ .
7 Бале́т _____ почти́ три часа́.
8 Не _____, он найдёт для вас биле́ты.
9 О́пера зака́нчивается _____ десяти́ де́сять.

9

5 Complete the times with **утра́**, **дня**, **ве́чера**, or **но́чи**.

1 12 midnight – двена́дцать часо́в _____
2 2 p.m. – два часа́ _____
3 7.30 p.m. – семь три́дцать _____
4 10 a.m. – де́сять часо́в _____
5 10 p.m. – де́сять часо́в _____
6 5 a.m. – пять часо́в _____

6

6 How would you do the following in Russian?
  (2 points if correct, 1 point if only one error)

1 Ask what the time is.
2 Say it's eight o'clock in the morning.
3 Say it's half past seven in the evening.
4 Ask what time the train to Kazan leaves?
5 Ask for one ticket for [the] ten o'clock [train].
6 Ask what time the box-office opens.
7 Ask what time the performance starts.
8 Ask how long the opera lasts.

16

TOTAL SCORE **50**

If you scored less than 40, re-read the Language Building
sections before completing the Summary on page 74.

Summary 5

Now try this final test summarizing the main points covered in this unit. You can check your answers on the recording.

How would you:
1 ask what the time is?
2 say it's five o'clock?
3 say it's ten past two?
4 say it's half past ten?
5 say it's twenty to three?
6 say it's ten to four?
7 say 'on Wednesday'?
8 ask what time the train to St Petersburg leaves?
9 ask what time the box-office opens?
10 ask what time the performance finishes?

REVISION

Practise what you have learned by asking yourself the time in Russian at various point during the day. Review your schedule for the day and the week in Russian: what time are you going shopping? what day? what hours do you work? what time is your bus or train? what time does that film you want to see start? Practising like this will keep your new language skills at the front of your mind.

6

Meeting people
Познако́мьтесь!

OBJECTIVES

In this unit you'll learn how to:

- ✓ introduce yourself
- ✓ ask what someone's name is
- ✓ talk to someone in a formal situation
- ✓ act when visiting someone at home
- ✓ accept and decline hospitality

And cover the following grammar and language:

- ✓ Russian patronymics and surnames
- ✓ the nominative of possessives
- ✓ familiar forms of first names
- ✓ the nominative of adjectives
- ✓ genitives in **-y** ('some', 'a bit of')

LEARNING RUSSIAN 6

Although learning a language entails much more than learning a few phrases off by heart, in the heat of the moment – when first meeting people, in a new situation or environment – it is often such stock phrases that come to our rescue.

Practise phrases such as 'pleased to meet you', 'have a seat', 'would you like some tea?', 'of course', 'I'd love to', 'yes, please', 'no, thank you', until you can produce them without effort. In informal social situations these phrases are essential. In formal situations, too, even though you might not yet be able to conduct your business entirely in Russian, your efforts at politeness are certain to be appreciated.

Now start the recording for Unit 6.

6.1 Introductions

Как вас зовут?

ACTIVITY 1 is on the recording.

ACTIVITY 2

Correct the statements which are false.

1 Maxim Shuisky is from the United States of America. T / F
2 He is from Washington, D.C.   T / F
3 He works for the firm *New Electronics*.   T / F
4 He has been studying Russian for a long time.   T / F
5 His family lives in Tomsk.   T / F

DIALOGUE 1

○ Здра́вствуйте. Моя́ фами́лия – Шу́йский. А как вас зову́т?

■ Меня́ зову́т Алексе́й Семёнович Гага́рин. О́чень рад с
   ва́ми познако́миться. Как ва́ше и́мя и о́тчество?

○ Меня́ зову́т Макси́м. О́тчество – Бори́сович, но я обы́чно
   его́ не употребля́ю.

■ А вы отку́да?

○ Я из США, из Нью-Йо́рка. Я рабо́таю на фи́рме «Нью
   Электро́никс». Вот, пожа́луйста, моя́ визи́тная ка́рточка.

■ Спаси́бо. Вы о́чень хорошо́ говори́те по-ру́сски. Давно́
   изуча́ете ру́сский язы́к?

○ Вы зна́ете, моя́ семья́ ру́сская, из То́мска. Но вся семья́ –
   ма́ма, па́па, ба́бушка, де́душка – уже́ давно́ живёт в США,
   в Чика́го.

VOCABULARY	
как вас зову́т?	what is your name?
меня́ зову́т ...	my name is ...
о́чень ра́д(а) с ва́ми познако́миться	pleased to meet you
обы́чно	usually, normally
употребля́ть Ia	to use
отку́да?	from where?
на фи́рме	in the firm
визи́тная ка́рточка	(business) card
давно́	for a long time
семья́	family
па́па	Dad
вся	whole, all

✓ Russian patronymics

Russians have a first name (**и́мя**), a patronymic (**о́тчество**), and a surname (**фами́лия**). The patronymic is formed from the father's name plus the suffix **-ович/-евич** for a son and **-овна/-евна** for a daughter.

Алексе́й Семёнович Гага́рин (father's name: **Семён**)
Ни́на Ива́новна Гага́рина (father's name: **Ива́н**)

The safest way of addressing someone politely is by their first name and patronymic. Note, however, that these days many Russians under about forty do not use their patronymics: **Макси́м Шу́йский, Ни́на Гага́рина.**

✓ Russian surnames

Russian surnames have different forms for male and female family members. If the male surname looks like a noun, **-a** is added to make the female form; if it looks like an adjective, the feminine form of the adjective is used as the female form (see 6.2). A plural form indicates the whole family. Titles such as **господи́н** ('Mr') and **госпожа́** ('Mrs') are not generally used, although they are becoming more common in official style.

Husband: **Алексе́й Семёнович Гага́рин** *Wife*: **Ни́на Ива́новна Гага́рина**
Husband: **Лев Никола́евич Толсто́й** *Wife*: **Со́фья Андре́евна Толста́я**
Whole family: **Ла́рины** ('the Larins') **Толсты́е** ('the Tolstoys')

✓ The nominative of possessives

The words for 'my', 'your', and 'our' are similar to adjectives in Russian – they agree in gender, number, and case with what is possessed.

	m	*f*	*n*	*pl*
my	**мой**	**моя́**	**моё**	**мои́**
your (*sing.*)	**твой**	**твоя́**	**твоё**	**твои́**
our	**наш**	**на́ша**	**на́ше**	**на́ши**
your (*pl., polite*)	**ваш**	**ва́ша**	**ва́ше**	**ва́ши**

мой брат и **твоя́ тётя** my brother and your aunt
На́ше свида́ние сего́дня в три часа́. Our meeting is today at three.
Ва́ши газе́ты здесь. Your newspapers are here.

ACTIVITY 3

Fill the gap with the correct form of the possessives.

1 Вот, пожа́луйста, _____ газе́та. (ваш)
2 Э́то _____ кни́ги. (мой)
3 Когда́ _____ свида́ние? (наш)
4 _____ фами́лия – Ге́ргиев? (твой)
5 Вот _____ визи́тная ка́рточка. (мой)
6 Где _____ сувени́ры? (наш)

🎧 Now do activities 4 and 5 on the recording.

What a lovely restaurant!

Какой красивый ресторан!

🎧 **ACTIVITY 6** is on the recording.

ACTIVITY 7

Fill in the missing information in the following summary.

1 The restaurant serves _____ and _____ cuisine.
2 Entertainment is provided by _____ .
3 The waiter recommends a very good _____ wine
   from _____ .
4 Kolya's mother say the prices are _____ .

DIALOGUE 2

○ Коля, какой красивый ресторан!

■ Красивый, правда? Это мой любимый ресторан.

○ А еда хорошая?

■ Мама, еда здесь замечательная. Венгерская и русская кухня. Очень вкусная.

○ А что это за музыка?

■ Цыганская. Здесь играет цыганский оркестр.

○ Цыганский оркестр!

▲ Пожалуйста, меню и карта вин. У нас очень хорошее венгерское вино, красное. Рекомендую.

○ Колька, но цены здесь такие высокие! Ресторан очень дорогой.

■ Мамочка, не волнуйся. У меня есть деньги.

VOCABULARY

какой	what a … !
любимый	favourite
еда	food
кухня	cuisine
венгерский	Hungarian
вкусный	tasty
что это за (+ *nom.*)	what (sort of …) is that … ?
музыка	music
цыганский	gypsy
карта вин	wine list
рекомендовать Ia	to recommend
цена	price
высокий	high, tall
деньги (*pl.; gen. pl.* **денег**)	money

✅ Familiar forms of first names

Russians often use short or 'familiar' forms of first names. Further suffixes may be added to make diminutive forms, or to indicate affection, annoyance, or reproof, and so on. Some of these suffixes may also be added to other nouns, e.g. **мама**: affectionate **мамочка**.

Николай: **Коля** (short), **Коленька** (affectionate), **Колька** (annoyed)
Елена: **Лена** (short form), **Леночка** (diminutive)

✅ The nominative of adjectives

There are two main types of adjectives in Russian: adjectives with 'hard' endings (the majority) and adjectives with 'soft' endings (a small group).

Most hard adjectives have the following endings:

	m	*f*	*n*	*pl*
'red'	**красный**	**красная**	**красное**	**красные**

красивый ресторан   a beautiful restaurant
хорошая еда   good food

Some hard adjectives have the stressed ending **-ой** in the m sing.

'pale blue'	**голубой**	**голубая**	**голубое**	**голубые**

голубая книга   a pale blue book
молодой студент   a young student

Spelling Rules 1 & 2 (see Grammar Summary, page 221) affect the endings of some forms: e.g. **русский** (*m*), **русские** (*pl*), **хорошее** (*n*).

'Russian'	**русский**	**русская**	**русское**	**русские**

русский язык   the Russian language
хорошие вина   good wines

Soft adjectives have the following endings:

'dark blue'	**синий**	**синяя**	**синее**	**синие**
сегодняшний	today's	**вечерний**	evening
вчерашний	yesterday's	**последний**	last
утренний	morning	**домашний**	home, home-made

вечерний поезд a night train
домашний торт a home-made cake

ACTIVITY 8

1	_____ организация	(большой)
2	_____ автобусы	(новый)
3	_____ сторона	(другой)
4	_____ вино	(венгерский)
5	_____ газета	(сегодняшний)

🔊 Now do activities 9 and 10 on the recording.

6.3 Come in!

Входи́те!

ACTIVITY 11 is on the recording.

ACTIVITY 12

1 How does Svetlana describe the flat?
2 How does Gleb describe the flat?
3 What is wrong with the slippers Svetlana tries to put on?
4 What is wrong with the chair Svetlana tries to sit on?

DIALOGUE 3

○ Све́та, здра́вствуйте!
■ Здра́вствуйте!
○ Входи́те-входи́те! Раздева́йтесь!
■ Спаси́бо.
○ Вот где я живу́. Э́то кварти́ра бра́та – он то́же здесь живёт.
■ Ой, э́то о́чень краси́вая кварти́ра.
○ Она́ о́чень ма́ленькая. Пожа́луйста, наде́ньте та́почки. Нет, не э́ти, э́то его́ та́почки! Вот э́ти для вас.
■ Спаси́бо, извини́те.
○ Вы хоти́те ча́ю?
■ Да, с удово́льствием.
○ И́ли мо́жет быть коньяку́?
■ Нет, спаси́бо. Я не пью конья́к.
○ Све́та, сади́тесь, пожа́луйста. Нет, не там, э́то его́ ме́сто.
■ О, извини́те.
○ А вот и он сам идёт. Познако́мьтесь, пожа́луйста. Све́та, э́то мой брат Бори́с. Бори́с, э́то Светла́на.
■ О́чень ра́да с ва́ми познако́миться.
▲ О́чень прия́тно. Све́та, вы то́же лю́бите футбо́л?

VOCABULARY

раздева́ться Ia	to take one's coat/hat/gloves/scarf off
наде́ньте	put on [imperative]
та́почки	slippers
с удово́льствием	yes, please
сади́тесь!	have a seat!
ме́сто	place, seat
сам	himself
познако́мьтесь, пожа́луйста	said when making introductions
о́чень прия́тно	pleased to meet you

LANGUAGE BUILDING

✓ Indeclinable possessives

The possessives **егó** 'his' or 'its', **её** 'her' or 'its', and **их** 'their' are indeclinable: they do not change form to agree with the noun. Unlike **мой** (**моя́**, **моё**, etc), **твой**, **наш**, and **ваш**, they reflect the gender of the possessor, not the thing possessed.

Э́то **егó та́почки.** Those are his slippers.
её брат her brother
их кварти́ра their flat

✓ -y 'a bit of'

A few masculine nouns have a special genitive form which ends in **-y** or **-ю**, used to express 'some', 'a bit of'. Note the following: **ча́ю** or **ча́йку** ('some tea'), **кофейку́** ('some coffee'), **коньяку́** or **коньячку́** ('some brandy'), **сы́ру** ('some cheese').

Вы хоти́те **ча́ю?** Would you like some tea?
И́ли мо́жет быть **коньяку́**? Or maybe some brandy?

ACTIVITY 13

Complete the sentences with **егó**, **её**, or **их** as appropriate.

1 Э́то _____ ма́ма (his)
2 Э́то _____ брат (his)
3 Э́то _____ стихи́ (her)
4 Э́то _____ окно́ (his)
5 Э́то _____ брат (her)
6 Э́то _____ такси́ (their)

ACTIVITY 14

Which phrase might you hear in each of the situations below?

1 You're about to be introduced to someone's family.
2 You're being offered something to drink.
3 Your host is waiting to take your coat, scarf, etc.
4 You're being shown to a seat.
5 You're being welcomed into the house.

a Сади́тесь, пожа́луйста.
b Раздева́йтесь, пожа́луйста.
c Входи́те!
d Вы хоти́те ча́ю?
e Познако́мьтесь, пожа́луйста.

🎧 Now do activities 15 and 16 on the recording.

(6.4) Family tree

Генеалоги́ческое дре́во

ACTIVITY 17

Look at the Larin family tree and make sure you understand the system of patronymics and different surnames. What are the full names of the members of the family we have already met in the story? Complete the table.

1 _____ _____ _____ (p. 1935)
2 _____ _____ _____ (p. 1963)
3 _____ _____ _____ (p. 1993)
4 _____ _____ _____ (p. 1967)

ACTIVITY 18

Look at the oldest generation — two sets of Lenochka's great-grandparents. What were their fathers' first names? If you need some help, see page 77.

ACTIVITY 19

Look at the first names and patronymics below, then match the children with their fathers. Check your answers on the Larin family tree.

child
Ю́рий Григо́рьевич
Еле́на Миха́йловна
Оле́г Ива́нович
Евге́ния Па́вловна

father
Па́вел Па́влович
Ива́н Григо́рьевич
Григо́рий Влади́мирович
Михаи́л Алексе́евич

CULTURE

Ла́рины

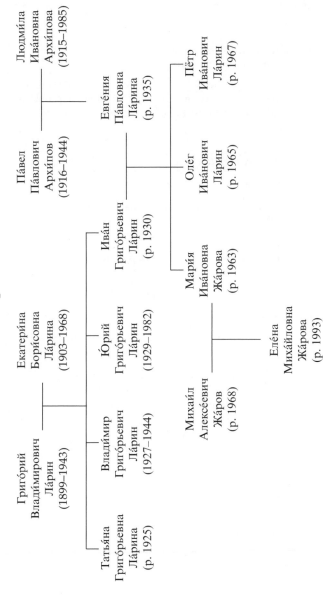

Григо́рий Влади́мирович Ла́рин (1899–1943)

Екатери́на Бори́совна Ла́рина (1903–1968)

Па́вел Па́влович Архи́пов (1916–1944)

Людми́ла Ива́новна Архи́пова (1915–1985)

Евге́ния Па́вловна Ла́рина (р. 1935)

Татья́на Григо́рьевна Ла́рина (р. 1925)

Влади́мир Григо́рьевич Ла́рин (1927–1944)

Ю́рий Григо́рьевич Ла́рин (1929–1982)

Ива́н Григо́рьевич Ла́рин (р. 1930)

Пётр Ива́нович Ла́рин (р. 1967)

Оле́г Ива́нович Ла́рин (р. 1965)

Мари́я Ива́новна Жа́рова (р. 1963)

Михаи́л Алексе́евич Жа́ров (р. 1968)

Еле́на Миха́йловна Жа́рова (р. 1993)

р. [= роди́лся, родила́сь] born

6.5 Ла́рины

Мо́йра идёт в го́сти
Moira comes to visit

Oleg – Ivan and Evgeniya's elder son – teaches Russian as a foreign language. He has formed a friendship with one of his students, Moira, and has invited her to the Larins' flat to meet his family.

VOCABULARY

ко́мната	room
институ́т	institute
ми́лости про́сим!	welcome!
сестра́	sister
вме́сте	together
часть (f)	part
да нет!	no! [emphatic]
отде́льный	separate
страна́	country
не стесня́йтесь!	don't be shy

ACTIVITY 20

Listen to the story and decide whether the following statements are true or false. Correct the statements which are false.

1 The Larins' flat is big – it has four rooms.
2 Mariya and Lenochka don't live in the flat anymore.
3 Moira accepts a cup of tea.
4 Moira accepts some cake.
5 The cake is old – yesterday's.
6 Ivan asks if Scotland is a part of England.

ACTIVITY 21

Listen to the story again and decide who's speaking: Oleg, Moira, Evgeniya, or Ivan?

1 Мо́йра, скажи́те, а вы отку́да?
2 О́чень прия́тно.
3 Ми́лости про́сим!
4 Входи́те, пожа́луйста. Раздева́йтесь!
5 Кака́я больша́я кварти́ра!
6 Шотла́ндия – отде́льная страна́.
7 Вы все вме́сте живёте?
8 Вы хоти́те ча́ю?

ACTIVITY 22

The story contains a number of adjectives. Write out the adjectives used to describe the following nouns.

кварти́ра –	1 _____	2 _____	
торт –	3 _____	4 _____	
страна́ –	5 _____		

STORY TRANSCRIPT

Oleg	Мо́йра, здра́вствуйте!
Moira	Здра́вствуйте, Оле́г.
Oleg	Входи́те, пожа́луйста. Раздева́йтесь!
Moira	Спаси́бо. Кака́я больша́я кварти́ра! Она́ ста́рая?
Oleg	Да, ста́рая и больша́я. Четы́ре ко́мнаты. Познако́мьтесь, пожа́луйста. Ма́ма, э́то Мо́йра, моя́ студе́нтка из институ́та. Мо́йра, э́то моя́ ма́ма, Евге́ния Па́вловна.
Moira	О́чень ра́да с ва́ми познако́миться.
Evgeniya	Ми́лости про́сим!
Oleg	А э́то мой па́па, Ива́н Григо́рьевич.
Moira	О́чень прия́тно.
Ivan	Здра́вствуйте.
Oleg	Здесь ещё живу́т моя́ сестра́ Мари́я и её до́чь Ле́ночка, но их сейча́с нет.
Moira	Вы все вме́сте живёте?
Oleg	Да, коне́чно.
Evgeniya	Мо́йра, сади́тесь, пожа́луйста. Вы хоти́те ча́ю?
Moira	С удово́льствием.
Evgeniya	Мо́йрочка, возьми́те торт.
Moira	Спаси́бо. Ммм, он о́чень вку́сный. Он дома́шний?
Evgeniya	Да, коне́чно, дома́шний.
Ivan	Мо́йра, скажи́те, а вы отку́да?
Moira	Я – шотла́ндка, из Гла́зго.
Ivan	Шотла́ндия – э́то часть А́нглии?
Evgeniya	Да нет, Ива́н. Шотла́ндия – отде́льная страна́.
Ivan	Гм, интере́сно.
Evgeniya	Мо́йрочка, возьми́те ещё торт. Ку́шайте-ку́шайте, не стесня́йтесь!

Test

Now it's time to test your progress in Unit 6.

1 Match the following with their English equivalents.

1 как ва́ше и́мя и о́тчество?	a don't be shy!
2 раздева́йтесь!	b please, have a seat
3 не стесня́йтесь!	c is the food Russian?
4 э́то ру́сская ку́хня?	d *said when making introductions*
5 познако́мьтесь, пожа́луйста	e what's your first name and patronymic?
6 сади́тесь, пожа́луйста	f the restaurant is small
7 наде́ньте та́почки	g take your things off
8 co ресторан ма́ленький	h put these slippers on

8

2 Pair up 1–6 with an appropriate response from a–f.

1 Вы отку́да?
2 Меня́ зову́т Дми́трий Ива́нович Вла́сов.
3 Вы хоти́те коньяку́?
4 Рестора́н дорого́й?
5 Здра́вствуйте! Как вас зову́т?
6 Возьми́те ещё торт.

a Меня́ зову́т О́льга Владисла́вовна Бори́сова.
b Да, с удово́льствием.
c Спаси́бо, он о́чень вку́сный.
d Дорого́й. Но не волну́йтесь – у меня́ есть де́ньги.
e Я из Кана́ды.
f О́чень ра́да с ва́ми познако́миться.

6

3 Complete the phrases with the correct form of the adjective.

1	_____ пло́щадь	(Кра́сный)
2	_____ бана́н	(ма́ленький)
3 мой	_____ рома́ны	(люби́мый)
4	_____ апельси́ны	(хоро́ший)
5	_____ собра́ние	(друго́й)
6	_____ газе́та	(вчера́шний)

6

4 Match 1–6 with the correct response from a–f.

1 Еда́ хоро́шая?   a Нет, она́ о́чень больша́я.
2 Там есть орке́стр?   b Она́ замеча́тельная.
3 У вас есть кра́сное вино́?   c Да, це́ны там высо́кие.
4 Рестора́н дорого́й?   d Да, там игра́ет цыга́нский орке́стр.
5 У вас есть де́ньги?   e Да, венге́рское.
6 Гости́ница ма́ленькая?   f Да, у меня́ есть де́ньги.

6

5 Complete the phrases with the correct form of the possessive adjective.

1 _____ откры́тка   (мой)
2 _____ письмо́   (мой)
3 _____ ча́йник   (твой)
4 _____ ма́рки   (твой)
5 _____ моро́женое   (наш)
6 _____ посу́да   (наш)
7 _____ гре́йпурут   (ваш)
8 _____ де́ньги   (ваш)
9 _____ гости́ница   (их)

9

6 How would you do the following in Russian?
(2 points if correct, 1 point if only one error)

1 Ask what someone's patronymic is.
2 Ask if the prices are high.
3 Ask if the flat is big.
4 Say 'yes, please', when offered a drink.
5 Say 'here is my card'.
6 Say 'pleased to meet you'.
7 Say 'what an expensive restaurant!'
8 Say 'it's very tasty', referring to cake.

16

TOTAL SCORE   **51**

If you scored less than 41, re-read the Language Building sections before completing the Summary on page 88.

Summary 6

Now try this final test summarizing the main points covered in this unit. You can check your answers on the recording.

How would you:
1 give your name?
2 ask someone her name?
3 say 'pleased to meet you'?
4 introduce two people to each other?
5 say 'please have a seat'?
6 say 'my brother'?
7 say 'my hotel'?
8 say 'their flat?
9 say 'today's paper'?

REVISION

To revise the language learned in this unit, imagine yourself visiting some Russian friends at home. How will they greet you? How should you respond? How will they introduce their family? What will you say? What will they say as they offer you a drink or some food? How should you respond politely?

If you are learning Russian with someone, this activity can be done as a role-play. If you are learning alone it is still just as useful – you play both roles and have double the practice!

Personal information
Кто я?

OBJECTIVES

In this unit you'll learn how to:

✓ say where you live and where you come from

✓ talk about your family

✓ talk about learning and speaking languages

✓ ask how to say something in Russian

✓ make comparisons

And cover the following grammar and language:

✓ the prepositional singular of nouns

✓ prepositions taking the prepositional

✓ the prepositional singular of adjectives, possessives, and pronouns

✓ comparatives

✓ superlatives

LEARNING RUSSIAN 7

If you have not already done so, it is worth considering buying a good Russian–English, English–Russian dictionary. One-volume dictionaries are the easiest to use, but you should buy the largest one you can afford, as this is most likely to contain the fullest information about each word – what gender it is, what pattern of endings it takes, different possible meanings, phrases in which it may occur, and so on. Make sure as well that the dictionary has both a Russian–English and an English–Russian section, for translating both ways.

Now start the recording for Unit 7.

Вы отку́да?

🎧 **ACTIVITY 1** is on the recording.

ACTIVITY 2

1 What does Valery say about the name 'Olga'?
2 What does Valery say about Belorussian girls?
3 Is Olga in fact Belorussian?
4 What is Olga doing in Moscow?
5 What is Olga's paper on?

DIALOGUE 1

○ Здра́вствуй! Меня́ зову́т Вале́рий. А тебя́ как зову́т?

■ Меня́ зову́т О́льга.

○ О́льга! Како́е краси́вое и́мя! Ты отку́да, О́ля?

■ Я из Ми́нска, но давно́ там не живу́.

○ А где ты живёшь?

■ Я живу́ в А́нглии, в О́ксфорде. Я рабо́таю в университе́те.

○ О́ля, ты – белору́ска? Белору́сские де́вушки – таки́е краса́вицы!

■ Нет, я – ру́сская. А мой муж – англича́нин.

○ Муж англича́нин? И он то́же здесь, в Москве́?

■ Нет, к сожале́нию, он в О́ксфорде. Он там рабо́тает.

○ Поня́тно. О́ля, скажи́, а что ты де́лаешь в Москве́?

■ Я здесь на конфере́нции в Институ́те Социоло́гии при Акаде́мии нау́к. Извини́те, но уже́ по́здно, а за́втра я чита́ю докла́д на конфере́нции.

○ О́ля, куда́ же ты идёшь? Скажи́, о чём докла́д?

■ О фемини́зме и о мужско́м шовини́зме. Споко́йной но́чи!

VOCABULARY	
краса́вица	beauty, good-looker
муж	husband
к сожале́нию	unfortunately
конфере́нция	conference
по́здно	late
чита́ть докла́д	to give a paper
же	*emphasizes the preceding word*
о чём?	about what?
мужско́й	male
шовини́зм	chauvinism
споко́йной но́чи!	good night!

✓ The prepositional singular of nouns

The prepositional case only occurs after certain prepositions.

Masculine nouns ending in

consonant	add **-e**	вокза́л<u>е</u>, феминиз́м<u>е</u>, го́род<u>е</u>
-ь	replace with **-е**	рубл<u>е́</u>, го́ст<u>е</u>, преподава́тел<u>е</u>

Feminine nouns ending in

-а	replace with **-е**	ви́з<u>е</u>, у́лиц<u>е</u>, гости́ниц<u>е</u>
-ь	replace with **-и**	пло́щад<u>и</u>, двер<u>и́</u>
-ия	replace with **-ии**	револю́ц<u>ии</u>, ста́нц<u>ии</u>

Neuter nouns ending in

-о	replace with **-е**	сло́в<u>е</u>, пи́в<u>е</u>, вин<u>е́</u>
-ие	replace with **-ии**	свида́н<u>ии</u>

✓ Prepositions taking the prepositional

The prepositions **в** 'in' and **на** 'on, at' are used idiomatically with the prepositional to express location, in answer to the question **где** 'where?'. Other prepositions taking the prepositional are **о** (**об** before a vowel and **обо** before a few isolated words) 'about' and **при** 'by, at, attached to'.

Я живу́ **в Москве́.** I live in Moscow.
Я здесь **на конфере́нции.** I am here at a conference.
докла́д **об Австра́лии** a paper about Australia
Институ́т Социоло́гии при Акаде́мии нау́к the Institute of Sociology at the Academy of Sciences

✓ Countries and nationalities

country	adjective	woman	man	people
Австра́лия	австрали́йский	австрали́йка	австрали́ец	австрали́йцы
Аме́рика (США)	америка́нский	америка́нка	америка́нец	америка́нцы
А́нглия	англи́йский	англича́нка	англича́нин	англича́не
Кана́да	кана́дский	кана́дка	кана́дец	кана́дцы
Ирла́ндия	ирла́ндский	ирла́ндка	ирла́ндец	ирла́ндцы
Уэ́льс	валли́йский	валли́йка	валли́ец	валли́йцы
Шотла́ндия	шотла́ндский	шотла́ндка	шотла́ндец	шотла́ндцы
Росси́я	ру́сский	ру́сская	ру́сский	ру́сские
Белару́сь	белору́сский	белору́ска	белору́с	белору́сы
Украи́на	украи́нский	украи́нка	украи́нец	украи́нцы

🎧 Now do activities 3 and 4 on the recording.

7.2 You know all about me

Вы всё знаете обо мне

ACTIVITY 5 is on the recording.

ACTIVITY 6

Nina is Russian, but her husband is _____ . They live
in _____ in a large _____ . Her parents live in a
_____ house far from the centre. The man lives on
_____ Street, but his son lives in _____ .

DIALOGUE 2

○ Скажите, Нина, у вас есть семья?

■ Да, у меня есть муж и сын. Муж – украинец, а я – русская.

○ А где вы живёте?

■ Мы живём в Казани, в большой квартире. Мои родители
тоже живут в Казани, но хотя в нашей квартире пять
комнат, родители не хотят там жить. Они живут в
маленьком доме далеко от центра города.

○ Почему?

■ Они не очень любят город. Для них город слишком
шумный.

○ Ну, понятно.

■ А я люблю Казань. В ней есть всё. Парки, река, кремль,
театры, кино... Теперь вы уже всё знаете обо мне, а я о
вас ничего не знаю! Скажите, вы тоже живёте в Казани?

○ В Казани. Я живу в маленькой квартире на улице
Пушкина.

■ А семья у вас есть?

○ У меня есть сын, но я не хочу говорить о нём. Он живёт в
Америке, в Нью-Йорке или в Вашингтоне – я не помню.
У него там хорошая работа, много денег, но он не пишет,
не звонит.

VOCABULARY

сын	son
родители	parents
хотя	although
почему?	why?
шумный	noisy
теперь	now
река	river
ничего ... не	nothing

✓ The prepositional singular of adjectives

Hard and soft adjectives take the following endings.

	m	*f*	*n*
red (*hard*)	кра́сном	кра́сной	кра́сном
dark blue (*soft*)	си́нем	си́ней	си́нем

Они́ живу́т в **ма́леньком** до́ме. They live in a small house.
Це́рковь нахо́дится на **Кра́сной** пло́щади. The church is on Red Square.
Статья́ в **сего́дняшней** газе́те. The article is in today's paper.

✓ The prepositional singular of possessives

my	мо́ём	мо́ей	мо́ём
your (*sing.*)	тво́ём	тво́ей	тво́ём
our	на́шем	на́шей	на́шем
your (*pl., polite sing.*)	ва́шем	ва́шей	ва́шем

В **на́шей** кварти́ре пять ко́мнат. There are five rooms in our flat.
о **ва́шем** бра́те about your brother

✓ The prepositional of pronouns

nom.	*prep.*	*nom.*	*prep.*
я	мне	мы	нас
ты	тебе́	вы	вас
он	нём	они́	них
она́	ней		
оно́	нём		

В **ней** есть всё. It [Kazan] has everything.
Я ду́маю о **нём** всё вре́мя. I think about him all the time.

ACTIVITY 7

Put the word in brackets into the prepositional.

1 Она́ живёт в _____ кварти́ре. (большо́й)
2 Э́то докла́д о _____ шовини́зме. (мужско́й)
3 Он нахо́дится на _____ пло́щади. (Кра́сный)
4 Я ничего́ не зна́ю о _____ (ты)
5 В _____ кварти́ре две ко́мнаты. (наш)
6 Есть рестора́н в _____ гости́нице? (ваш)
7 Я не хочу́ говори́ть о _____ . (оно́)
8 Я ничего́ не зна́ю о _____ бра́те. (твой)
9 Э́то во _____ газе́те. (вчера́шний)
10 Что ты ду́маешь о _____ сы́не? (мой)

🎧 Now do activities 8 and 9 on the recording.

Я изучаю английский язык

🅐 **ACTIVITY 10** is on the recording.

ACTIVITY 11

1 Svetlana wants to read Byron in English.	T / F
2 Gleb says Byron is better than Pushkin.	T / F
3 Svetlana says that English spelling is more complex than Russian.	T / F
4 Gleb says Chinese is the most difficult language.	T / F
5 Gleb's brother asks Svetlana what she thinks of English football.	T / F

DIALOGUE 3

○ Света, вы студентка?

■ Да, я изучаю английский язык.

○ Английский? Зачем?

■ Потому что я хочу читать Байрона по-английски.

○ Байрона? Кто он такой?

■ Байрон – английский поэт. Я очень люблю его стихи.

▲ Но Пушкин, конечно, лучше! Пушкин – самый великий поэт!

○ А скажите, Света, английский язык трудный?

■ Русская грамматика, наверно, труднее, чем английская, но английская орфография – сложнее. Очень трудно писать по-английски. По-русски – гораздо легче.

▲ Самый трудный язык – это, конечно, китайский язык.

○ Света, а вы уже хорошо говорите по-английски? Например, как по-английски «футбол»?

VOCABULARY	
зачем?	why?
потому что	because
кто он такой?	who's he?
великий	great
трудный	difficult
грамматика	grammar
орфография	spelling
сложный	complex, complicated
трудно	difficult [adverb]
гораздо	much, by far
китайский	Chinese
как по-английски … ?	how do you say … in English?

✓ по-ру́сски or ру́сский язы́к?

по-ру́сски is an adverb meaning 'in Russian'.
ру́сский язы́к means 'the Russian language'.

Он говори́т **по-ру́сски**. He speaks Russian.
Как **по-ру́сски** «football»? How do you say 'football' in Russian?
Я изуча́ю **ру́сский язы́к**. I am studying Russian.
Ру́сский язы́к – тру́дный? Is Russian [i.e. the Russian language] difficult?

✓ Comparatives

To form the comparative of most adjectives, the ending **-ée** is added to the adjective stem: **тру́дный** – **трудне́е** ('more difficult'), **сло́жный** – **сложне́е** ('more complex'). These forms are indeclinable.

Alternatively, the indeclinable word **бо́лее** ('more') is added before the adjective: the adjective agrees with the noun it refers to.

Ру́сский – **бо́лее краси́вый** язы́к. Russian is a more beautiful language.

'than' is translated by **чем**. The two things compared are in the same case.

Ру́сский язы́к трудне́е, **чем** англи́йский. Russian is more difficult than English.

Comparatives ending in a single **-e**
Some adjectives have comparative forms with a single **-e** on the end.
There are also a few irregular comparatives with quite unexpected forms.

дешёвле	cheaper	**бо́льше**	bigger; more
доро́же	more expensive	**ме́ньше**	smaller; less, fewer
ле́гче	easier, lighter	**лу́чше**	better
вы́ше	taller, higher	**ху́же**	worse

✓ Superlatives

Superlatives can be formed by simply adding the word **са́мый** in the correct gender and case before the adjective.

Кита́йский – **са́мый тру́дный** язы́к. Chinese is the most difficult language.
Она́ **са́мая краси́вая**. She is the most beautiful (woman).

ACTIVITY 12

Match 1–5 with the correct English version from a–e.

1 ру́сский язы́к трудне́е
2 са́мый тру́дный язы́к
3 он вы́ше
4 там гора́здо дешёвле
5 бо́лее тру́дный язы́к

a a more difficult language
b he is taller
c it's much cheaper there
d the most difficult language
e Russian is more difficult

🎧 Now do activities 13 and 14 on the recording.

(7.4) Visa application form

Ви́зовая анке́та

ACTIVITY 15

Look at the visa application form below and see if you can work out the meanings of the questions, without looking at the vocabulary list. What information is such a form likely to ask for? What words do you recognize immediately? What words can you guess from their context?

CULTURE

ВИ́ЗОВАЯ АНКЕ́ТА			
1	Гражда́нство		
2.	Фами́лия		
3.	И́мя, о́тчество		
4.	(Е́сли изменя́ли, то Ва́ша фами́лия, и́мя и о́тчество до измене́ния)		
5.	Да́та рожде́ния	6.	Пол (М/Ж)
7.	Цель пое́здки в Росси́ю		
8.	Маршру́т сле́дования (в пу́нкты)		
9.	Да́та нача́ла де́йствия ви́зы		
10.	Да́та оконча́ния де́йствия ви́зы		
11.	Но́мер па́спорта		
12.	Ме́сто рабо́ты и́ли учёбы, а́дрес, но́мер телефо́на		
13.	А́дрес постоя́нного местожи́тельства, но́мер телефо́на		
14.	Ме́сто рожде́ния		
15.	Ско́лько раз бы́ли в Росси́и?	Да́та Ва́шей после́дней пое́здки	

16.	Де́ти до 16 лет	Фами́лия	И́мя, о́тчество	Да́та рожде́ния

17.	Ва́ши ро́дственники в Росси́и

Да́та	Ли́чная по́дпись

ви́зовый	visa [*adjective*]
анке́та	form
гражда́нство	citizenship
изменя́ли	changed
то	then
измене́ние	change
да́та	date
рожде́ние	birth
пол	sex
М/Ж	male/female
цель (*f*)	purpose, object
пое́здка	trip, journey
маршру́т сле́дования	route of journey
пункт	point (of destination)
нача́ло	beginning
де́йствие	validity, functioning
оконча́ние	end, termination
но́мер	number
па́спорт	passport
учёба	study
постоя́нный	permanent
местожи́тельство	residence
ско́лько раз?	how many times?
бы́ли	were
де́ти	children
ро́дственник	relative
ли́чный	personal
по́дпись (*f*)	signature

ACTIVITY 16

Fill in the form – in Russian as far as possible – as if you are Maxim Shuisky. Use the information below, and make up other details where necessary:

– Maxim (Borisovich) Shuisky, American of Russian extraction
– travelling to Moscow
– will be attending trade fair (so purpose of trip is business – делова́я)
– born in Chicago
– lives and works in New York
– all relatives live in Chicago
– fifth trip to Russia
– last trip was in 1998

7.5 Ла́рины

Мо́йра у Ла́риных
Moira at the Larins'

Moira, Oleg, Evgeniya Pavlovna, and Ivan Grigorevich continue to chat over tea and cake at the Larins' flat. They are all very impressed by her Russian.

VOCABULARY	
совсе́м	entirely, quite
акце́нт	accent
был	was
настоя́щий	real
свобо́дно	fluently
Брита́нская Колу́мбия	British Columbia
Ванку́вер	Vancouver
междунаро́дный	international
раз	time
и ..., и ...	both ... and ...
все (pl.)	all
но и	but also

ACTIVITY 17

Complete the summary.

Moira's surname is (1) _____ , but originally the name was (2) _____ . Her grandmother speaks fluent (3) _____ . Her grandmother and her parents live in (4) _____ , in a (5) _____ _____ in the centre of the city. Moira's brother lives in (6) _____ , not far from (7) _____ . This is Moira's (8) _____ trip to Russia, and she has been to St Petersburg (9) _____ times. Between Moscow and St Petersburg, she prefers (10) _____ .

ACTIVITY 18

What nationality are/were the following people?

1 Moira's grandfather
2 Moira's grandmother
3 Moira's brother's wife
4 Moira's brother's wife's mother?

ACTIVITY 19

Listen to the story again and fill in the missing comparative and superlative forms.

1 Санкт-Петербу́рг, мо́жет быть, _____, чем Москва́, но Москва́ и _____, и _____, и _____ .

2 Все мои́ студе́нты говоря́т, что ру́сский язы́к – _____ _____ язы́к, но и _____ _____!

STORY TRANSCRIPT

Evgeniya	Мо́йра, вы о́чень хорошо́ говори́те по-ру́сски, совсе́м без акце́нта.
Moira	Спаси́бо. Вы зна́ете, мой де́душка был ру́сский, из Москвы́.
Evgeniya	Пра́вда? А как ва́ша фами́лия?
Moira	Моя́ фами́лия – Пе́терс, но на́ша настоя́щая фами́лия – Петро́вы.
Evgeniya	Ба́бушка то́же ру́сская?
Moira	Нет, моя́ ба́бушка – англича́нка, но она́ свобо́дно говори́т по-ру́сски. Она́ и говори́т, и пи́шет, и чита́ет по-ру́сски.
Ivan	Она́ – англича́нка? Она́ живёт в А́нглии и́ли в Шотла́ндии?
Moira	В Шотла́ндии. Ба́бушка и мои́ роди́тели живу́т в Гла́зго, в большо́м до́ме в це́нтре го́рода.
Evgeniya	А у вас есть брат и́ли сестра́?
Moira	У меня́ есть брат. Но он живёт в Кана́де, в Брита́нской Колу́мбии, недалеко́ от Ванку́вера. Его́ жена́ – кана́дка, а её мать – украи́нка.
Evgeniya	Кака́я междунаро́дная семья́! Скажи́те, вы пе́рвый раз в Росси́и?
Moira	Нет, уже́ тре́тий раз. Я уже́ два ра́за была́ в Санкт-Петербу́рге.
Evgeniya	А како́й го́род вы бо́льше лю́бите – Москву́ и́ли Санкт-Петербу́рг?
Moira	Коне́чно, Москву́! Санкт-Петербу́рг, мо́жет быть, краси́вее, чем Москва́, но Москва́ и ста́рше, и бо́льше, и интере́снее.
Ivan	Гм, интере́сно. А скажи́те, Мо́йра, ру́сский язы́к – тру́дный?
Moira	Ой да, о́чень тру́дный. Но э́то о́чень краси́вый язы́к.
Oleg	Пра́вильно! Все мои́ студе́нты говоря́т, что ру́сский язы́к – са́мый тру́дный язы́к, но и са́мый краси́вый!

Before completing the test on pages 100–101 revise the prepositional case with the activity below.

ACTIVITY 20

Supply the prepositional case of the nouns in brackets.

1 Вы хоти́те жить в _____? (Москва́)
2 Татья́на чита́ет докла́д о _____ . (Пу́шкин)
3 Па́па на _____ . (рабо́та)
4 Мы говори́м о _____ . (письмо́)
5 У меня́ есть дом в _____ . (Ванку́вер)
6 Ле́ночка игра́ет на _____ . (у́лица)

Test

Now it's time to test your progress in Unit 7.

1 Match the following with their English equivalents.

1 спокойной ночи!	a I love reading Russian
2 я не помню	b she's Irish
3 я люблю читать по-русски	c it's the oldest city
4 мои родители – украинцы	d a more interesting newspaper
5 более интересная газета	e good night!
6 она – ирландка	f my parents are Ukrainian
7 это самый старый город	g I can't remember

7

2 Pair up 1–6 with an appropriate response from a–f.

1 О чём ты думаешь?
2 Что ты думаешь о его брате?
3 Что Дима делает в Москве?
4 Они американцы или канадцы?
5 Где вы живёте в Москве?
6 Русский язык труднее, чем английский?

a В большой гостинице на старой улице.
b Он здесь на конференции в Институте Социологии.
c О вашем письме.
d Да, конечно. Гораздо труднее.
e Он – американец, а она – канадка.
f Я ничего не знаю о нём.

6

3 Supply the prepositional singular of the nouns in brackets.

1 Он уже на _____ . (вокзал)
2 Вы живёте в _____? (Нью-Йорк)
3 Она – на _____ . (улица)
4 Церковь находится на _____ . (площадь)
5 Мы живём в _____ . (Англия)
6 Что ты думаешь о русском _____? (пиво)

6

4 Supply the nationalities in the correct form.

1 Áнна – _____ (a Canadian woman)
2 Я – _____ (an American man)
3 Они не _____ (English people)
4 _____ мýзыка (Irish – feminine adjective)
5 Óльга – _____ (a Russian woman)

5

5 Put the personal pronoun into the prepositional case.

1 Эти стихи́ о _____ . (ты)
2 Я хочý говори́ть о _____ . (вы)
3 Я люблю́ Москвý. В _____ есть всё. (она́)
4 Не говори́те о _____ . (они́)
5 Она́ всё зна́ет обо _____ . (я)

5

6 Complete 1–8 with the correct form of the words.

1 Она́ живёт в _____ кварти́ре. (краси́вый)
2 Сего́дня в _____ теа́тре (Большо́й)
3 Во _____ газе́те (вчера́шний)
4 В _____ стака́не (твой)
5 О _____ сы́не (ваш)
6 В _____ гости́нице (наш)
7 Я всё зна́ю о _____ . (ты)
8 Я дýмаю о _____ всё вре́мя. (она́)

8

7 How would you do the following in Russian?
(2 points if correct, 1 point if only one error)

1 Say you live in Moscow.
2 Say you are American.
3 Say you live in small flat.
4 Say St Petersburg is more beautiful than Moscow.
5 Say you want to read novels in Russian.
6 Say you can't remember.
7 Ask 'do you have a brother or sister?'

14

TOTAL SCORE   51

If you scored less than 41, revise the Language Building sections before completing the Summary on page 102.

Summary 7

 Now try this final test summarizing the main points covered in this unit. You can check your answers on the recording.

How would you:
1 say you live in New York?
2 say he's Russian?
3 say you live in a small house?
4 say Russian is more difficult than English?
5 ask what the Russian for 'caviar' is?
6 say you have a brother in Canada?
7 say your grandmother is Russian?
8 say goodnight?

REVISION

One of the most frequent conversations you will have in Russia will be all about you – you'll be asked where you're from ,whether you have a family, what you are are doing in Russia, and, of course, what you think of it. Imagine such conversations in your head, remembering to practise speaking out loud, so that you become confident and fluent talking about such things.

Review 2

VOCABULARY

1 Which is the odd one out in each group?

  1 америка́нка / ирла́ндка / украи́нец / ру́сская
  2 фами́лия / семья́ / и́мя / о́тчество
  3 суббо́та / среда́ / четве́рг / вре́мя
  4 та́почки / конце́рт / бале́т / о́пера
  5 голубо́й / кра́сный / си́ний / вку́сный

2 Match 1–5 with the correct English version from a–e.

  1 Он начина́ется в два   a It finishes at two o'clock.
    часа́.
  2 Он дли́тся два часа́.   b It begins at two o'clock.
  3 Сейча́с два часа́.   c It opens at two o'clock.
  4 Он зака́нчивается в   d It lasts two hours.
    два часа́.
  5 Он открыва́ется в   e It's two o'clock.
    два часа́.

GRAMMAR AND USAGE

3 Complete 1–5 with the genitive plural (or animate accusative plural) of the nouns in brackets.

  1 Там нет _____ . (рестора́н)
  2 Пять _____ . (у́лица)
  3 Шесть _____ . (письмо́)
  4 У Светла́ны мно́го _____ . (кни́га)
  5 Я не люблю́ _____ . (гость)

4 Complete the questions / sentences with the appropriate form of the possessive.

  1 Где _____ тапо́чки? (мой)
  2 Э́то _____ кварти́ра? (твой)
  3 Э́то _____ ме́сто. (наш)
  4 Вот, пожа́луйста, _____ конья́к. (ваш)
  5 Э́то _____ пробле́ма. (его́)

5 Complete the sentences with the appropriate form of the adjectives in brackets.

    1 Вы лю́бите _____ мю́зиклы? (но́вый)
    2 Она́ о́чень _____ . (молодо́й)
    3 _____ ма́рки о́чень краси́вые. (ру́сский)
    4 Э́то моя́ _____ ку́хня. (люби́мый)
    5 Вот её _____ письмо́. (после́дний)

6 Complete the sentences with the prepositional of the nouns in brackets.

    1 Писа́тель живёт в _____ . (Санкт-Петербу́рг)
    2 Ни́на на _____ . (рабо́та)
    3 Ты ду́маешь о её _____? (письмо́)
    4 Вокза́л нахо́дится на _____ . (пло́щадь)
    5 У меня́ сестра́ в _____ . (Австра́лия)

7 Complete the adjectives with the prepositional of the adjectives / possessives in brackets.

    1 Что ты ду́маешь о _____ тёте? (мой)
    2 В _____ до́ме есть телефо́н? (ваш)
    3 В _____ кио́ске есть то́лько газе́ты. (ма́ленький)
    4 Я не хочу́ жить в _____ гости́нице. (большо́й)
    5 Э́то в _____ газе́те. (вече́рний)

8 Complete the sentences with the prepositional of the pronouns in brackets.

    1 Что вы хоти́те знать обо _____ ? (я)
    2 Ма́ма всё вре́мя говори́т о _____ . (ты)
    3 Он поёт о _____ . (она́)
    4 Вы ничего́ не зна́ете о _____ . (мы)
    5 Я не могу́ говори́ть о _____ . (они́)

9 Supply the correct form of the noun **сло́во** ('word'), as required after the numbers.

    1 Одно́ _____
    2 Три _____
    3 Де́сять _____
    4 Со́рок два _____
    5 Сто два́дцать одно́ _____

10 Nina is at the market in Kazan, buying some fruit. Listen to her conversation with the stall-holder and write the prices in the gaps below.

1 bananas   _____ roubles per kilogram
2 oranges   _____ roubles per kilogram
3 black cherries _____ roubles per kilogram
4 grapefruit   _____ roubles per kilogram
5 apples   _____ roubles per kilogram

11 At the electronics trade-fair, Maxim Shuisky is trying to arrange a meeting with his new contact, Aleksei Semyonovich Gagarin. Listen to their conversation and fill in the gaps in Aleksei Semyonovich's diary below. You will need to find out the following information:

– when he is working
– when he is in St Petersburg
– what's happening on Monday
– what's happening on Friday
– the time / day of the meeting with Maxim

● понедéльник
_____

втóрник
_____

средá
_____

● четвéрг
_____

пя́тница
_____

суббóта
_____

● воскресéнье
_____

12 How you would ask the following questions? First of all
    write down the Russian, then try to do the activity using
    only the recording, without looking at your notes. Use
    polite forms (**вы**) wherever possible.

1 How much does this cost?
2 Is there anything cheaper?
3 How much is a stamp for a letter to England?
4 What time is it?
5 What time does the train to Moscow leave?
6 What time does the ticket office open?
7 How long does the show last?
8 What's your name?
9 How do you say 'salmon' in Russian?

13 Now it's time for you to answer some questions. Listen to
    the questions on the recording and give an appropriate
    response. You'll be asked about the following:

– where you live
– your name
– your family
– whether you want a drink
– the Russian language
– your nationality
– the time

8

Let's relax
Мы отдыхаем

OBJECTIVES

In this unit you'll learn how to:

- ✓ talk about future plans
- ✓ arrange to meet people
- ✓ make suggestions
- ✓ state when you are busy

And cover the following grammar and language:

- ✓ imperfective and perfective verbs
- ✓ the perfective future
- ✓ давайте to make suggestions
- ✓ the verbs мочь ('to be able to') and уметь ('to know how to')
- ✓ adjective short forms
- ✓ the verb быть ('to be')
- ✓ the imperfective future

LEARNING RUSSIAN 8

Try recording your own voice speaking Russian – for example, when doing the pronunciation practice activities. When you listen to it afterwards, you may not like what you hear. Don't worry! This is one of the best ways of evaluating your performance and improving on it if necessary. Compare your pronunciation with the master version, see how you can do better, and have another go. If you do this several times, you will find you improve each time.

Now start the recording for Unit 8.

8.1 Tomorrow we'll go into town
Завтра мы пойдём в город

🎧 **ACTIVITY 1** is on the recording.

ACTIVITY 2

It's Monday, and Kolya's mother is asking him about their plans for the week. What is planned for each day?

DIALOGUE 1

○ Коля, дорогой, что мы делаем завтра?

■ Завтра мы пойдём в город и сделаем покупки в Гостином дворе. Потом мы возьмём такси до Мариинского театра и пойдём на оперу.

○ Ой, как хорошо! Я люблю оперу. А билеты будут?

■ Я сначала позвоню и забронирую два билета в партер.

○ Хорошо! А что в среду?

■ В среду мы поедем в Петродворец. Там мы проведём весь день, потом вернёмся в гостиницу.

○ Замечательно! Коля, а какие планы у нас на четверг и пятницу?

■ В четверг мы пойдём в Русский музей, а в пятницу на экскурсию в Эрмитаж.

○ А что в субботу?

■ В субботу? Мама, в субботу я тебя провожу на вокзал. Ты же уезжаешь домой, правда?

VOCABULARY	
Гостиный двор	Gostiny Dvor [a *department store*]
Мариинский театр	the Mariinsky Theatre
сначала	first, at first
забронировать Ib *perf.* (забронирую)	to book, to reserve
провести Ib *perf.* (проведу)	to spend, to pass [*time*]
Петродворец	Petrodvorets [a *palace*]
вернуться Ib *perf.*	to return
замечательно	wonderful
экскурсия	excursion
Эрмитаж	the Hermitage Museum
уезжать Ia *imperf.*	to leave

✅ Imperfective and perfective verbs

Most Russian verbs actually exist as not one, but two verbs: an imperfective verb and a perfective verb. These two verbs are used as the basis for different tenses. For example, the present tense can only be formed from the imperfective, whereas adding the normal verb endings to a perfective creates a future tense. Both imperfective and perfective are used to form past tenses, although with slightly different meanings.

Most of the verbs you have met so far have been imperfective, and these all have perfective counterparts differing in conjugation type or prefix, or even having quite different stems. Here are some imperfective and perfective pairs.

	imperfective	*perfective*
to see	**ви́деть** (II)	**уви́деть** (II)
to do, make	**де́лать** (Ia)	**сде́лать** (Ia)
to go (*by transport*)	**е́хать** (Ib)	**пое́хать** (Ib)
to wait	**ждать** (Ib)	**подожда́ть** (Ib)
to telephone	**звони́ть** (II)	**позвони́ть** (II)
to go (on foot)	**идти́** (Ib)	**пойти́** (Ib)
to write	**писа́ть** (Ib)	**написа́ть** (Ib)
to listen	**слу́шать** (Ia)	**послу́шать** (Ia)
to look, to watch	**смотре́ть** (II)	**посмотре́ть** (II)
to leave	**уезжа́ть** (Ia)	**уе́хать** (Ib)
to read	**чита́ть** (Ia)	**прочита́ть** (Ia)
to buy	**покупа́ть** (Ia)	**купи́ть** (II)
to take	**брать** (Ib)	**взять** (Ib)
to return	**возвраща́ться** (Ia)	**верну́ться** (Ib)
to say	**говори́ть** (II)	**сказа́ть** (Ib)
to understand	**понима́ть** (Ia)	**поня́ть** (Ib)
to spend	**проводи́ть** (II)	**провести́** (Ib)

✅ The perfective future

As you have already seen, adding Ia, Ib, or II endings to an imperfective infinitive gives the present tense. Adding the same endings to a perfective infinitive gives the perfective future. This tense is used to refer to a one-off event in the future, or to stress the result or completion of a future action.

За́втра мы **сде́лаем** поку́пки. Tomorrow we will go shopping.
Мы **возьмём** такси́. We will take a taxi.
Я снача́ла **позвоню́**. I'll call first.
Они́ **послу́шают** о́перу. They will listen to an opera.
Во ско́лько он **вернётся**? What time will he return?

 Now do activities 3 and 4 on the recording.

8.2 Let's go for a walk!

Дава́й пойдём на прогу́лку!

ACTIVITY 5 is on the recording.

ACTIVITY 6

1 Where and when does Gleb suggest they meet?
2 What does he suggest they do on Monday?
3 What is Svetlana's reaction to this suggestion?
4 What does she propose they do instead?
5 What feature of the gallery does Gleb mention?

DIALOGUE 2

○ Све́та, дава́йте перейдём на «ты».

■ Да, коне́чно, так бу́дет лу́чше.

○ Све́та, скажи́, за́втра ты свобо́дна?

■ За́втра воскресе́нье? Я свобо́дна весь день.

○ Дава́й пойдём на прогу́лку.

■ Да, с удово́льствием. Где мы встре́тимся?

○ Дава́й встре́тимся здесь, о́коло метро́, в пятна́дцать часо́в.

■ Хорошо́.

○ А в понеде́льник дава́й пойдём на като́к.

■ К сожале́нию, я не уме́ю ката́ться на конька́х.

○ Как жа́лко!

■ Дава́й лу́чше пойдём в Центра́льный дом худо́жника. Э́то моя́ люби́мая галере́я.

○ Ну ла́дно. Там о́чень хоро́шее кафе́.

■ А во вто́рник дава́й пойдём в Музе́й древнеру́сской культу́ры.

○ Нет, к сожале́нию, во вто́рник я не могу́. Я о́чень за́нят.

■ А когда́ ты смо́жешь?

○ Наве́рное, я бу́ду свобо́ден в сре́ду и́ли в четве́рг. Но я ещё то́чно не зна́ю.

VOCABULARY

перейти́ (Ib *perf.*) на «ты»	to move from **вы** to **ты**
так бу́дет лу́чше	that will be better
встре́титься II *perf.*	to meet
като́к	skating-rink
ката́ться на конька́х	to ice-skate
как жа́лко!	what a pity!
лу́чше	rather, instead
то́чно	exactly

✔ Дава́йте to make suggestions

дава́й (*sing.*) or **дава́йте** (*pl., polite*) followed by the first person plural form of a verb expresses the idea 'let's do something'.

Дава́йте перейдём на «ты». Let's move from **вы** to **ты**.
Дава́й пойдём на прогу́лку. Let's go for a walk.

✔ 'to be able to' and 'to know how to'

The type Ib verb **мочь** (*imperf.*), **смочь** (*perf.*) means 'I can' in the sense of being available to do something or of being physically able to do it. 'I can' in the sense of 'I know how to' is expressed by the type Ia verb **уме́ть** (*imperf.*), **суме́ть** (*perf.*).

я **могу́**	я **уме́ю**
ты **мо́жешь**	ты **уме́ешь**
он, она́, оно́ **мо́жет**	он, она́, оно́ **уме́ет**
мы **мо́жем**	мы **уме́ем**
вы **мо́жете**	вы **уме́ете**
они́ **мо́гут**	они́ **уме́ют**

К сожале́нию, в пя́тницу я не **могу́**. Unfortunately I can't make Friday.
Когда́ вы **смо́жете**? When will you be able to?
Я не **уме́ю** ката́ться на конька́х. I can't skate.

✔ Adjective short forms

Most adjectives have special 'short' forms (as well as the 'long' forms you have already met) which can only be used in certain contexts. Short forms have four different forms, agreeing with the noun/pronoun they refer to.

	m	*f*	*n*	*pl*
busy	за́нят	занята́	за́нято	за́няты
free	свобо́ден	свобо́дна	свобо́дно	свобо́дны

Я **свобо́дна** весь день. I'm free all day. [*a woman speaking*]
Она́ о́чень **занята́**. She's very busy.
Вы **за́няты**? Are you busy?

ACTIVITY 7

Match 1–4 with the appropriate response from a–d.

1 Дава́йте перейдём на «ты».
2 Ты мо́жешь сего́дня туда́ пойти́?
3 Вы уме́ете ката́ться на конька́х?
4 А когда́ вы смо́жете?

a Нет, я не уме́ю.
b В понеде́льник и́ли во вто́рник.
c Да, коне́чно, так бу́дет лу́чше.
d Могу́.

Now do activities 8 and 9 on the recording.

8.3 What are you going to do there?

Что вы там бу́дете де́лать?

🎧 **ACTIVITY 10** is on the recording.

ACTIVITY 11

What will Nina be doing on holiday? Fill in the gaps.

1 _____ on the beach   2 reading _____
3 _____ the sea   4 going to _____
5 buying _____

DIALOGUE 3

■ Ни́на, скажи́те, где вы проведёте о́тпуск?

○ В а́вгусте мы пое́дем на Ма́льту.

■ На Ма́льту? А что вы там бу́дете де́лать?

○ Я бу́ду весь день лежа́ть на пля́же, чита́ть кни́ги, смотре́ть на мо́ре – там о́чень краси́вое мо́ре.

■ А где вы бу́дете жить?

○ У на́ших друзе́й. Они́ ру́сские из Каза́ни, но у них есть дом на Ма́льте.

■ А где вы бу́дете пита́ться?

○ Мы бу́дем ходи́ть в рестора́ны. На Ма́льте о́чень хоро́шие ма́ленькие рестора́нчики, совсе́м недороги́е.

■ А вы бу́дете покупа́ть сувени́ры?

○ Да, коне́чно.

■ Когда́ вы вернётесь, то непреме́нно заходи́те ко мне в го́сти и расскажи́те о ва́шем о́тдыхе.

○ Спаси́бо, с удово́льствием.

VOCABULARY

провести́ о́тпуск	to spend one's holidays, to spend one's vacation
лежа́ть II *imperf.*	to lie
пляж	beach
мо́ре	sea
друг (*gen. pl.* друзе́й)	friend
у на́ших друзе́й	at our friends' house
пита́ться Ia *imperf.*	to have meals, to eat
недорого́й	inexpensive
непреме́нно	without fail, make sure you …
заходи́те ко мне в го́сти	come and visit me
рассказа́ть Ib *perf.*	to tell, to recount
о́тдых	holiday, vacation; rest, relaxation

✓ The verb быть 'to be'

As you know, the verb 'to be' is omitted in the present tense. The future tense is formed from **быть** (Ib), as shown below.

я **бу́ду**	I will be	мы **бу́дем**	we will be
ты **бу́дешь**	you will be	вы **бу́дете**	you will be
он, она́, оно́ **бу́дет**	he, she, it will be	они́ **бу́дут**	they will be

Он там **бу́дет**. He will be there.

✓ The imperfective future

As well as the perfective future, Russian also has an imperfective future. The imperfective future refers to repeated events in the future or stresses the ongoing or habitual nature of a future event. It is formed from the appropriate form of **быть** followed by the imperfective infinitive.

я **бу́ду лежа́ть**	I will lie / will be lying
ты **бу́дешь лежа́ть**	you will lie / will be lying
он, она́, оно́ **бу́дет лежа́ть**	he, she, it will lie / will be lying
мы **бу́дем лежа́ть**	we will lie / will be lying
вы **бу́дете лежа́ть**	you will lie / will be lying
они́ **бу́дут лежа́ть**	I will lie / they will be lying

✓ The months

The months are all masculine, as is the word for 'month' itself, **ме́сяц**. To say 'in' a particular month, **в** + the prepositional case is used.

янва́рь	January	**ию́ль**	July
февра́ль	February	**а́вгуст**	August
март	March	**сентя́брь**	September
апре́ль	April	**октя́брь**	October
май	May	**ноя́брь**	November
ию́нь	June	**дека́брь**	December

в январе́ in January
в а́вгусте in August

ACTIVITY 12

Add the correct form of **быть** to make an imperfective future.

1 Они́ _____ писа́ть откры́тки.
2 Я _____ жить у друзе́й.
3 Она́ _____ лежа́ть на пля́же.
4 Мы не _____ покупа́ть сувени́ры.
5 Ты _____ ходи́ть в рестора́ны.
6 Вы _____ ката́ться на конька́х?

🎧 Now do activities 13 and 14 on the recording.

Óтдых

ACTIVITY 15

See if you can recognize the holiday destinations mentioned in the adverts below. Make a list in Russian, then add English translations. Check your answers with the vocabulary list on the next page.

РЕКЛА́МА

Автóбусные тýры.
Евро́па и Скандина́вия.
Замеча́тельный óтдых в
любóй странé.
Тел. 206-22-49.

Экскýрсии, óтдых, шоп-
тýры. От 2 дней. Тра́нспорт
– а́виа, автóбус. Еги́пет – от
$265. Тенери́фе – от $607.
Пра́га – от $260. Ита́лия –
от $590. Испа́ния, Туни́с,
Гре́ция (Шоп-тýр и óтдых)
– $150. Большóй вы́бор.
Тел. 259-14-90.

Шоп-тýр и óтдых в
Гре́ции – $50.
Тел. (095) 203-55-59.

Фра́нция, А́встрия,
Швейца́рия, Болга́рия,
Тýрция. Ло́ндон, Пари́ж,
Пра́га. Óтдых, экскýрсии,
шоп-тýры. Це́ны – от $245.
Тел. 250-27-04.

Ма́льта, Еги́пет, весь
Тайла́нд. Óтдых на мóре,
экскýрсии. За́втрак - ýжин.
Апартаме́нты. От 7 дней.
Ви́зы США, вся Евро́па,
Кана́да, Ме́ксика. Цена́ –
недóрого.
Тел. (095) 380-10-05.

Еги́пет. Круи́зы, óтдых
на мóре. Óчень ни́зкие
це́ны.
Тел. 209-41-40.

Экскýрсии. Росси́я,
Белару́сь. Украи́на.
1 день и бóлее.
Тел. (095) 209-55-65.

Замеча́тельный óтдых
на Кýбе и в Ме́ксике.
Ви́зы. Апартаме́нты.
Большóй вы́бор
гости́ниц. Цена́ –
недóрого.
Тел. 288-41-48.

Круи́зы с Ки́пра в
Изра́иль. Прода́жа
авиабиле́тов. Ви́зы в
стра́ны Евро́пы, в
Австра́лию, Кана́ду,
Кита́й.
Тел. 280-30-31.

Санкт-Петербýрг,
Сýздаль, Но́вгород.
Гости́ницы, апартаме́нты,
санато́рии. Экскýрсии,
óтдых, лече́ние. Цена́ –
от $100.
Тел. (095) 288-39-52.

Пра́га. Недóрого.
Говори́м по-рýсски.
Тел. 8-10-420604433859

CULTURE

рекла́ма	advertisment
авто́бусный	bus [*adjective*]
тур	tour
любо́й	any
шоп-ту́р	shopping tour
а́виа	by air
вы́бор	choice
на мо́ре	by the sea
за́втрак	breakfast
у́жин	dinner
апартаме́нт	apartment
недо́рого	inexpensive
круи́з	cruise
ни́зкий	low
авиабиле́т	airline ticket
санато́рий	sanatorium
лече́ние	(medical) treatment
А́встрия	Austria
Болга́рия	Bulgaria
Ме́ксика	Mexico
Гре́ция	Greece
Пари́ж	Paris
Евро́па	Europe
Пра́га	Prague
Еги́пет	Egypt
Изра́иль (*m*)	Israel
Тайла́нд	Thailand
Испа́ния	Spain
Ита́лия	Italy
Туни́с	Tunisia
Кипр	Cyprus
Ту́рция	Turkey
Кита́й	China
Фра́нция	France
Швейца́рия	Switzerland

ACTIVITY 16

Your firm has sent you to Moscow for three months. At the end of this time you will have two weeks holiday, which you'd like to use to travel around Russia. Write down the telephone numbers of adverts specifically mentioning Russia or Russian cities.

ACTIVITY 17

Alternatively, you are considering a trip to the Czech capital, Prague. Write down the telephone numbers of adverts which mention this city.

Oleg and Moira at the Institute
Оле́г и Мо́йра в институ́те

Oleg is chatting to Moira at the Institute about her plans for the future.

VOCABULARY

ско́ро	soon
сно́ва	again
приезжа́ть Ia *imperf.*, приéхать Ib *perf.*	to come [*by transport*]
учи́ться II *imperf.*	to study
бесе́да	talk, conversation
зна́чить II *imperf.*	to mean
пу́сто	empty
друг дру́га	each other
к нам	to us
да́ча	dacha, holiday cottage, country house
день рожде́ния	birthday
до́брый	good
дое́хать Ib *perf.*	to get to [*by transport*]

ACTIVITY 18

Listen to the the story and decide whether the following statements are true or false. Correct the statements which are false.

1 Moira plans to stay two more months in Moscow. T / F
2 Moira doesn't know when she's coming back to Russia. T / F
3 Oleg suggests that they move from **вы** to **ты**. T / F
4 Oleg tells Moira that his family really like her. T / F
5 Oleg invites Moira to their dacha. T / F
6 They arrange to meet at the entrance to the institute at 10 a.m. T / F

ACTIVITY 19

Listen to the the story again and fill the gaps with the missing verbs. Mark whether each is the imperfective future or perfective future.

1 В сентябре́ я _____ домо́й в Шотла́ндию. *imperf./perf.*
2 А когда́ вы сно́ва _____ в Росси́ю? *imperf./perf.*
3 С сентября́ я _____ _____ в Гла́зго. *imperf./perf.*
4 Э́то далеко́, мы туда́ _____ вме́сте. *imperf./perf.*
5 Хорошо́. А где мы _____? *imperf./perf.*

ACTIVITY 20

Now translate the sentences in Activity 19 into English.

STORY TRANSCRIPT

Oleg	Мо́йра, ско́лько вре́мени вы ещё бу́дете в Москве́?
Moira	Наве́рное, ещё три ме́сяца, до сентября́. В сентябре́ я верну́сь домо́й в Шотла́ндию.
Oleg	Так ско́ро? А когда́ вы сно́ва прие́дете в Росси́ю?
Moira	Я ещё не зна́ю. С сентября́ я бу́ду учи́ться в Гла́зго. Там я бу́ду о́чень занята́.
Oleg	Как жа́лко. На́ши бесе́ды, на́ши прогу́лки так мно́го зна́чат для меня́. Без вас в институ́те бу́дет о́чень пу́сто.
Moira	Оле́г, дава́йте перейдём на «ты», ла́дно? Мы же хорошо́ зна́ем друг дру́га.
Oleg	Коне́чно! Мы уже́ давно́ друзья́. Мо́йра, ты зна́ешь, вся моя́ семья́ тебя́ о́чень лю́бит. Приезжа́й, пожа́луйста, к нам на да́чу. В суббо́ту у ма́мы бу́дет день рожде́ния. Ей испо́лнится шестьдеся́т пять лет. Ты прие́дешь?
Moira	С удово́льствием. Я о́чень люблю́ Евге́нию Па́вловну. Она́ така́я ми́лая, така́я до́брая.
Oleg	Она́ тебя́ то́же о́чень лю́бит.
Moira	А где нахо́дится да́ча? Как туда́ дое́хать?
Oleg	Э́то далеко́, мы туда́ пое́дем вме́сте.
Moira	Хорошо́. А где мы встре́тимся?
Oleg	Дава́й встре́тимся у вхо́да в институ́т в де́вять утра́.

Test

Now it's time to test your progress in Unit 8.

1 Match 1–8 with the appropriate English version.

1 я заброни́рую два биле́та	a I'm busy all day
2 в сре́ду мы сде́лаем поку́пки	b unfortunately, I don't know how to
3 когда́ ты свобо́дна?	c we will do the shopping on Wednesday
4 я за́нят весь день	d when shall we meet?
5 когда́ мы встре́тимся?	e when will you be able to?
6 к сожале́нию, я не уме́ю	f I'll reserve two tickets
7 как жа́лко!	g when are you free?
8 когда́ вы смо́жете?	h what a pity!

8

2 Pair up 1–6 with an appropriate response from a–f.

1 Дава́йте перейдём на «ты».
2 Каки́е пла́ны у нас на четве́рг?
3 Когда́ мы вернёмся в гости́ницу?
4 Дава́йте встре́тимся в понеде́льник.
5 Где вы бу́дете жить?
6 Ско́лько вре́мени вы ещё бу́дете в Москве́?

a В четрве́рг мы пойдём на экску́рсию.
b К сожале́нию, в понеде́льник я не могу́.
c Ещё два ме́сяца, до ию́ня.
d В пятна́дцать часо́в.
e Коне́чно, так бу́дет лу́чше.
f В недорого́й гости́нице.

6

3 Supply the correct form of **за́нят** or **свобо́ден**.

1 Она́ _____ . (за́нят)
2 Бори́с Петро́вич, вы _____? (за́нят)
3 И́горь, когда́ ты _____? (свобо́ден)
4 Раи́са Алекса́ндровна сейча́с _____ . (свобо́ден)
5 В суббо́ту мы _____ весь день. (свобо́ден)

5

4 Fill the gap with the month, in the correct form: nominative, genitive (after **до** or **с**), or prepositional (after **в**).

1 В _____ я поéду в Кѝев. (February)
2 _____ – мой любѝмый мéсяц. (April)
3 В _____ мы поéдем на Мáльту. (June)
4 До _____ он бýдет в Лóндоне. (August)
5 В _____ онѝ вернýтся домóй. (October)
6 С _____ онá бýдет рабóтать в США. (December)

	6

5 Use the verb in brackets to make a perfective future.

1 Мы _____ покýпки. (сдéлать, Ia)
2 Он _____ в США. (поéхать, Ib)
3 Я _____ таксѝ. (взять, Ib)
4 Вы _____ «Áнну Карéнину»? (прочитáть, Ia)
5 Онá скóро _____ . (уéхать, Ib)
6 Когдá ты _____ ? (позвонѝть, II)

	6

6 Add **быть** to make an imperfective future.

1 Вы _____ говорѝть по-рýсски.
2 Скóлько врéмени ты _____ ждать?
3 Мáма, я _____ звонѝть кáждый день.
4 Онѝ _____ отдыхáть.
5 Мы _____ покупáть апельсѝны и банáны.
6 Онá _____ слýшать óперу кáждый день.

	6

7 How would you do the following in Russian?
(2 points if correct, 1 point if only one error)

1 Suggest going for a walk.
2 Suggest meeting on Thursday.
3 Say you can't make Wednesday.
4 Say you're very busy.
5 Say you'll be staying in a hotel'.
6 Say 'in September'.

	12

TOTAL SCORE | 49 |

If you scored less than 39, re-read the Language Building sections before completing the Summary on page 120.

Summary 8

Now try this final test summarizing the main points in this unit. You can check your answers on the recording.

How would you:
1 ask 'when will we go to St Petersburg? '?
2 say 'let's move from **вы** to **ты**'?
3 suggest meeting on Sunday?
4 say you can't make Tuesday?
5 say you're busy all day?
6 ask a friend where he'll be staying?
7 say 'in August'?
8 say 'in November'?

REVISION

Before moving on to the next unit, play Unit 8 through again and check your progress. Make sure you understand the difference between the perfective future and the imperfective future – how each is formed, and when each is used. To practise the perfective future, work out a series of activities that you will carry out (and finish) – I'll go to the shop, buy a newspaper, come home, read the newspaper, and so on. Practise the imperfective future by working out what you will be doing as ongoing activities during your next holiday – I'll be lying on the beach, reading books, buying souvenirs, eating in restaurants, studying Russian …

This contrast in usage – *perfective* for one-off events, stressing result or successful completion, *imperfective* for repeated events, stressing the ongoing nature of an event – is found in Russian not only in the future, but also in the past tense, as you will learn in Unit 11.

High days and holidays
Пра́здники

LEARNING RUSSIAN 9

When speaking a foreign language, it is impossible to translate everything word for word from your native language, so it is important to think directly in the foreign language. This unit contains many examples illustrating this point. For instance, the Russian for 'I am cold' is **мне хо́лодно**, literally 'to me it is cold', and the Russian for 'you are sad' is **тебе́ гру́стно**, literally 'to you it is sad'. Keeping that in mind will help you to progress more easily and to start sounding Russian more quickly.

Now start the recording for Unit 9.

Что подари́ть па́пе?

ACTIVITY 1 is on the recording.

ACTIVITY 2

1 When does Kolya say he will probably come to the dacha?
2 What does Kolya's father like to happen on his birthday?
3 How does Kolya's mother describe his father?
4 What is Kolya planning to give his father for his birthday?
5 When will Kolya's mother call him at work?

DIALOGUE 1

○ Ко́ля, дорого́й, когда́ ты прие́дешь на да́чу? Па́па о́чень скуча́ет по тебе́, а ты так ре́дко к нам приезжа́ешь.

■ Я зна́ю, ма́ма. Но я о́чень за́нят. Я, наве́рное, прие́ду к вам в ию́ле.

○ Ко́лька, но ты же зна́ешь, что в ию́не у па́пы день рожде́ния. Он лю́бит, когда́ вся семья́ собира́ется на да́че в э́тот день.

■ Ну да, коне́чно. Éсли смогу́, то прие́ду.

○ Ко́ля, я наде́юсь, что ты бу́дешь там. Э́то так ва́жно для него́. Ведь он уже́ стари́к, а ста́рость – не ра́дость. А что ты пода́ришь ему́ на день рожде́ния?

■ Я хочу́ подари́ть ему́ что́-нибудь для да́чи, но я ещё не зна́ю, что и́менно.

○ Тогда́ лу́чше я его́ снача́ла спрошу́, а пото́м тебе́ скажу́. Я тебе́ позвоню́ на рабо́ту в понеде́льник и́ли во вто́рник и скажу́, что он хо́чет. Ведь ему́ так тру́дно угоди́ть.

VOCABULARY

скуча́ть (Ia *imperf.*) **по**	to miss
ре́дко	rarely
собира́ться Ia *imperf.*	to gather
ва́жно	it is important
ведь	you know, you see
стари́к	old man
ста́рость – не ра́дость	old age is no joy [*Russian proverb*]
дари́ть II *imperf.* (+ *dat.*), подари́ть II *perf.*	to give a present
спроси́ть II *perf.* (**спрошу́**)	to ask
угоди́ть II *perf.* (+ *dat.*)	to please

✓ The dative case

The dative case is used for the indirect object, the person or thing to whom something is given, said, etc., after verbs such as **дать**, **звони́ть**, **говори́ть**, **дари́ть**. It is also used after the prepositions **к** 'to, towards' and **по** 'along'.

Я позвоню́ **Ива́ну** на рабо́ту. I'll call Ivan at work.
Я о́чень скуча́ю по **ма́ме**. I really miss Mum.

✓ The dative singular of nouns

masculine nouns ending in

consonant	add **-у**	вокза́лу, го́роду
-ь	replace with **-ю**	рублю́, го́стю, преподава́телю

feminine nouns ending in

-а	replace with **-е**	ви́зе, у́лице, гости́нице
-ь	replace with **-и**	пло́щади, двери́
-ия	replace with **-ии**	револю́ции, ста́нции

neuter nouns ending in

-о	replace with **-у**	сло́ву, вину́
-ие	replace with **-ию**	свида́нию

✓ The dative of pronouns

Dative pronouns often come before the verb.

Я **тебе́** позвоню́. I will call you.

nom.	dat.	nom.	dat.
я	**мне**	мы	**нам**
ты	**тебе́**	вы	**вам**
он	**(н)ему́**	они́	**(н)им**
она́	**(н)ей**		
оно́	**(н)ему́**		

The forms **ему́**, **ей**, and **им** gain an initial **н-** when used after prepositions, becoming **нему́**, **ней**, **ним**.

Они́ скуча́ют по **ней**. They miss her.

ACTIVITY 3

1 Дава́йте пойдём на прогу́лку по _____ . (го́род)
2 Ле́ночка скуча́ет по _____ . (ба́бушка)
3 Ты скуча́ешь по _____ ? (он)
4 Позвони́те _____ на рабо́ту. (Бори́с)
5 Я сейча́с приду́ к _____ . (вы)

⓵ Now do activities 4 and 5 on the recording.

9.2 A present for my aunt

Пода́рок для тёти

ACTIVITY 6 is on the recording.

ACTIVITY 7

1 How many packets of cigarettes does Maxim have?
2 What alcohol does Maxim have?
3 Why does the customs official at first think the samovar (Russian tea-urn) cannot be exported?
4 On what item does Maxim have to pay duty?

DIALOGUE 2

○ Ско́лько у вас багажа́?

■ Оди́н чемода́н и две су́мки.

○ Откро́йте су́мки. … Ско́лько у вас сигаре́т?

■ Три-четы́ре па́чки, не бо́льше. И одна́ буты́лка во́дки.

○ А э́то что тако́е?

■ Самова́р. Пода́рок для тёти на день рожде́ния.

○ Не ва́жно для кого́. Ста́рые ве́щи нельзя́ вывози́ть.

■ Да вы что? Он не ста́рый, а совсе́м но́вый, электри́ческий.

○ Ну ла́дно. А э́то что тако́е?

■ Э́то компью́тер. Ра́зве нельзя́ его́ вывози́ть?

○ Мо́жно, но ну́жно заплати́ть по́шлину. Вам на́до ещё раз запо́лнить деклара́цию.

VOCABULARY

бага́ж	luggage
чемода́н	suitcase
су́мка	bag
откро́йте	open [*imperative*]
три-четы́ре	three or four
па́чка	packet, pack(age)
э́то что тако́е?	what's that?
кого́ (*acc./gen. of* кто)	whom
вещь (*f*)	thing
вывози́ть II *imperf.*	to export
да вы что?	but what do you mean?
электри́ческий	electric
заплати́ть II *perf.*	to pay
по́шлина	duty
ещё раз	once again
запо́лнить II *perf.*	to fill in
деклара́ция	declaration

✓ Invariable modal forms

These modal forms can be used on their own or with a noun or pronoun in the dative.

мóжно	it is possible; it is permitted
нáдо/нýжно	it is necessary to; one should
не нáдо + *imperf.*	one should not; don't; one does not need
нельзя́ + *imperf.*	it is not permitted
нельзя́ + *perf.*	it is impossible

Ста́рые ве́щи **нельзя́** вывози́ть. It is not permitted to export antiques.
Мóжно, но **нýжно** заплати́ть пóшлину. You can, but it is necessary to pay duty.
Мне **мóжно** идти́? Can I go?
Не нáдо говори́ть так бы́стро. You shouldn't/Don't speak so quickly.
Вам **нáдо** идти́? Do you have to go?

✓ рáзве

The word **рáзве**, which means something like 'can it really be … ?', indicates that a neutral or negative answer is expected to the question. When followed by a negative construction, it indicates that a positive answer is expected.

Рáзве он придёт? Do you think he'll come?
Рáзве так мóжно? You can't do that!
Рáзве нельзя́ его вывози́ть? Surely it can be exported? [Can it really be that it is not permitted to export it?]

ACTIVITY 8

Complete the sentences with the appropriate modal form:
мóжно, нельзя́, нáдо/нýжно, or не нáдо.

1 Здесь _____ игра́ть в футбóл. (it is not permitted to)
2 Тудá _____ идти́ пешкóм. (it is possible to)
3 Егó _____ уви́деть. (it is impossible to)
4 Вам _____ отдыхáть. (it is necessary to)
5 _____ его вывози́ть? (is it permitted to?)
6 _____ говори́ть так ти́хо. (don't)

🎧 Now do activities 9 and 10 on the recording.

Какой твой любимый праздник?

ACTIVITY 11 is on the recording.

ACTIVITY 12

1 Which two church festivals does Svetlana mention?
2 Where does she normally spend these holidays?
3 Which Soviet holidays does Gleb mention?
4 How old is Svetlana's father?
5 What happens on 8th March (International Women's Day)?

DIALOGUE 3

○ Света, какой праздник ты больше всего любишь?

■ Мне очень нравятся церковные праздники, например Пасха и Рождество Христово. Обычно тогда я езжу к бабушке. Ей восемьдесят три года, она очень верующая и отмечает все церковные праздники.

○ А тебе не нравится праздник Первого мая или Октябрьской революции?

■ Нет, они мне совсем не нравятся. Мне кажется, что все эти демонстрации на Красной площади – просто глупость. Но мой папа их очень любит. Он всегда отмечает советские праздники.

○ Сколько ему лет?

■ Ему пятьдесят пять лет. Во время этих праздников ему всегда очень весело, а мне просто скучно и даже грустно.

○ А Восьмое марта ты любишь?

■ Люблю. В этот день мужчины дарят нам цветы, маленькие подарки. Да, это мой любимый праздник.

VOCABULARY

например	for example
Пасха	Easter
Рождество Христово	Christmas
ездить II *imperf.* (езжу)	to go [by transport]
верующий	religious [of a person]
отмечать Ia *imperf.*	to celebrate
советский	Soviet
во время (+ *genitive*)	during
даже	even
мужчина (*m*)	man
цветы	flowers

✅ Impersonal constructions with the dative

Feelings, emotions

There are a number of impersonal constructions made up of a noun/pronoun in the dative and a word with an **-o** on the end.

Мне ве́село/гру́стно/ску́чно. I am happy/sad/bored.
Вам хо́лодно/тепло́/жа́рко? Are you cold/warm/hot?
Оле́гу хорошо́. Oleg is doing fine.

Ages

Ages are expressed by a noun or pronoun in the dative, followed by the number of years + **год** 'year' (gen. sing. **го́да**, gen. pl. **лет**).

Ей во́семьдесят три го́да. She is eighty-three years old.
Па́пе пятьдеся́т пять лет. My dad's fifty-five.
Ско́лько вам лет? How old are you?

нра́виться ('*to like*')

With the verb **нра́виться** (II, *imperf.*) 'to like', the person doing the liking is in the dative, and the thing which he or she likes is in the nominative.

Мне нра́вятся церко́вные пра́здники. I like church festivals.
Ива́ну не нра́вится францу́зская ку́хня. Ivan doesn't like French cuisine.

Мне ка́жется, что ... ('*I think that, it seems to me that ...*')

The verb **каза́ться** (Ib, *imperf.*) 'to seem' also requires the dative.

Мне ка́жется, что э́то глу́пость. I think that's silly.
Ему́ ка́жется, что э́то пра́вда. He thinks it's true.

ACTIVITY 13

Complete 1–4 using impersonal constructions with the dative.

1 Ему́ _____ . (hot)   2 Ма́ме _____ . (bored)
3 Вам _____ ? (cold)   4 Мне _____ . (sad)

ACTIVITY 14

Match 1–5 with the appropriate English version from a–e. Underline the dative form in each Russian example.

1 Ско́лько Ива́ну лет?   a She's thirty-one.
2 Вам нра́вится э́та му́зыка?   b Do you like this music?
3 Мне ка́жется, что э́то он.   c How old is Ivan?
4 Ему́ не нра́вится ру́сская   d He doesn't like Russian
   ку́хня.   food.
5 Ей три́дцать оди́н год.   e I think it's him.

🎧 Now do activities 15 and 16 on the recording.

(9.4) Happy holiday!

С праздником!

ACTIVITY 17

Below is a page from a Russian diary listing major state and religious holidays. Look through the information and try to identify the Russian for the following English words. Give the words in their dictionary forms.

1 New Year's
2 sovereignty
3 federation
4 constitution
5 unofficial
6 Slav, Slavonic

Государственные праздники

Новогодний праздник	1-ое и 2-ое января
Рождество Христово	7-ое января
Международный Женский День	8-ое марта
Праздник весны и труда	1-ое и 2-ое мая
День Победы	9-ое мая
День принятия декларации о государственном суверенитете Российской Федерации	12-ое июня
День согласия и примирения (бывший праздник Великой Октябрьской революции)	7-ое ноября
День конституции Российской Федерации	12-ое декабря

Неофициальные праздники

Старый новый год	14-ое января
День защитников Отечества	23-ое февраля
Пасха	30-ое апреля
День славянской культуры	24-ое мая
Пушкинский день России	6-ое июня

госуда́рственный	State, public
пра́здник	(public) holiday; (religious) festival
нового́дний	New Year's
же́нский	women's, feminine
весна́	spring
побе́да	victory
приня́тие	adoption
суверените́т	sovereignty
росси́йский	Russian
федера́ция	federation
согла́сие	agreement, harmony
примире́ние	reconciliation
бы́вший	former
конститу́ция	constitution
неофициа́льный	unofficial
защи́тник	defender, protector
оте́чество	native land, fatherland
славя́нский	Slav, Slavonic
пу́шкинский	Pushkin [*adjective*]

There will be more on dates in Unit 11.

ACTIVITY 18

What holidays fall on the following dates?

1 6th June
2 12th December
3 1st and 2nd May
4 7th November
5 24th May

ACTIVITY 19

What date are the following holidays?

1 Victory Day
2 Easter
3 Defenders of the Fatherland Day
4 (Orthodox) Christmas
5 Old (Orthodox) New Year

На да́че
At the dacha

It is Evgeniya Pavlovna's birthday party at the Larins' dacha just outside Moscow. All the family are there – Evgeniya Pavlovna, Ivan Grigorevich, Auntie Tanya, Mariya Ivanovna and Lenochka, Pyotr, Oleg – plus their guests Rustam and Moira.

VOCABULARY	
сиде́ть II *imperf.*	to sit
холо́дный	cold
пла́кать, Ib *imperf.* пла́чу	to cry
ку́хня	kitchen
с утра́	since morning
убира́ть Ia *imperf.*	to clean up
гото́вить II *imperf.*	to cook
помо́чь Ib *perf.* (+ *dat.*)	to help
прекрати́	stop [*imperative*]
ушла́	gone out
что случи́лось?	what's the matter? what happened?
катастро́фа	catastrophe

ACTIVITY 20

Listen to the the story and answer the following questions.

1 How does Evgeniya Pavlovna describe the dacha?
2 What does Ivan Grigorevich suggest?
3 Where is Lenochka?
4 Why is she crying?
5 Where is Mariya?
6 What has she being doing since morning?

ACTIVITY 21

Listen to the story again and say whether the following statements are true or false. Correct the statements which are false.

1	Moira wants to go and help Mariya.	T / F
2	Oleg wants Moira to stay with him.	T / F
3	Oleg says he is sad when they are together.	T / F
4	Oleg says Evgeniya is a nice, good woman.	T / F
5	Oleg tells Moira he loves her.	T / F
6	Moira tell Oleg that she loves him too.	T / F

STORY TRANSCRIPT

Moira	Кака́я замеча́тельная да́ча! Така́я больша́я и краси́вая!
Evgeniya	И о́чень холо́дная. Мне всегда́ здесь хо́лодно, а мне уже́ шестьдеся́т пять лет. Я ста́рая, мне нельзя́ сиде́ть в холо́дном до́ме.
Ivan	А мне жа́рко! Дава́йте откро́ем ещё окно́.
Evgeniya	Да нет, Ива́н! Я говорю́, что мне хо́лодно, а ты хо́чешь ещё окно́ откры́ть?
Oleg	Ма́ма, а где Ле́ночка?
Evgeniya	Она́ в друго́й ко́мнате. Сиди́т и пла́чет.
Moira	Почему́ же она́ пла́чет?
Evgeniya	Она́ говори́т, что ей ску́чно. Ей совсе́м не нра́вится на да́че. И мне то́же и ску́чно, и гру́стно. Ведь мне уже́ шестьдеся́т пять лет. Я уже́ совсе́м ста́рая.
Moira	А где Мари́я?
Ivan	Она́ на ку́хне. С утра́ там рабо́тает – убира́ет, гото́вит.
Moira	Я пойду́ к ней.
Oleg	Нет, Мо́йра. Пожа́луйста, посиди́ здесь. Когда́ мы вме́сте, мне о́чень хорошо́, а без тебя́ мне о́чень ску́чно.
Moira	Нет, Оле́г. На́до помо́чь Мари́и.
Oleg	Мо́йра, Мо́йрочка моя́. Ты же така́я ми́лая, така́я до́брая. Мо́йрочка, я тебя́ люблю́!
Moira	Да что ты говори́шь, Оле́г!?
Oleg	Но э́то же пра́вда, Мо́йра! Я тебя́ люблю́, люблю́, люблю́!!!
Moira	Оле́г, прекрати́!
Ivan	А куда́ ушла́ Мо́йра? Что случи́лось?
Evgeniya	Ой-ой-ой! Мой день рожде́ния – настоя́щая катастро́фа!

Test

Now it's time to test your progress in Unit 9.

1 Match 1–8 with the appropriate English version from a–h.

1 роди́тели скуча́ют по мне	a I don't know what to give them
2 е́сли смогу́, то прие́ду	b that can't be exported
3 не на́до говори́ть так гро́мко	c I have to go
4 я не зна́ю, что им подари́ть	d he'll call you on Wednesday
5 он тебе́ позвони́т в сре́ду	e I'll come if I can
6 э́то нельзя́ вывози́ть	f you need to pay duty
7 ну́жно заплати́ть по́шлину	g my parents miss me
8 мне на́до идти́	h don't speak so loudly

8

2 Pair up 1–6 with an appropriate response from a–f.

1 Это что тако́е?
2 Почему́ Ле́ночка пла́чет?
3 Ему́ нра́вится здесь?
4 Мне жа́рко.
5 Како́й ваш люби́мый пра́здник?
6 Вам нра́вится пра́здник Пе́рвого ма́я?

a Дава́йте откро́ем ещё окно́.
b Нет, ему́ здесь совсе́м не нра́вится.
c Нет. Мне нра́вятся церко́вные пра́здники.
d Буты́лка во́дки. Пода́рок для бра́та на день рожде́ния.
e Ей ску́чно.
f Ста́рый но́вый год.

6

3 Complete the sentences with the dative form of the noun.

1 Я скуча́ю по _____ . (ма́ма)
2 Экску́рсия по _____ . (Санкт-Петербу́рг)
3 Да́йте э́то _____ . (гость)
4 Скажи́ _____ . (Ива́н)
5 Я позвоню́ _____ . (Мари́я)
6 Ты пойдёшь к_____ ? (ба́бушка)

6

4 Complete the sentences with the dative form of the pronouns in brackets.

1 Когда́ вы _____ позвони́те? (мы)
2 Я _____ напишу́ письмо́. (ты)
3 _____ не нра́вится э́та ко́мната. (он)
4 Да́йте _____ э́ти де́ньги. (я)
5 _____ хо́лодно? (вы)
6 Наве́рное _____ ску́чно. (они́)
7 Позвони́ _____ за́втра. (я)
8 _____ нельзя́ там сиде́ть. (она́)
9 _____ на́до идти́ домо́й. (вы)

9

5 How would you do the following in Russian?
(2 points if correct, 1 point if only one error)

1 Ask if you can export it (a samovar – **он**).
2 Ask if you can go.
3 Ask how old he is.
4 Say 'I miss you' to a close friend.
5 Say 'I'll call you tomorrow'.
6 Say 'we need to rest'.
7 Say you're cold.
8 Say you like this music.

16

6 Answer the questions, using the English prompts as a guide. (2 points if correct, 1 point if only one error)

1 Ско́лько у вас багажа́?	(Say one suitcase.)
2 Вам хо́лодно?	(Say no, you're hot.)
3 Ско́лько ей лет?	(Say she's forty-three.)
4 Мо́жно игра́ть в футбо́л?	(Say no, it's not permitted.)
5 Э́то что тако́е?	(Say it's a present for your mother.)

10

TOTAL SCORE 55

If you scored less than 45, re-read the Language Building sections before completing the Summary on page 134.

Summary 9

 Now try this final test summarizing the main points covered in this unit. You can check your answers on the recording.

How would you:
1 ask if you can go?
2 ask a friend how old she is?
3 ask your mother if she's cold?
4 ask your boss if she likes the hotel?
5 ask if it's possible to go there on foot?
6 say 'I'll call you on Thursday'?
7 say 'we miss Moscow'?
8 say it's a birthday present?

REVISION

Before moving on to the next unit, play Unit 9 through again and check your progress. As you have seen, the dative is used in many useful constructions. Practise forms by giving your own age and the ages of your friends and family. Say what you like and don't like. Say how you're feeling (cold? hot? bored?). Say what people have to do (**на́до**), and what they mustn't do (**нельзя́**).

Look at the noun and pronoun tables in the grammar section at the end of this book and see how the dative forms you have learnt fit in. Revise the uses of the various cases you have encountered so far. You'll be pleased to hear you only have one more case to learn – the instrumental; it's introduced in the next unit.

10

Public transport
Городско́й тра́нспорт

In this unit you'll learn how to:

✓ ask how to get somewhere by bus, tram, metro, and local train

✓ buy tickets for public transport

✓ find the right bus stop, platform, etc.

✓ take a taxi

And cover the following grammar and language:

✓ the instrumental case

✓ the instrumental singular of nouns

✓ the instrumental of pronouns

✓ the dative, instrumental, and prepositional plural of nouns, adjectives, and possessives

LEARNING RUSSIAN 10

Although speaking and listening is very important, don't forget that writing in Russian can also be of use. The activities in this book provide plenty of written practice, but you may also find it helpful to write your own sentences, even keep a simple diary, using the Russian you already know. Writing is a good consolidation exercise, since you can take your time to consider what you want to say. Start off simply, choosing appropriate vocabulary. Use your dictionary to look up any words you don't know. As you learn more vocabulary and grammar your writing will become more fluent.

Now start the recording for Unit 10.

(10.1) By metro

На метро́

ACTIVITY 1 is on the recording.

ACTIVITY 2

1 Which does the receptionist recommend – bus or metro?
2 Where is the entrance to the metro station?
3 Where can tokens for the metro be bought?
4 Is the university far from the metro station?

DIALOGUE 1

○ Скажи́те, пожа́луйста, как мне добра́ться до
   университе́та?

■ Мо́жно дое́хать авто́бусом, и́ли на метро́.

○ А как лу́чше?

■ Лу́чше на метро́. Вы зна́ете, где нахо́дится ста́нция метро́?

○ Э́то здесь, напро́тив гости́ницы, о́коло кио́сков?

■ Да-да. Вход в метро́ за кио́сками. Сади́тесь на по́езд,
   кото́рый идёт в центр. Че́рез две ста́нции бу́дет
   «Театра́льная». Там на́до пересе́сть на по́езд, кото́рый
   идёт из це́нтра к университе́ту. На шесто́й и́ли седьмо́й
   ста́нции вам на́до вы́йти.

○ А где мо́жно купи́ть биле́ты на метро́?

■ Не биле́ты, а жето́ны. Их мо́жно купи́ть там же в метро́, в
   ка́ссе и́ли в автома́те.

○ А университе́т далеко́ от метро́?

■ Далекова́то. От метро́ мо́жно дое́хать авто́бусом.

○ А каки́м авто́бусом?

■ Ой, я не зна́ю. На́до спроси́ть там, на ме́сте.

○ Спаси́бо.

■ Не́ за что.

VOCABULARY	
как мне добра́ться до	how do I get to ...?
сади́ться (II *imperf.*) на	to get on [*public transport*]
че́рез (+ *acc.*)	after [*with spatial expressions*]
пересе́сть (Ib *perf.*) на	to change [*public transport*]
направле́ние	direction
жето́н	token
автома́т	machine
далекова́то	quite far
на ме́сте	at that place, on the spot
не́ за что	don't mention it

ⓥ The instrumental case

The instrumental case has a number of different uses. It is used for means of transport – **автобусом** ('by bus'), **поездом** ('by train') – and times of the day – **утром** ('in the morning'), **вечером** ('in the evening'). It is also used after the following prepositions:

с/со	with	перед	in front of, before
над	above, over	под	underneath, under [location]
между	between	за	behind [location]

между гостиницей и **магазином** between the hotel and the shop.
чай **с молоком** tea with milk

ⓥ The instrumental singular of nouns

masculine nouns ending in

consonant	add **-ом**	вокза́л**ом**, го́род**ом**,
-ь	replace with **-ем**	го́ст**ем**, преподава́тел**ем**
	(if stressed, **-ём**	рубл**ём**)

feminine nouns ending in

-а	replace with **-ой**	ви́з**ой**, кни́г**ой**
-ь	add **-ю**	пло́щадь**ю**, две́рь**ю**
-ия	replace with **-ией**	револю́ц**ией**, ста́нц**ией**

neuter nouns ending in

-о	add **-м**	сло́во**м**, вино́**м**
-ие	add **-м**	свида́ние**м**

Note the effect of Spelling Rule 2 – see page 221 of the Grammar Summary: **у́лицей, гости́ницей, ме́сяцем**.

ACTIVITY 3

Supply the instrumental form of the noun in brackets.

1 Она́ говори́т с _____ . (преподава́тель)
2 Магази́н за _____ . (гости́ница)
3 За́втра _____ мы пойдём на прогу́лку. (у́тро)
4 Мо́жно дое́хать _____ . (авто́бус)
5 Ко́ля лю́бит борщ со _____ . (смета́на)

ACTIVITY 4

Translate the following phrases.

1 in front of the theatre
3 behind the church
5 coffee with milk
2 above the door
4 over the city
6 under the house

ⓐ Now do activities 5 and 6 on the recording.

137

Where's the bus-stop?

Где тут автобусная остановка?

ACTIVITY 7 is on the recording.

ACTIVITY 8

Correct the statements which are false.

1 Most buses go to the university.	T / F
2 Bus tickets are sold by the bus-driver.	T / F
3 Tram tickets can only be bought from kiosks.	T / F
4 Olga should either get out at the next stop but one …	T / F
5 … or the next stop, and walk from there.	T / F

DIALOGUE 2

○ Молодой человек, где тут автобусная остановка?

■ А вы куда едете?

○ Мне надо доехать до университета.

■ Остановка на другой стороне улицы, перед киоском с книгами.

○ Спасибо.

■ Пожалуйста.

...

○ Скажите, пожалуйста, на каком автобусе можно доехать до университета?

▲ На любом.

○ А где можно купить билеты?

▲ Талоны можно купить у водителя, как в трамвае.

...

○ Девушка, вы не скажете, сколько остановок до университета?

◇ Вам надо выйти через одну остановку. Или выйти на следующей и пройти пешком.

VOCABULARY

остановка (*gen. pl.* **остановок**)	stop [*e.g. bus stop*]
талон	ticket [*for buses, trams, etc.*]
водитель (*m*)	driver
трамвай	tram, streetcar
выйти Ib *perf.*	to get off
через одну остановку	the next stop but one
следующий	next

✓ The instrumental of pronouns

nom.	instr.	nom.	instr.
я	**мной**	мы	**на́ми**
ты	**тобо́й**	вы	**ва́ми**
он	**(н)им**	они́	**(н)и́ми**
она́	**(н)ей** or **(н)е́ю**		
оно́	**(н)им**		

Он пойдёт с **ва́ми**. He'll go with you.

The forms **им, ей/е́ю**, and **и́ми** gain an initial **н-** when used after prepositions, becoming **ним, ней/не́ю, ни́ми**.

Я не хочу́ говори́ть с **ни́ми**. I don't want to talk to them.

✓ The dative, instrumental, and prepositional plural of nouns

masculine nouns ending in

	dat. pl.	instr. pl.	prep. pl.
consonant	add **-ам**	add **-ами**	add **-ах**
	вокза́л**ам**	вокза́л**ами**	вокза́л**ах**
-ь	replace with **-ям**	replace with **-ями**	replace with **-ях**
	рубл**я́м**	рубл**я́ми**	рубл**я́х**

feminine nouns ending in

-а	replace with **-ам**	replace with **-ами**	replace with **-ах**
	ви́з**ам**	ви́з**ами**	ви́з**ах**
-ь	replace with **-ям**	replace with **-ями**	replace with **-ях**
	площад**я́м**	площад**я́ми**	площад**я́х**
-ия	replace with **-иям**	replace with **-иями**	replace with **-иях**
	револю́ц**иям**	револю́ц**иями**	револю́ц**иях**

neuter nouns ending in

-о	replace with **-ам**	replace with **-ами**	replace with **-ах**
	слов**а́м**	слов**а́ми**	слов**а́х**
-ие	replace with **-иям**	replace with **-иями**	replace with **-иях**
	свида́н**иям**	свида́н**иями**	свида́н**иях**

ACTIVITY 9

Supply the instrumental of the pronouns in brackets.

1 Пе́ред _____ – гости́ница «Метропо́ль». (вы)

2 Почему́ ты не говори́шь со _____ по-ру́сски? (я)

3 Мы придём с _____ за́втра. (он)

4 Па́па игра́ет с _____ . (они́)

5 Я не могу́ пойти́ с _____ (ты)

6 Вот по́чта, а за _____ – телефо́н-автома́т. (она́)

🎧 Now do activities 10 and 11 on the recording.

10.3 Local trains

Электри́чка

ACTIVITY 12 is on the recording.

ACTIVITY 13

Kolya and his mother are taking a (1) _____ train to
(2) _____ , arriving at (3) _____ . The train will leave
from platform (4) _____ , track (5) _____ .

DIALOGUE 3

○ Ко́ля, где мы ку́пим биле́ты на электри́чку?

■ Не волну́йся, ма́ма, у меня́ уже́ есть биле́ты.

○ А во ско́лько отхо́дит по́езд?

■ Я не зна́ю. Дава́й посмо́трим на расписа́ние. Там вся
   информа́ция о при́городных поезда́х.

   ...

○ Ко́ля, во ско́лько мы бу́дем в Петербу́рге?

■ В восемна́дцать три́дцать пять.

○ А нам ну́жно де́лать переса́дку?

■ Нет, э́то прямо́й по́езд.

   ...

■ Ма́ма, дава́й пройдём на платфо́рму.

○ А как нам туда́ пройти́?

■ Наве́рное, на́до сюда́ – ви́дишь, тут напи́сано «К
   поезда́м».

○ А с како́й платфо́рмы отхо́дит по́езд?

■ По́езд прибыва́ет на пе́рвую платфо́рму, второ́й путь.

   ...

○ Ко́ля, ра́зве э́то уже́ наш по́езд?

■ Я не зна́ю. Сейча́с спрошу́. Молодо́й челове́к, э́тот по́езд
   идёт в Петербу́рг?

▲ Да.

○ Ко́ля, э́то наш?

■ Наш, ма́ма. Бежи́м!

VOCABULARY	
расписа́ние	timetable
при́городный	suburban
де́лать la *imperf.* переса́дку	to change [*trains*]
прямо́й	direct
платфо́рма	platform
бежи́м	hurry!

✅ Dative, instrumental, prepositional plural of adjectives

	hard adj.	*soft adj.*
dat.	кра́сным	си́ним
instr.	кра́сными	си́ними
prep.	кра́сных	си́них

о кра́сных я́блоках about red apples

с си́ними паспорта́ми with dark blue passports

✅ Dative, instrumental, prepositional plural of possessives

Except for differences in stress, the endings for **мой, твой, наш**, and **ваш** are the same as the endings for soft adjectives (such as **си́ний**).

	my	*your (sing.)*	*our*	*your (pl., polite)*
dat.	мои́м	твои́м	на́шим	ва́шим
instr.	мои́ми	твои́ми	на́шими	ва́шими
prep.	мои́х	твои́х	на́ших	ва́ших

к **твои́м** роди́телям to your parents

пе́ред **на́шими** дома́ми in front of our houses

ACTIVITY 14

Complete 1–6 with the correct form of the adjective.

1 по _____ у́лицам (шу́мный, *dat. pl.*)
2 к _____ де́вушкам (молодо́й, *dat. pl.*)
3 с _____ о́кнами (откры́тый, *instr. pl.*)
4 пе́ред _____ проблéмами (тру́дный, *instr. pl.*)
5 о _____ я́блоках (вку́сный, *prep. pl*)
6 в _____ газéтах (сего́дняшний, *prep. pl.*)

ACTIVITY 15

Match 1–3 with the correct English version from a–c.

1 С како́й платфо́рмы отхо́дит по́езд?
2 Э́тот по́езд идёт в Москву́?
3 Во ско́лько отхо́дит по́езд?

a Is this the train for Moscow?
b What platform does the train go from?
c What time does the train go?

🎧 Now do activities 16 and 17 on the recording.

(10.4) An excursion

Экску́рсия

ACTIVITY 18

Look at the information on the leaflet below advertising a sightseeing excursion on the Moscow metro and answer the following questions.

1 What time does the excursion begin?
2 On what days does it take place?
3 How long does it last?
4 How much does it cost?
5 Where exactly does it start?

Экску́рсия по ста́нциям Моско́вского Метро́

Цена́ экску́рсии – 75 рубле́й.

Экску́рсия дли́тся два часа́.

Нача́ло в де́сять часо́в и в пятна́дцать часо́в, по суббо́там и воскресе́ньям.

Ме́сто сбо́ра – ста́нция метро́ «Пло́щадь Револю́ции» Замоскворе́цкой ли́нии, в це́нтре за́ла.

Маршру́т экску́рсии: мы начнём экску́рсию на ста́нции метро́ «Пло́щадь Револю́ции» Замоскворе́цкой ли́нии. Зате́м перейдём пешко́м на ста́нцию «Театра́льная» и прое́дем две остано́вки до ста́нции метро́ «Маяко́вская». Зате́м прое́дем до ста́нции «Белору́сская». Здесь переся́дем на Кольцеву́ю ли́нию и прое́дем две остано́вки до ста́нции метро́ «Ки́евская». Сле́дующая остано́вка в на́шей экску́рсии – «Парк Культу́ры». Здесь перейдём на Соко́льническую ли́нию и ся́дем на по́езд, кото́рый идёт в центр до ста́нции метро́ «Кропо́ткинская». Зате́м прое́дем до ста́нции «Комсомо́льская». Зате́м сно́ва перейдём на Кольцеву́ю ли́нию и прое́дем до ста́нции метро́ «Тага́нская». Здесь перейдём на Кали́нинскую ли́нии (на ста́нцию «Маркси́стская») и дое́дем до ста́нции метро́ «Третьяко́вская». По перехо́ду вы́йдем на ста́нцию метро́ «Новокузне́цкая». От ста́нции метро́ «Новокузне́цкая» вернёмся на ста́нцию метро́ «Пло́щадь Револю́ции», где зако́нчится на́ша экску́рсия.

NB Metro stations which are served by different lines often have a different name on each line. Pedestrian passageways (**перехо́ды**) connect the different sections of the station.

VOCABULARY	
сбор	assembly
ли́ния	line
зал	station concourse
нача́ть Ib *perf.* (начну́)	to begin
зате́м	after that, next
прое́хать Ib *perf.*	to go [*a certain distance by transport*]
пересе́сть Ib *perf.*	to change [*trains*]
перейти́ (Ib *perf.*) **на** (+ *acc.*)	to cross over [*on foot*]
зако́нчиться II *perf.*	to end

ACTIVITY 19

Your guidebook lists the following metro stations as the most interesting and worth visiting. Tick off which ones you will see if you take the excursion.

Новокузне́цкая, Пло́щадь Револю́ции, Кита́й-Го́род, Белору́сская, Парк Побе́ды, Маяко́вская, Пло́щадь Суво́рова, Комсомо́льская, Парк Культу́ры, Чи́стые Пруды́.

ACTIVITY 20

Fill in the missing words in the sentences below, paying attention to the endings. Refer back to the leaflet only if necessary.

1 Мы начнём _____ (excursion) на ста́нции метро́ «Пло́щадь Револю́ции».
2 Зате́м перейдём пешко́м на _____ (station) «Театра́льная».
3 Мы прое́дем _____ _____(two stops) до ста́нции метро́ «Ки́евская».
4 _____ (Next) остано́вка в на́шей экску́рсии – «Парк Культу́ры».
5 Здесь мы _____ (we will cross) на Соко́льническую ли́нию.
6 От ста́нции метро́ «Новокузне́цкая» _____ (we will return) на ста́нцию метро́ «Пло́щадь Револю́ции».

(10.5) Ла́рины

Мо́йра возвраща́ется в го́род
Moira goes back to the city

Having left the dacha in an agitated state, Moira is having difficulty finding her way back to the city and to her hostel.

VOCABULARY

что мне де́лать?	what should I do?
обра́тный	opposite, reverse
вам придётся …	you will have to …
до́лго	a long time

ACTIVITY 21

Listen to the story and decide whether the following statements are true or false. Correct the statements which are false.

1 The train Moira is on is going to Moscow.
2 Moira will have to wait a long time for a train going in the other direction.
3 Moira needs to get off the trolleybus at the next stop.
4 The bus stop Moira needs is between the kiosks and the post-office.
5 Moira can take any bus to Prospekt Vernadskogo.
6 The second man says that Moira can take a bus or a tram.
7 Moira finally decides on a taxi.

ACTIVITY 22

Listen to the story again and fill in the missing verbs.

1 Прости́те, э́тот по́езд _____ в Москву́?
2 Что же мне _____?
3 Но вам придётся до́лго _____.
4 Авто́бус _____ на проспе́кт Верна́дского?
5 Авто́бусная остано́вка _____ на друго́й стороне́ у́лицы.
6 Молодо́й челове́к, как мне _____ на проспе́кт Верна́дского?
7 Ну́жно _____ на метро́?!
8 Спаси́бо, я _____ такси́.

STORY TRANSCRIPT

Moira	Прости́те, э́тот по́езд идёт в Москву́?
Passenger 1	Нет, из Москвы́.
Moira	Бо́же мой! Что же мне де́лать?
Passenger 1	Вам ну́жно вы́йти на сле́дующей ста́нции и пересе́сть на по́езд, кото́рый идёт в обра́тном направле́нии. Но вам придётся до́лго ждать.
	...
Moira	Скажи́те, пожа́луйста, э́тот авто́бус е́дет на проспе́кт Верна́дского?
Passenger 2	Не понима́ю.
Moira	Авто́бус е́дет на проспе́кт Верна́дского?
Passenger 2	Э́то не авто́бус, а тролле́йбус. Вам на́до пересе́сть на сле́дующей остано́вке. Авто́бусная остано́вка нахо́дится на друго́й стороне́ у́лицы, ме́жду кио́сками и магази́ном «Молоко́». Вы дое́дете до проспе́кта Верна́дского на любо́м авто́бусе.
Moira	Спаси́бо.
Passenger 2	Не́ за что.
	...
Moira	Молодо́й челове́к, как мне пройти́ на проспе́кт Верна́дского?
Passerby	Проспе́кт Верна́дского? Э́то о́чень далеко́. Лу́чше дое́хать авто́бусом и́ли на метро́, но до ста́нции метро́ то́же далекова́то.
Moira	Ну́жно е́хать на метро́?! Спаси́бо, я возьму́ такси́.
	...
Moira	Прости́те, вы свобо́дны? Пожа́луйста, проспе́кт Верна́дского.

Before completing the test on pages 146–147 revise the dative, instrumental, and prepositional plural forms of nouns with the activity below.

ACTIVITY 23

Supply the correct form of the nouns in brackets.

1 Экску́рсия по _____ Росси́и. (го́род, *dat.pl.*)
2 Да́йте э́тот пода́рок _____ . (роди́тели, *dat. pl.*)
3 Э́то пе́ред _____ . (кио́ск, *instr. pl.*)
4 На́до говори́ть с _____ об э́том. (гость, *instr. pl.*)
5 Они́ живу́т в _____ . (дом, *prep. pl.*)
6 Я чита́ю о _____ Росси́и. (река́, *prep. pl.*)

Test

Now it's time to test your progress in Unit 10.

1 Match 1–4 with the appropriate English version from a–d.

1 с какóй платфóрмы   a can one get there by
  отхóдит пóезд?   metro?

2 э́тот пóезд идёт в   b what platform does the
  Москвý?   train go from?

3 нé за что   c does this train go to
                         Moscow?

4 мóжно доéхать на метрó? d don't mention it

4

2 Pair up 1–6 with an appropriate response from a–f.

1 Где мóжно купи́ть жетóны?
2 Как мне добрáться до пáрка?
3 На какóм автóбусе мóжно доéхать до гости́ницы?
4 Нам нýжно дéлать пересáдку?
5 Музéй нахóдится далекó от останóвки?
6 Скóлько останóвок до теáтра?

a Далековáто.
b Ещё две останóвки.
c Нет, э́то прямóй пóезд.
d В кáссе и́ли в автомáте.
e На любóм.
f Мóжно доéхать трамвáем.

6

3 Complete these sentences with the instrumental form of the pronouns in brackets.

1 Он не мóжет пойти́ с _____ . (ты)
2 Э́то мéжду _____ . (мы)
3 Вот магази́н «Ры́ба», а за _____ – стáнция метрó. (он)
4 Э́та америкáнка со _____ . (я)
5 Они́ не хотя́т говори́ть с _____ . (онá)
6 Подожди́те, пожáлуйста, с _____ . (они́)

6

4 Supply the instrumental singular of the nouns.

1 Он позвони́т за́втра _____ (ве́чер)
2 Она́ придёт с _____ (ба́бушка)
3 Кио́ск с газе́тами за _____ (вокза́л)
4 Я говорю́ с _____ (преподава́тель)
5 Ру́сские пьют чай с _____? (молоко́)
6 Они́, наве́рное, прие́дут _____ (по́езд)
7 Мо́жно дое́хать _____ (тролле́йбус)
8 Вот молодо́й челове́к с _____ (кни́га)
9 Сего́дня _____ у нас бу́дет свида́ние (у́тро)

9

5 How would you do the following in Russian?
   (2 points if correct, 1 point if only one error)

1 Ask if you can get there by bus.
2 Ask where you can buy bus tickets.
3 Ask where the bus stop is.
4 Ask which bus goes to the Kremlin.
5 Ask if this trolleybus goes to the Kremlin.
6 Ask if it's a direct train.
7 Ask if you need to change.
8 Ask a taxi-driver if he's free.

16

6 Answer the questions, using the English prompts as a
   guide. (2 points if correct, 1 point if only one error)

1 Где нахо́дится ста́нция метро́?
   Say it's behind the kiosks.
2 Когда́ мы пойдём в музе́й?
   Say tomorrow, in the morning.
3 Куда́ вы е́дете?
   Say you need to get to the university.
4 Где мы ку́пим биле́ты?
   Say you already have the tickets.
5 Э́то прямо́й по́езд?
   Say you don't know.

10

TOTAL SCORE **51**

If you scored less than 41, re-read the Language Building
sections before completing the Summary on page 148.

Summary 10

Now try this final activity summarizing the main points in this unit. You can find the answers on the recording.

How would you:
1 ask where you can buy tokens?
2 ask which bus goes to the university?
3 ask if you need to change?
4 ask what platform the train goes from?
5 ask if this train goes to Moscow?
6 say 'with me'? 'with him'?
7 say 'in the morning', 'in the evening'?
8 say 'by bus'? 'by train'?

REVISION

You have now met all the cases in Russian. Before you try Review 3, try making a list from memory of all the prepositions you have encountered so far, arranging them according to the cases they require. You will probably find you have forgotten quite a few – check back through earlier units to see which ones you missed. This information can be found in Units 3 (genitive), 4 (accusative), 7 (prepositional), 9 (dative), and 10 (instrumental).

As well as occurring after prepositions, the cases often have other uses. For example, the accusative is the case used for the direct object of a verb. The genitive is used to express possession and quantities with 'of'. The dative expresses the indirect object, and is used in expressing feelings, emotions, ages, and the like. The instrumental can express a means of transport, times of the day, 'in a season', and so on. The prepositional is the only case with no other uses than its occurrence after certain prepositions.

Try writing out a list of the different uses of the different cases, with example sentences for each. You will find more information and examples in the Grammar Summary at the end of the book.

Review 3

1 Which is the odd one out in each group?

1 Гре́ция / Еги́пет / Ту́рция / Пари́ж
2 ба́бушка / тётя / па́па / сестра́
3 Восьмо́е ма́рта / Рождество́ / Кра́сная пло́щадь / Па́сха
4 тролле́йбус / автома́т / электри́чка / трамва́й
5 ноя́брь / сентя́брь / янва́рь / календа́рь

2 Match 1–5 with the correct English version from a–e.

1 О́льга уме́ет ката́ться на конька́х. a Olga is very religious.
2 О́льга сего́дня о́чень занята́. b Olga is very busy today.
3 О́льга о́чень ве́рующая. c Olga is looking at the timetable.
4 О́льге не нра́вятся цветы́. d Olga can skate.
5 О́льга смо́трит на расписа́ние. e Olga doesn't like the flowers.

GRAMMAR AND USAGE

3 Complete the sentences with the correct form of the verb in brackets (these are all perfective verbs), making a perfective future.

1 Ты _____ такси́? (взять, Ib)
2 Когда́ ты _____ на по́чту? (пойти́, Ib)
3 Они́ _____ в суббо́ту. (уе́хать, Ib)
4 Ива́н _____ поку́пки. (сде́лать, Ia)
5 Я _____ «А́нну Каре́нину». (прочита́ть, Ia)

4 Complete the sentences with the correct form of **быть**, making an imperfective future.

1 Вы _____ лежа́ть на пля́же?
2 Ра́зве они́ _____ ходи́ть в рестора́ны?
3 Я не _____ звони́ть ка́ждый день.
4 Она́ _____ говори́ть по-францу́зски.
5 Мы _____ де́лать поку́пки ка́ждый день.

5 Complete the sentences with the dative singular of the nouns in brackets.

1 Я хочу́ пойти́ на прогу́лку по _____ . (го́род)
2 Сёстры скуча́ют по _____ . (ма́ма)
3 Да́йте э́то _____ . (гость)
4 Дава́йте пойдём на экску́рсию по _____ . (Москва́)
5 Скажи́ _____ об э́том. (Бори́с)

6 Complete the sentences with the dative forms of the pronouns in brackets.

1 _____ не о́чень нра́вится гости́ница. (он)
2 Да́йте _____, пожа́луйста, «Пра́вду». (я)
3 _____ гру́стно? (ты)
4 Я _____ позвоню́ за́втра у́тром. (вы)
5 _____ на́до идти́ домо́й. (она́)

7 Complete the sentences with the appropriate modal form.

1 _____ его́ вывози́ть? (is it permitted to?)
2 _____ говори́ть по-англи́йски. (don't)
3 Её _____ уви́деть. (it is impossible to)
4 Мне _____ сиде́ть в холо́дном до́ме. (not allowed to)
5 Им _____ войти́? (can they?)

8 Complete the sentences with the instrumental singular of the nouns in brackets.

1 Мо́жно дое́хать _____? (по́езд)
2 Вы пойдёте с _____ . (ма́ма)
3 Он придёт за́втра _____ . (ве́чер)
4 Магази́н за _____ . (по́чта)
5 Я не люблю́ чай с _____ . (молоко́)

9 Complete the sentences with the instrumental forms of the pronouns in brackets.

1 О́чень ра́да с _____ познако́миться. (вы)
2 Я не могу́ пойти́ с _____ . (ты)
3 Вот по́чта, а за _____ – магази́н. (она́)
4 Он пое́дет со _____ . (я)
5 Э́то ме́жду _____ . (мы)

10 It's your first day in Moscow and your Intourist guide is telling you about your sight-seeing programme for the next few days. Listen to what she says and answer the questions below.

1 Where, and at what time, do you meet tomorrow?
2 What will you be able to do in GUM (the State Department Store)?
3 What two things are planned for Wednesday?
4 What is happening on Thursday morning?
5 What is happening at 8 p.m. on Thursday?
6 What time is the night-train to St Petersburg?
7 How long will you be staying in St Petersburg?
8 What two excursions are planned for there?
9 On what does the visit to the Mariinsky Theatre depend?

11 You've asked at your hotel reception for directions to V.V.Ts., the All-Russia Exhibition Centre. Listen to the instructions and decide whether the statements below are true or false.

1 It's quicker to go by bus.   T / F
2 The Okhotny Ryad metro station is opposite
   the hotel.   T / F
3 You can also walk to the Turgenevskaya metro
   station from the hotel.   T / F
4 At Turgenevskaya you need to take a train
   coming from the centre.   T / F
5 You need to get out at the fifth station –
   V.D.N.Kh.   T / F
6 You cannot walk to V.V.Ts. from the metro.   T / F

12 You're on an Intourist package holiday to Moscow. To find out everything you want to know, you need to ask a lot of questions.

Ask your guide about the planned sightseeing: in particular you want to know when you'll return to the hotel (1), and what your plans are for Tuesday and Wednesday (2).

At dinner, you get chatting to another hotel guest. Ask her if she likes the hotel (3). She's off to St Petersburg tomorrow – ask her where she'll be staying (4). She tells you she's bought a samovar as a souvenir – ask her if she'll be able to export it (5).

Next morning, you decide to do some independent sight-seeing. Ask at reception how to get to the Kremlin (6). The receptionist suggests a bus – but where can you buy tickets (7)? How many stops is it (8)? Do you need to change (9)? Perhaps, after all, it would be easier to go with the group…

13 Now it's time for you to answer some questions. Listen to the questions on the recording and give an appropriate answer. You'll be asked – though not necessarily in this order – about:

    – your holiday plans
    – how you're feeling
    – your age
    – your plans for the week
    – whether you like certain food

11

Do you remember?

Ты по́мнишь?

OBJECTIVES

In this unit you'll learn how to:

✓ talk about past experiences

✓ make a telephone call

✓ give the date

And cover the following grammar and language:

✓ the past tense: the perfective and imperfective past

✓ further uses of the instrumental

✓ impersonal constructions with the dative in the past

✓ the accusative and genitive of adjectives and possessives

✓ adjectives after numbers

✓ ordinal numbers for dates

LEARNING RUSSIAN 11

When learning a language, it is important to recycle vocabulary and structures so that you can use what you have learnt in as many different contexts as possible. This has been done throughout the course, but you can do more yourself to suit your own needs and interests. At the end of each unit, see how you can combine what you have just learnt with what you already know. For example, once you have learnt the past tense in this unit, you can combine it with the language of Unit 5 and talk about what you have done at different times and on different days, or with the language of Unit 9 and say how you felt on a particular occasion.

Now start the recording for Unit 11.

(11.1) Oh, what times they were!

Какие это были времена!

🔊 **ACTIVITY 1** is on the recording.

ACTIVITY 2

1 The man lived with his parents in a communal flat.	T / F
2 His mother worked in a factory.	T / F
3 In the winter they would go to Sochi or Yalta.	T / F
4 He moved to Kazan because he got work there.	T / F

DIALOGUE 1

○ Вы всегда жили в Казани?

■ Нет, не всегда. Я родился в Москве. Мы там жили с родителями в большой коммунальной квартире на улице Большая Полянка. Кроме нас там жили ещё три семьи – Ивановы, Скороходовы, а третья – кто они были? Не помню. Ой, как давно это всё было!

○ Чем занимались ваши родители?

■ Мой папа работал на фабрике, а мама работала в продовольственном магазине. Это была очень хорошая работа. У нас всегда была колбаса, были фрукты …

○ А где вы проводили отпуск?

■ Летом мы ездили в Сочи или в Ялту в санаторий от фабрики, где работал папа. Боже, какие это были времена!

○ А когда вы переехали в Казань?

■ После учёбы я получил работу в Казани. Я приехал сюда, женился, да и остался здесь. Наверное, здесь и умру.

VOCABULARY	
мы … с родителями	my parents and I
кроме (+ gen.)	apart from
давно	a long time ago
чем [instr. of что]	what
заниматься Ia imperf. (+ inst.)	to work (on, in)
фабрика	factory
продовольственный	food, grocery [adjective]
колбаса	Continental sausage, salami
фрукты (pl.)	fruit
переехать (Ib perf.) в (+ acc.)	to move to
получить II perf.	to receive, to get
жениться II perf./imperf.	to get married [of a man]
остаться Ib perf.	to remain
умереть Ib perf. (умру)	to die

✅ The past tense: the perfective and imperfective past

The past tense can be formed from both perfective and imperfective verbs. The *perfective past* is used to refer to a one-off event or stresses the result or successful completion of an action. The *imperfective past* refers to repeated events in the past or stresses the ongoing or habitual nature of a past event.

The past tense is formed from the infinitive of the verb: the final -ть is replaced by -л, plus a feminine, neuter, or plural ending if required. If the verb is reflexive, the ending -ся (after a consonant) or -сь (after a vowel) appears at the very end of the form.

	m	*f*	*n*	*pl*
жить	жил	жила́	жи́ло	жи́ли
быть	был	была́	бы́ло	бы́ли
рабо́тать	рабо́тал	рабо́тала	рабо́тало	рабо́тали
роди́ться	роди́лся	родила́сь	родило́сь	родили́сь

Я **жил** (*imperf.*) в Ло́ндоне. I lived in London.
Она́ **была́** (*imperf.*) в Москве́. She was in Moscow.
Вы **родили́сь** (*perf.*) в Москве́? Were you born in Moscow?

✅ The seasons

To say 'in' a particular season, the instrumental is used without a preposition: **весно́й** 'in spring', **ле́том** 'in summer', **о́сенью** 'in autumn', **зимо́й** 'in winter'.

Зимо́й он лю́бит ката́ться на конька́х. He loves skating in winter.

✅ бы́ло + the dative

Impersonal constructions with a noun or pronoun in the dative add **бы́ло** (invariable) in the past.

Ему́ **бы́ло** два́дцать два го́да. He was twenty-two.
Мо́жно **бы́ло** рабо́тать. You could work.

ACTIVITY 3

Put the verb in brackets into the past. Note the difference in emphasis/meaning between imperfective and perfective past.

1 Она́ всегда́ _____ в Росси́и. (жить) (*imperf.*)
2 Чем он там _____? (занима́ться) (*imperf.*)
3 Что вы там _____ о́сенью? (де́лать) (*imperf.*)
4 Они́ уже́ _____ поку́пки. (сде́лать) (*perf.*)
5 Она́ _____ в Санкт-Петербу́рге. (роди́ться) (*perf.*)
6 Когда́ он _____ в Москву́? (перее́хать) (*perf.*)

🔊 Now do activities 4 and 5 on the recording.

Два но́вых пле́да

ACTIVITY 6 is on the recording.

ACTIVITY 7

1 What happened to Kolya's mother on the train?
2 What is Kolya's father glad about?
3 What exactly did Kolya's father say he wanted?
4 What does Kolya's mother think he should in fact buy?

DIALOGUE 2

○ Алло́!

■ Здра́вствуйте! Мо́жно попроси́ть Никола́я Никола́евича?

○ Приве́т, ма́ма.

■ Ко́ля, э́то ты? Я тебя́ не узна́ла. Как ты пожива́ешь?

○ Хорошо́, ма́ма. А ты как? Как ты добрала́сь? Норма́льно?

■ Да, спаси́бо, всё в поря́дке. В по́езде я познако́милась с о́чень интере́сной же́нщиной. Её зову́т Ли́дия Васи́льевна... и́ли Влади́мировна, я не по́мню – нет, то́чно Васи́льевна, и она́ ...

○ Ма́ма, прости́, я сего́дня о́чень за́нят. Скажи́, ты спроси́ла па́пу о пода́рке?

■ Коне́чно, спроси́ла. Он о́чень рад, что ты прие́дешь на его́ день рожде́ния. По́мнишь, ты обеща́л?

○ Да, ма́ма, я по́мню. А скажи́, что ему́ подари́ть?

■ Вот он говори́т, что хо́чет но́вый плед. «Большо́й, тёплый плед» – так он сказа́л. Но мне ка́жется, что лу́чше купи́ть два но́вых пле́да, пра́вда?

○ Пра́вда, ма́мочка. Хорошо́, я куплю́ два больши́х тёплых пле́да. Ма́ма, я тебе́ за́втра позвоню́, ла́дно?

■ Хорошо́. Всё, Ко́ля, пока́!

○ Пока́, ма́ма!

VOCABULARY	
узна́ть Iа *perf.*	to recognize
норма́льно	OK, all right
же́нщина	woman
то́чно	definitely
обеща́ть Iа	to promise
плед	rug [*for keeping warm*]
тёплый	warm

✓ The accusative and genitive of adjectives

	m	f	n	pl
acc.	кра́сный	кра́сную	кра́сное	кра́сные
gen.	кра́сного	кра́сной	кра́сного	кра́сных
acc.	си́ний	си́нюю	си́нее	си́ние
gen.	си́него	си́ней	си́него	си́них

Я ви́дел **Кра́сную** пло́щадь. I've seen Red Square.
Вы чита́ли **сего́дняшнюю** газе́ту? Have you read today's paper?
Э́то о́коло **Большо́го** теа́тра. It's near the Bolshoi Theatre.

✓ The accusative and genitive of possessives

твой ('your') is declined like **мой** ('my') and **ваш** ('your' plural/polite) is declined like **наш** ('our').

	m	f	n	pl
acc.	мой	мою́	моё	мои́
gen.	моего́	мое́й	моего́	мои́х
acc.	наш	на́шу	на́ше	на́ши
gen.	на́шего	на́шей	на́шего	на́ших

Кто взял **мою́** кни́гу? Who has taken my book?
Вот дом **твоего́** дру́га. There is your friend's house.

✓ Adjectives after numbers

Nouns after numbers (other than **оди́н**) either go into the genitive singular or genitive plural. Adjectives after numbers *always* go into the genitive plural, even if followed by a noun in the genitive singular.
два **но́вых** (*gen. pl.*) пле́да (*gen. sing.*) two new rugs
три **больши́х** (*gen. pl.*) **тёплых** (*gen. pl.*) пле́да (*gen. sing.*)
three big warm rugs
пять **но́вых** (*gen. pl.*) рестора́нов (*gen. pl.*) five new restaurants

---

ACTIVITY 8

Supply the correct form of the adjective or possessive.

1 Дай _____ су́мку (большо́й – *f acc. sing.*)
2 О́коло _____ до́ма (пе́рвый – *m gen. sing.*)
3 Четы́ре _____ пле́да (тёплый – *gen. pl.*)
4 Оди́ннадцать _____ книг (но́вый – *gen. pl.*)
5 Она́ зна́ет _____ рабо́ту (мой – *f. acc. sing.*)
6 И́мя _____ го́стя (твой – *m gen. sing.*)

🎧 Now do activities 9 and 10 on the recording.

11.3 Can I speak to Gleb, please?
Мóжно Глéба?

🎧 **ACTIVITY 11** is on the recording.

ACTIVITY 12

The first call Svetlana makes is a wrong number. The second time she calls she gets through to (1) _____ . Gleb isn't in – he's gone to (2) _____ . The third time she calls, she gets through to (3) _____ . Gleb says their trip is planned for (4) _____ .

DIALOGUE 3

○ Здрáвствуйте, мóжно Глéба?
■ Когó?
○ Глéба.
■ Нет, вы не тудá попáли.
○ Извинѝте, пожáлуйста.

...

○ Здрáвствуйте, мóжно Глéба?
▲ Привéт, Свéта, э́то Борѝс. Глéба сейчáс нéт. Он пошёл на стадиóн.
○ А когдá он бýдет?
▲ Навéрное, чéрез час.
○ Спасѝбо, я позвоню́ попóзже. До свидáния.
▲ Ну покá.

...

○ Здрáвствуйте, мóжно Глéба?
◇ Слýшаю.
○ Привéт, Глеб. Говорѝт Светлáна.
◇ Привéт, Свéта. Как делá?
○ Хорошó, спасѝбо. Глеб, я забы́ла, когдá мы поéдем к твоѝм родѝтелям – двенáдцатого ѝли девятнáдцатого ию́ня?
◇ Мы поéдем во вторýю суббóту в ию́не. Э́то бýдет двенáдцатого.
○ Двенáдцатого ию́ня, хорошó. Ну всё, покá.
◇ Покá.

VOCABULARY	
пошёл	went [*past tense of* **пойтѝ**]
стадиóн	stadium
попóзже	a bit later
как делá?	how's things?
забы́ть Ib *perf.*	to forget

158

✅ Giving the date

The neuter form of the ordinal number is used, and the month is in the genitive.

Како́е сего́дня число́? What's the date?
Сего́дня **трина́дцатое апре́ля**. It's the 13th of April.
Сего́дня **два́дцать восьмо́е ию́ня**. It's the 28th of June.

	nom. (neuter)	*gen.*
13th	трина́дцатое	трина́дцатого
14th	четы́рнадцатое	четы́рнадцатого
15th	пятна́дцатое	пятна́дцатого
16th	шестна́дцатое	шестна́дцатого
17th	семна́дцатое	семна́дцатого
18th	восемна́дцатое	восемна́дцатого
19th	девятна́дцатое	девятна́дцатого
20th	двадца́тое	двадца́того
21st	два́дцать пе́рвое	два́дцать пе́рвого
30th	тридца́тое	тридца́того

To say 'on' a particular date, the ordinal number is simply put into the genitive – no preposition is used.

Он прие́хал **восьмо́го февраля́**. He arrived on the 8th of February.
Я верну́сь **пе́рвого ма́рта**. I'm coming back on the 1st of March.

ACTIVITY 13

Match the dates with the appropriate English version.

1	двена́дцатого ма́рта	a	on the 16th of March
2	два́дцать пе́рвое ма́рта	b	the 18th of March
3	два́дцать пе́рвого ма́я	c	the 21st of March
4	шестна́дцатого ма́рта	d	on the 21st of May
5	восемна́дцатое ма́рта	e	on the 12th of March

ACTIVITY 14

Match 1–5 with the appropriate English version from a–e.

1	мо́жно Мари́ю?	a	I'll call later
2	слу́шаю	b	wrong number
3	вы не туда́ попа́ли	c	when will she be in?
4	я позвоню́ попо́зже	d	speaking
5	когда́ она́ бу́дет?	e	can I speak to Mariya, please?

🎧 Now do activities 15 and 16 on the recording.

11.4 Vera Nikolaevna Gorenko
Ве́ра Никола́евна Го́ренко

ACTIVITY 17

Look at the interview below with Vera Nikolaevna Gorenko, a
93-year-old Muscovite, about her memories of Moscow in
days gone by. Match the Russian words below with their
English translations, using the text to help you.

1	разгово́р	a	school
2	большеви́к	b	tsar
3	экипа́ж	c	motor-car
4	царь (*m*)	d	carriage
5	полити́ческий	e	conversation
6	шко́ла	f	Bolshevik
7	автомоби́ль (*m*)	g	political

Разгово́р с Ве́рой Никола́евной Го́ренко

Ве́ре Никола́евне Го́ренко сего́дня исполня́ется 93 го́да.
Она́ прожила́ всю жизнь в Москве́. Уже́ 55 лет она́
живёт в Спасопеско́вском переу́лке о́коло Арба́та.

К.П. Ве́ра Никола́евна, вспо́мните, пожа́луйста, Ва́ше де́тство.
Как Вы тогда́ жи́ли?

В.Н. Я родила́сь в Москве́. Э́то бы́ло до револю́ции, ещё при
царе́. Мне бы́ло де́сять лет, когда́ большевики́ пришли́ к
вла́сти. Я по́мню, что в Москве́ бы́ли больши́е беспоря́дки.
Да́же шко́лы бы́ли закры́ты. Не́которое вре́мя я вообще́ не
ходи́ла в шко́лу.

К.П. Как тогда́ вы́глядела Москва́?

В.Н. Я по́мню, что бы́ло о́чень мно́го экипаже́й с лошадьми́.
Автомоби́лей тогда́ бы́ло ма́ло. Я о́чень люби́ла лошаде́й
и по́сле шко́лы всегда́ ходи́ла корми́ть их. За на́шим
до́мом была́ коню́шня.

К.П. А каки́е полити́ческие собы́тия Вы по́мните?

В.Н. Пе́рвое, что я по́мню, э́то когда́ у́мер Ле́нин. Я по́мню,
что я стоя́ла на у́лице и пла́кала. Все тогда́ пла́кали. Вся
страна́ была́ в тра́уре.

К.П. А как Вы вспомина́ете Ста́лина?

В.Н. Снача́ла мы его́ о́чень люби́ли. Вы по́мните ло́зунги:
«Ста́лин – Ле́нин сего́дня!», «Ста́лин – наш Оте́ц и
Учи́тель»? А пото́м, коне́чно, пришли́ стра́шные времена́.
Тридца́ть седьмо́й, три́дцать восьмо́й год… Ка́ждый боя́лся
– кто же бу́дет сле́дующий? Весь мир как бу́дто сошёл с ума́.

CULTURE

ACTIVITY 18

Now read the interview again and answer the following questions.

1 Where, and when, was Vera Nikolaevna born?
2 What happened when she was ten?
3 Why did she stop going to school for a while?
4 What does she remember about how Moscow looked in those days?
5 What is her first political memory?
6 How did people feel about Stalin at first?
7 What are the slogans she mentions?
8 Which years does she describe as terrible?

VOCABULARY

переу́лок	lane, narrow street
Арба́т	the Arbat [*a street in Moscow*]
вспо́мнить II *perf.*, вспомина́ть Ia *imperf.*	to recall, to remember
де́тство	childhood
при (+ *prep.*)	during the reign of, under
пришли́ к вла́сти	came to power
вла́сть (*f*)	power
беспоря́дки	disturbances
не́которое вре́мя	for some time
вы́глядеть II *imperf.*	to look
ло́шадь (*f*) (*inst. pl.* лошадьми́)	horse
корми́ть II *imperf.*	to feed
коню́шня	stable
собы́тие	event
у́мер	died
стоя́ть II *imperf.*	to stand
все	everyone
тра́ур	mourning
ло́зунг	slogan
оте́ц	father
учи́тель (*m*)	teacher
стра́шный	terrible
боя́ться II *imperf.*	to be afraid
мир	world
как бу́дто	as if, as though
сойти́ Ib *perf.* с ума́	to go mad

Разгово́р о про́шлом
A conversation about the past

Ivan Grigorevich and Evgeniya Pavlovna are back in the flat in Moscow. As they sit drinking tea and eating jam, they discuss how Russia has changed since they were young.

VOCABULARY	
Же́ня	*short form of the name Evgeniya*
про́шлое	the past [*adjective*]
измени́ться II *perf.*	to change
больни́ца	hospital
зараба́тывать Ia *imperf.*	to earn
не́ было	there wasn't, there weren't
проду́кты	foodstuffs, produce
круго́м	all around
кефи́р	kefir [*a sour milk product*]
голода́ть Ia *imperf.*	to starve
нали́ть Ib *perf.*	to pour
варе́нье	jam; whole fruit preserve
пе́нсия	pension
хвата́ть Ia *imperf.*	to be enough
на жизнь не хвата́ет	it's not enough to live on
хулига́нство	hooliganism
выходи́ть II *imperf.*	to leave, go out
НКВД	NKVD [*forerunner of KGB*]
сиде́ть II *imperf.*	to sit, to be imprisoned
ГУЛА́Г	GULAG [*corrective labour camp*]
те	those
прошли́	passed [*past tense of* пройти́]
лю́ди, (*instr.* людьми́)	people
путеше́ствовать Ib *imperf.* (путеше́ствую)	to travel
знако́миться II *imperf.*	to meet, to get acquainted
впереди́	ahead

ACTIVITY 19

Listen to the story and answer the following questions.

1 Where did Ivan use to work?
2 Where did Evgeniya use to work?
3 What examples does Evgeniya give of the problems with foodstuffs?
4 What does Ivan say about their pensions?
5 What does Evgeniya say about Ivan's brother?
6 What does Evgeniya say about what their children can do?

ACTIVITY 20

Listen to the story again and fill in the missing past tense verbs.

1 Же́ня, как всё _____ !
2 Ты по́мнишь, когда́ мы _____ ?
3 Норма́льно _____ .
4 И что же мо́жно _____ купи́ть на на́ши де́ньги?
5 Но мы же не _____ !
6 А ты не по́мнишь, как мы тогда́ _____ НКВД?
7 Я о́чень ра́да, что те времена́ _____ .

STORY TRANSCRIPT

Ivan	Же́ня, как всё измени́лось! Ты по́мнишь, когда́ мы познако́мились? Мы бы́ли таки́е молоды́е! Ка́жется, что мир тогда́ был совсе́м друго́й, лу́чше.
Evgeniya	Да что ты говори́шь, Ва́ня! Как же э́то – лу́чше ?
Ivan	Ты по́мнишь, я тогда́ рабо́тал в метро́, а ты в больни́це. Норма́льно зараба́тывали, не́ было пробле́м с деньга́ми.
Evgeniya	И что же мо́жно бы́ло купи́ть на на́ши де́ньги? По́мнишь, каки́е тогда́ бы́ли пробле́мы с проду́ктами – вхо́дишь в магази́н, а круго́м пу́сто. И́ли хо́чешь купи́ть смета́ну – есть то́лько кефи́р. Хо́чешь кефи́р – есть то́лько смета́на.
Ivan	Но мы же не голода́ли!
Evgeniya	Ну и сейча́с не голода́ем. Ва́ня, тебе́ ещё ча́ю нали́ть?
Ivan	Да, пожа́луйста. Дай ещё варе́нья. А что же мо́жно купи́ть сего́дня на на́ши пе́нсии? Да́же на жизнь не хвата́ет. А како́е хулига́нство круго́м! Я да́же бою́сь выходи́ть из кварти́ры.
Evgeniya	А ты не по́мнишь, как мы тогда́ боя́лись НКВД? Ведь твой брат, Ю́рий, сиде́л в ГУЛА́Ге. Нет, Ва́ня, я о́чень ра́да, что те времена́ прошли́. Коне́чно, нам, ста́рым лю́дям, жить тру́дно. Но посмотри́ на на́ших дете́й, на Мари́ю, Оле́га, Петра́. Они́ путеше́ствуют, знако́мятся с интере́сными людьми́ – с Мо́йрой, наприме́р. Кака́я у них интере́сная жизнь! Они́ уже́ забыва́ют, как всё тогда́ бы́ло.
Ivan	Да, Же́ня, ты права́. У них всё впереди́.

Test

Now it's time to test your progress in Unit 11.

1 Match 1–6 with the correct English version from a–f.

1 о́сенью у нас бы́ли фру́кты
2 не́ было пробле́м с деньга́ми
3 я не ходи́ла в шко́лу
4 когда́ у́мер Ста́лин?
5 я познако́мился с интере́сной же́нщиной
6 мир был совсе́м друго́й

a I've met an interesting woman
b I didn't go to school
c when did Stalin die?
d money wasn't a problem
e we had fruit in autumn
f the world was quite different

| 6 |

2 Pair up 1–6 with an appropriate response from a–f.

1 Мо́жно Бори́са?
2 Вы не туда́ попа́ли.
3 Алло́!
4 Мо́жно попроси́ть Мари́ю.
5 Когда́ она́ бу́дет?
6 Он бу́дет че́рез час.

a Слу́шаю.
b В семь часо́в ве́чера.
c Хорошо́, я позвоню́ попо́зже.
d Её сейча́с нет.
e Извини́те, пожа́луйста.
f Здра́вствуйте!

| 6 |

3 Supply the correct form of the adjective.

1 Я чита́л _____ газе́ту (сего́дняшний)
2 Он взял _____ су́мку (большо́й)
3 И́мя _____ преподава́теля (но́вый)
4 Недалеко́ от _____ пло́щади (Кра́сный)
5 Два _____ самова́ра (новый)
6 Три́дцать _____ домо́в (ста́рый)

| 6 |

4 Supply the correct form of the possessive.

1 Вы зна́ете _____ сестру́ (мой)
2 Вы взя́ли _____ газе́ту (наш)
3 Фами́лия _____ го́стя (твой)
4 Дом _____ тёти (ваш)
5 Без _____ паспорто́в (ваш)
6 У _____ друзе́й (мой)

6

5 Supply the past imperfective or perfective.

1 Они́ _____ тогда́ в Чика́го. (жить, *imperf.*)
2 Чем вы _____? (занима́ться, *imperf.*)
3 Евге́ния _____ в больни́це. (рабо́тать, *imperf.*)
4 Зимо́й он _____ на конька́х. (ката́ться, *imperf.*)
5 Ле́том мы _____ квас. (пить, *imperf.*)
6 Вы _____ на́ше письмо́? (получи́ть, *perf.*)
7 Где вы _____ ? (роди́ться, *perf.*)
8 Тётя _____ поку́пки. (сде́лать, *perf.*)
9 Татья́на _____ в Каза́нь. (перее́хать, *perf.*)

9

6 How would you say the following things in Russian?
(2 points if correct, 1 point if only one error)

1 Ask a new work colleague if he has always lived in Moscow.
2 Ask your boss when she moved to St Petersburg.
3 Ask to speak to Gleb on the phone.
4 Ask a close friend how he is getting on.
5 Say your mother worked in a hospital.
6 Say it was a good job.
7 Say you'll call later.
8 Say 'wrong number'.

16

TOTAL SCORE **49**

If you scored less than 39, re-read the Language Building sections before completing the Summary on page 166.

Summary 11

Now try this final test summarizing the main points covered in this unit. You can check your answers on the recording.

How would you:
1 ask to speak to Nikolai on the phone?
2 ask when he'll be in?
3 ask someone you don't know well where he was born?
4 ask a close friend if she got there all right?
5 say you played football?
6 say 'in winter'? 'in spring'?
7 say 'today is the 12th of March'?
8 say 'on the 18th of September'?

REVISION

Look through your diary and say what you did on different dates: 'on 30th of June I had a meeting with X'; 'the 12th of July was X's birthday – he was forty'; 'on the 3rd of May I was working'; 'on the 5th of May I was travelling'; and so on. You could practise the seasons too, with the imperfective past; 'in spring I played football', 'in winter I read books', and so on.

Before moving on to the next unit, play Unit 11 through again and check your progress. See how the new endings you have learnt for adjectives and possessives fit into the tables along with those you know already. If you feel your memory for endings is getting to saturation point, don't worry – the end is in sight! By the end of the next unit you will have met all the endings for nouns, adjectives and possessives, as well as all the forms of pronouns and verbs.

12

Eating out
В рестора́не и в кафе́

OBJECTIVES

In this unit you'll learn how to:

- ✔ book a table in a restaurant
- ✔ order in a café
- ✔ agree and disagree
- ✔ pay the bill

And cover the following grammar and language:

- ✔ the dative and instrumental singular of adjectives and possessives
- ✔ что́-то and что́-нибудь ('something')
- ✔ the verbs есть ('to eat') and дать ('to give')
- ✔ э́тот ('this'), тот ('that')
- ✔ согла́сен ('I agree')

LEARNING RUSSIAN 12

Good language learners take risks and don't mind making mistakes. Making some mistakes with endings in a language like Russian is inevitable, but even if in the heat of the moment you get most of your endings wrong it is usually possible to make yourself understood somehow. Taking risks and making mistakes is the only way to make progress.

Re-doing the activities in this book at your leisure, when you have time to look back over the grammar sections and check the tables of endings, will help to consolidate your knowledge and identify your weak areas. Do this regularly so that you know where you need to do more work and can improve accordingly.

Now start the recording for Unit 12.

Now start the recording for Unit 12.

Я хочу́ заказа́ть сто́лик

(1 A) **ACTIVITY 1** is on the recording.

ACTIVITY 2

Complete the summary

Reservation made for:

1 _____ (day / date)
2 _____ (time)
3 _____ (number of people)
4 _____ (dining-area)

DIALOGUE 1

○ Алло́!

■ Здра́вствуйте. Э́то рестора́н «Пра́га»?

○ Да, слу́шаю.

■ Я хочу́ заказа́ть сто́лик.

○ Подожди́те.

...

△ «Пра́га», слу́шаю.

■ Здра́вствуйте. Я хочу́ заказа́ть сто́лик.

△ На како́й день?

■ На вто́рник, пятна́дцатого ию́ня.

△ Пятна́дцатого ию́ня. На кото́рый час?

■ На девятна́дцать часо́в.

△ Девятна́дцать часо́в. А на ско́лько челове́к?

■ На четырёх челове́к.

△ В како́м за́ле?

■ Я не зна́ю. Каки́е у вас есть за́лы?

△ Ра́зные. Вы хоти́те смотре́ть шо́у?

■ Да, коне́чно.

△ Хорошо́, э́то бу́дет второ́й зал. Фами́лия?

■ Га-га-рин, Алексе́й Семёнович.

VOCABULARY

заказа́ть Ib *perf.*	to book, to reserve
сто́лик	table [*diminutive of* **стол** *table*]
подожда́ть Ib *perf.*	to wait
на ско́лько челове́к?	for how many people?
на четырёх челове́к	for four people
зал	dining-area, hall
ра́зный	different, various
шо́у	floor-show, cabaret

✅ The dative and instrumental singular of adjectives

	m	*f*	*n*
dat.	кра́сному	кра́сной	кра́сному
instr.	кра́сным	кра́сной	кра́сным
dat.	си́нему	си́ней	си́нему
instr.	си́ним	си́ней	си́ним

Как пройти́ к **Большо́му** теа́тру? Which way is it to the Bolshoi Theatre?
Мы ходи́ли по **Кра́сной** пло́щади. We walked around Red Square.
По́чта за **после́дним** до́мом. The post office is behind the last house.

✅ The dative and instrumental singular of possessives

Except for differences in stress, the possessives **мой, твой, наш**, and **ваш** have the same endings as the soft adjective **си́ний**.

	m	*f*	*n*
dat.	моему́	мое́й	моему́
instr.	мои́м	мое́й	мои́м
dat.	на́шему	на́шей	на́шему
instr.	на́шим	на́шей	на́шим

Он дал де́ньги **твоему́** бра́ту. He gave the money to your brother.
Ты написа́ла письмо́ **мое́й** сестре́. You wrote a letter to my sister.
ме́жду **на́шим** и **ва́шим** до́мом between our house and yours

---

ACTIVITY 3

Complete the sentences with the correct form of the adjective/possessive in brackets.

1 Я дал кни́гу _____ преподава́телю. (но́вый)
2 Он позвони́л _____ ба́бушке. (ста́рый)
3 Э́то под _____ газе́той. (сего́дняшний)
4 Что ты сказа́ла _____ бра́ту?. (мой)
5 Мы написа́ли _____ ма́ме. (ваш)
6 Кни́га над _____ компью́тером. (твой)

🎧 Now do activities 4 and 5 on the recording.

(12.2) In the café

В кафе́

ACTIVITY 6 is on the recording.

ACTIVITY 7

Make a list of all the food and drink mentioned in the dialogue.

DIALOGUE 2

○ Све́та, что ты бу́дешь есть?

■ Я не зна́ю. Что здесь вку́сное?

○ Здесь всё о́чень вку́сно. Ты хо́чешь что́-нибудь горя́чее и́ли холо́дное?

■ Наве́рное, что́-нибудь горя́чее.

○ Здесь о́чень вку́сные грибы́ в смета́не.

■ Хорошо́, я возьму́ грибы́.

○ А на второ́е я рекоменду́ю котле́ты и́ли ры́бу.

■ Лу́чше ры́бу. Я не ем мясно́е.

○ Де́вушка, принеси́те, пожа́луйста, две по́рции грибо́в в смета́не …

▲ Грибо́в нет. Зато́ есть щи и́ли суп-лапша́.

○ Тогда́ да́йте, пожа́луйста, две по́рции щей и две ры́бы.

▲ Лю́ся, ры́ба есть?

◇ Ры́ба ко́нчилась.

○ А что у вас есть без мя́са?

▲ Без мя́са? Омле́т и́ли яи́чница.

○ Да́йте яи́чницу и котле́ту.

▲ А что вы пить бу́дете?

○ Есть компо́т?

▲ Есть сли́вовый и гру́шевый.

○ Да́йте, пожа́луйста, два сли́вовых компо́та.

VOCABULARY	
гриб	mushroom
второ́е	main course
котле́та	cutlet; burger; rissole
суп-лапша́	noodle-soup
щей (*gen. pl.* of **щи**)	cabbage soup
мя́со	meat
яи́чница	fried eggs
компо́т	compote [*drink with stewed fruits*]
сли́вовый	plum [*adjective*]
гру́шевый	pear [*adjective*]

✅ что́-то, что́-нибудь

что́-то is used when referring to something in particular, although you may not know what it is; **что́-нибудь** refers to something indefinite – 'something or other' or 'anything'.

Что́-то случи́лось. Something's happened.

Ты хо́чешь **что́-нибудь** горя́чее? Do you want something hot?

Что́-нибудь для да́чи. Something or other for the dacha.

✅ есть ('to eat') and дать ('to give') – irregular verbs

есть (*imperf.*) – to eat		дать (*perf.*) – to give	
я **ем**	I eat	я **дам**	I will give
ты **ешь**	you eat	ты **дашь**	you will give
он, она́, оно́ **ест**	he, she, it eats	он, она́, оно́ **даст**	he, she, it will give
мы **еди́м**	we eat	мы **дади́м**	we will give
вы **еди́те**	you eat	вы **дади́те**	you will give
они́ **едя́т**	they eat	они́ **даду́т**	they will give

Я не **ем** мясно́е. I don't eat meat.

Когда́ он **даст** мне де́ньги? When will he give me the money?

ACTIVITY 8

Match 1–5 with the appropriate response from a–e.

1 Что у вас есть без мя́са?   a Ко́фе.
2 Что вы пить бу́дете?   b Здесь всё о́чень вку́сное.
3 Я возьму́ котле́ту.   c Сли́вовый.
4 Како́й у вас компо́т?   d Нет котле́т.
5 Что здесь вку́сное?   e Есть то́лько омле́т.

ACTIVITY 9

Complete 1–7 with the correct form of the verb **есть** (present tense) or **дать** (perfective future).

1 Он _____ пломби́р. (есть)
2 Я _____ щи. (есть)
3 Вы _____ мясно́е? (есть)
4 Они́ _____ бу́лочки. (есть)
5 Они́ вам _____ факс. (дать)
6 Я тебе́ _____ сигаре́ту. (дать)
7 Он мне _____ де́ньги. (дать)

🎧 Now do activities 10 and 11 on the recording.

Счёт, пожа́луйста

(A) **ACTIVITY 12** is on the recording.

ACTIVITY 13

1 Aleksei Semyonovich orders dessert for his colleague. T / F
2 Aleksei Semyonovich then orders coffee and liqueurs. T / F
3 The restaurant accepts his form of payment. T / F
4 The waiter calls them a taxi. T / F

DIALOGUE 3

○ Я хочу́ заказа́ть вам э́то моро́женое. Вы согла́сны?
■ Коне́чно, согла́сна.
▲ Что вы зака́жете на десе́рт?
○ Моро́женое, пожа́луйста.
   …
▲ Ещё ко́фе, ликёр?
○ Нет. Счёт, пожа́луйста.
▲ Сейча́с принесу́.
   …
▲ Вот, пожа́луйста, счёт.
○ Вы креди́тные ка́рточки принима́ете?
▲ Да, коне́чно.
   …
▲ Пожа́луйста, подпиши́те здесь.
○ Вот, пожа́луйста. А э́то для вас.
▲ Большо́е спаси́бо.
○ Бу́дьте добры́, вы́зовите такси́.
▲ Такси́ стоя́т пе́ред вхо́дом в рестора́н.
○ Спаси́бо. До свида́ния!
▲ Споко́йной но́чи!

VOCABULARY	
я хочу́ вам заказа́ть …	I want to order … for you
ликёр	liqueur
счёт	bill, check
сейча́с	right away, now
креди́тная ка́рточка	credit card
принима́ть Ia *imperf.*	to take, to accept
подписа́ть Ib *perf.*	to sign
бу́дьте добры́	would you be so kind … ?

LANGUAGE BUILDING

✓ э́тот, тот

э́тот 'this' and **тот** 'that' change form, taking the gender, number, and case of the noun they stand for – their forms are listed in the Grammar Summary on page 228.

Ты чита́ла **э́ту** кни́гу? Have you read this book?
Те времена́ прошли́. Those days are gone.

Note that **тот же** means 'the same' and **не тот** means 'the wrong (one)'.

Я сел **не** на **тот** по́езд. I took the wrong train.

✓ согла́сен

согла́сен ('agreeable'), is another example of an adjective short form, like **за́нят** and **свобо́ден** (see Unit 8). Like **за́нят** and **свобо́ден** it has four forms only, agreeing with the subject.

	m	*f*	*n*	*pl*
agree	**согла́сен**	**согла́сна**	**согла́сно**	**согла́сны**

Вы **согла́сны**? Do you agree?
Нет, я не **согла́сна**. No, I don't agree. [*a woman speaking*]

ACTIVITY 14

Match 1–6 with the appropriate English version from a–f.

1	что вы зака́жете на второе?	a	more coffee, tea?
2	счёт, пожа́луйста	b	sign here, please
3	пожа́луйста, подпиши́те здесь	c	what main course will you have?
4	ещё ко́фе, чай?	d	the bill, please
5	сейча́с принесу́	e	this is for you
6	э́то для вас	f	right away

ACTIVITY 15

Complete the sentences with the correct form of **согла́сен**.

1 Он _____ .
2 Я не _____ . (a woman speaking)
3 Вы _____ ?
4 Ты _____ ? (said to a man)
5 Мы все _____ .
6 Она́ не _____ .

🎧 Now do activities 16 and 17 on the recording.

Меню́

ACTIVITY 18

Match the Russian words below with their English equivalents. Use the menu below to help you.

1	бефстро́ганов		a	omelette
2	карп		b	steak
3	шпро́ты		c	cutlets
4	котле́ты		d	beef Stroganoff
5	омле́т		e	salad
6	бифште́кс		f	carp
7	сала́т		g	trout
8	форе́ль (f)		h	sprats

КАФЕ́-РЕСТОРА́Н «ЖАР-ПТИ́ЦА»
МЕНЮ́

ЗАКУ́СКИ		Шашлы́к 150 гр	53, –
Икра́ кра́сная 100 гр	150, –	Котле́ты 150 гр	40, –
Икра́ чёрная 100 гр	220, –	**ПТИ́ЦА**	
Винегре́т	20, –	Инде́йка жа́реная 150 гр	85, –
Шпро́ты	25, –	У́тка жа́реная с	
Сала́т «Столи́чный»	35, –	я́блоками 150 гр	75, –
Сала́т из све́жих овоще́й	23,50	**РЫ́БНЫЕ БЛЮ́ДА**	
Сала́т из помидо́ров	28, –	Форе́ль 150 гр	53,50
Грибы́ в смета́не	48,50	Карп с миндалём 180 гр	82, –
ПЕ́РВЫЕ БЛЮ́ДА			
Борщ	32,50	Омле́т	22, –
Щи	32,50	Яи́чница	15, –
Соля́нка	45, –	Ка́ша	12, –
Рассо́льник	45, –	Карто́фель отварно́й	22, –
МЯСНЫ́Е БЛЮ́ДА		Карто́фель фри	25, –
Бефстро́ганов 150 гр	75, –	Морко́вь с горо́шком	12,50
Бифште́кс 150 гр	65, –	Свёкла	14,50
Бли́нчики с мя́сом 180 гр	60, –	Ква́шеная капу́ста	11, –
Пе́чень по-францу́зски		Кисе́ль	10, –
150 гр	55, –	Компо́т	10, –
Пельме́ни 180 гр	43,50	Моро́женое	18, –

Notice that for certain dishes in Russian restaurants, prices are usually given per portion of a certain weight (**гр** = grams). If your particular serving comes up smaller or bigger than this, you will be charged accordingly.

жар-птица	firebird
закуска	hors-d'oeuvre, snack
икра	caviar
чёрный	black
винегрет	Russian salad [boiled vegetables in vinaigrette]
салат «Столичный»	'Capital' salad [boiled vegetables and egg in mayonnaise]
свежий	fresh
овощи	vegetables
помидор	tomato
первые блюда	first courses, starters, appetizers
блюдо	dish
солянка	solyanka [a spicy meat soup with vegetables]
рассольник	rassolnik [a meat soup with pickled cucumbers]
блинчик	pancake, fritter
печень (f)	liver
пельмени	pelmeni [a kind of ravioli]
шашлык	kebab
птица	bird, fowl
индейка	turkey
жареный	roast
утка	duck
рыбный	fish [adjective]
миндаль (m)	almonds
каша	kasha [a dish of cooked grain or groats]
картофель (m)	potatoes
отварной	boiled
картофель фри	chips, French fries
морковь (f)	carrots
горошек	peas
свёкла	beetroot
квашеная капуста	pickled cabbage, sauerkraut
кисель (m)	kissel [a kind of blancmange]

ACTIVITY 19

Look at the menu on page 174 and pick out a starter, main course, and dessert for yourself.

ACTIVITY 20

You're with a friend who is a strict vegetarian – she eats no meat and no fish products. You want to order a selection of hors-d'oeuvres. Which ones will be suitable?

В рестора́не
In the restaurant

Pyotr and Rustam have invited Moira out to a restaurant.

VOCABULARY	
немно́жко	a little bit [*diminutive of* **немно́го**]
расстро́енный	upset
побежа́ть II *perf.*	to run
догна́ть II *perf.*	to catch up (with)
сожале́ть Ia *imperf.*	to regret
всё так случи́лось	it happened like that
встреча́ться Ia *imperf.*	to meet
минера́льная вода́	mineral water
Оле́г идёт!	here comes Oleg!
поговори́ть II *perf.*	to have a talk
страсть (*f*)	passion
пря́мо как	just as

ACTIVITY 21

Listen to the story and decide whether the following statements are true or false. Correct those which are false.

1 Pyotr and Rustam ran after Moira when she left the dacha.
2 Moira wants to meet Oleg one more time.
3 Pyotr says they want to be present at this meeting too.
4 Pyotr and Rustam really like Moira.
5 Oleg arrives saying he needs to speak to Moira.
6 Pyotr says that the scene could be straight out of a soap-opera.

ACTIVITY 22

Make a list of the food and drink they order. There are eight different items.

ACTIVITY 23

Supply the missing pronouns in the following extracts from the story.

1 Мойра, _____ так ра́ды, что вы позвони́ли.
2 Мойра, а мы же с _____ бу́дем встреча́ться, пра́вда?
3 Мы _____ о́чень лю́бим.
4 А для _____ два рассо́льника.
5 Извини́те, _____ на́до идти́.
6 Мойра, Мо́йрочка! Куда́ _____ идёшь?
7 Мне на́до поговори́ть с _____ !

STORY TRANSCRIPT

Pyotr	Мойра, мы так ра́ды, что вы позвони́ли. Ведь мы не по́няли, что тогда́ случи́лось. А как вы добрали́сь домо́й?
Moira	Норма́льно. То́лько я была́ немно́жко расстро́ена и се́ла не на тот по́езд.
Pyotr	Бо́же мой! Ведь мы с Руста́мом тогда́ побежа́ли за ва́ми, но не догна́ли вас. Мы о́чень сожале́ем, что всё так случи́лось.
Moira	Я поняла́, что бо́льше не могу́ встреча́ться с Оле́гом.
Pyotr	Мойра, а мы же с ва́ми бу́дем встреча́ться, пра́вда? Мы вас о́чень лю́бим.
Moira	Коне́чно, бу́дем встреча́ться.
Waitress	Что вы бу́дете есть?
Moira	Я возьму́ сала́т из све́жих овоще́й, инде́йку и моро́женое.
Pyotr	А для нас два рассо́льника, бефстро́ганов … Руста́м, ты бли́нчики бу́дешь на второ́е? И бли́нчики, пожа́луйста.
Waitress	А пить что бу́дете?
Pyotr	Да́йте, пожа́луйста, большу́ю буты́лку минера́льной воды́ и два пи́ва.
Waitress	Сейча́с принесу́.
Moira	О, Бо́же! Смотри́те, Оле́г идёт! Извини́те, мне на́до идти́.
Oleg	Мойра, Мо́йрочка! Куда́ ты идёшь? Иди́ сюда́, Мо́йрочка. Мне на́до поговори́ть с тобо́й!
Pyotr	Бо́же мой, стра́сти пря́мо как в о́пере. Пра́вда, Руста́м!

Test

Now it's time to test your progress in Unit 12.

1 Match 1–8 with the appropriate English version from a–h.

1 буты́лка минера́льной воды́   a I got on the wrong train
2 сейча́с принесу́   b there are no more carrots
3 я сел не в тот по́езд   c have you got caviar?
4 инде́йка жа́реная   d a bottle of mineral water
5 есть икра́?   e for how many people?
6 подпиши́те здесь   f sign here
7 морко́вь ко́нчилась   g right away
8 на ско́лько челове́к?   h roast turkey

                                                          | 8 |

2 Pair up 1–6 with the correct response from a–f to make six mini-dialogues.

1 Что ты бу́дешь есть?   a Пи́ва нет.
2 Принеси́те, пожа́луйста, пи́во.   b Есть.
3 Что вы пить бу́дете?   c Гру́шевый.
4 Вы согла́сны?   d Да, я согла́сен.
5 Есть кисе́ль?   e Чай.
6 Како́й у вас компо́т?   f Щи и пельме́ны.

                                                          | 6 |

3 Complete the sentences with the correct form of **есть** (present tense) or **дать** (perfective future).

1 Он не _____ мясно́е. (есть)
2 Мы _____ апельси́ны. (есть)
3 Они́ _____ грибы́. (есть)
4 Они́ мне _____ биле́ты. (дать)
5 Я тебе́ _____ та́почки. (дать)
6 Ра́зве он нам _____ де́ньги? (дать)

                                                          | 6 |

4 Add the correct form of the adjective or possessive.

1 Как пройти́ к _____ теа́тру? (Большо́й)
2 Что ты сказа́л _____ австрали́йке? (молодо́й)
3 Они́ ходи́ли по _____ пло́щади. (Кра́сный)
4 Э́то за _____ до́мом. (но́вый)
5 Э́то пе́ред _____ гости́ницей. (ста́рый)
6 Са́ша написа́л письмо́ _____ бра́ту. (мой)
7 Я пойду́ к_____ ма́ме. (твой)
8 Он пошёл вме́сте с _____ дру́гом. (наш)
9 Он прие́дет вме́сте с _____ семьёй. (ваш)

9

5 You've phoned the restaurant Aragvi to book a table.
Complete the conversation you have with the waiter.
(2 points if correct, 1 point if only one error)

1 Алло́! Say hello, is that the restaurant *Aragvi*?
2 Да, слу́шаю. Say you want to book a table.
3 На како́й день? Say for Saturday.
4 На кото́рый час? Say for 6.30 p.m. (18.30).
5 На ско́лько челове́к? Say for three people.
6 Как ва́ша фами́лия? Give your surname.
7 Хорошо́. До свида́ния! Say goodbye.

14

6 How would you do the following in Russian?
(2 points for each correct answer, 1 point if you make only
one error)

1 Say you don't eat meat.
2 Ask a friend what he's going to drink.
3 Ask 'what's good here? what do they do that's tasty?'
4 Ask for the bill.
5 Say 'this is for you' when tipping someone.

10

TOTAL SCORE **53**

If you scored less than 43, revise the Language Building
sections before completing the Summary on page 180.

Summary 12

Now try this final test summarizing the main points covered in this unit. You can check your answers on the recording.

How would you:
1 ask how to get (on foot) to the Bolshoi Theatre?
2 ask (in a café or restaurant) what they have without meat?
3 ask for the bill?
4 ask if they take credit cards?
5 say you'd like to book a table for four people?
6 say that you agree?
7 ask your boss what she's going to eat?'
8 say you want something hot?

REVISION

The next unit deals with the language of business. Before beginning this unit, look back at some of the language you have already met which can be used in a business context, for example in Unit 6 (introducing yourself) and Unit 8 (arranging to meet people, stating when you are busy).
The **А тепéрь – вы** ('Your Turn') exercises on the recording, particularly in Units 6, 9, and 11, also contain many business scenarios.

13

▷ ▷ ▷ ▷ ▷ ▷ ▷ ▷ ▷ ▷ ▷ ▷ ▷ ▷

And now to business
Бизнес есть бизнес

In this unit you'll learn how to:

- ✓ use job titles
- ✓ introduce yourself and your company
- ✓ use key business language
- ✓ write a letter

And cover the following grammar and language:

- ✓ **который** ('who', 'which')
- ✓ common gender nouns in **-a**
- ✓ the question word **ли**
- ✓ **друг друга** ('each other')

LEARNING RUSSIAN 13

There are various tactics for improving your listening and reading skills in Russian. For example, always try to see how much the context can help you understand. Train yourself to focus on the important words (times, amounts, places, directions, and so on), so that you can get the gist of what you're hearing or reading. Learn to recognize common patterns between Russian and English to help you guess unfamiliar words.

You can apply similar techniques when speaking or writing. For example, when you don't know a word, use a paraphrase or use familiar patterns to invent one!

Now start the recording for Unit 13.

13.1 Our new colleague

Наш но́вый колле́га

ACTIVITY 1 is on the recording.

ACTIVITY 2

What are the following people's jobs:

1 Boris Ivanovich
2 Sergei Konstantinovich
3 Mariya Denisovna
4 Mikhail Nikolaevich
5 Kostya
6 Lena and Olga?

DIALOGUE 1

○ Познако́мьтесь, пожа́луйста. Э́то наш но́вый колле́га, Рома́н Алекса́ндрович Мураве́нко. А э́то Бори́с Ива́нович. Он по специа́льности адвока́т, но у нас рабо́тает консульта́нтом.

■ О́чень прия́тно.

○ А вот здесь кабине́т Серге́я Константи́новича, президе́нта на́шей фи́рмы. Вы, коне́чно, уже́ с ним знако́мы.

■ Да-да, коне́чно.

○ О, познако́мьтесь, пожа́луйста. Мари́я Дени́совна, э́то наш но́вый колле́га, Рома́н Алекса́ндрович Мураве́нко. Мари́я рабо́тает перево́дчицей.

■ О́чень рад с ва́ми познако́миться.

○ У нас ещё рабо́тает бухга́лтер, Михаи́л Никола́евич, кото́рый прихо́дит то́лько по вто́рникам и четверга́м. И ещё Ко́стя, ваш води́тель, с кото́рым вы уже́ познако́мились. А вот на́ши секрета́рши, Ле́на и О́льга. Де́вушки, э́то наш но́вый колле́га Рома́н Алекса́ндрович.

■ О́чень прия́тно.

▲ Приве́т, Рома́н.

VOCABULARY

специа́льность (f)	profession, trade, speciality
рабо́тать Ia (+ *instr.*)	to work as
кабине́т	office
знако́мы с (+ *instr.*)	acquainted with
по (+ *dat. pl.*)	on a day of the week

✅ Job titles

Where two forms are given, the second is used for women.

accountant	бухга́лтер	lawyer	адвока́т
actor	актёр, актри́са	manager	нача́льник
artist	худо́жник, -ница	musician	музыка́нт
banker	банки́р	nurse	медсестра́
businessman	бизнесме́н, -ка	policeman	милиционе́р
consultant	консульта́нт	receptionist	дежу́рный, -ая
dentist	зубно́й врач	secretary	секрета́рь, -а́рша
doctor	врач	sportsman	спортсме́н, -ка
driver	води́тель	school-teacher	учи́тель, -ница
guide	гид	translator	перево́дчик, -чица

✅ кото́рый ('who', 'which')

кото́рый ('who', 'which') changes form like a regular adjective. It agrees with the noun it refers to in gender and number, but its case is determined by the verb in the clause it introduces.

бухга́лтер, **кото́рый** (*m nom. sing.*) рабо́тает на на́шей фи́рме
the accountant who works for our firm

ваш води́тель, с **кото́рым** (*m inst. sing.*) вы уже́ познако́мились
your driver, whom you have already met

• Common gender nouns in -a

Russian has a number of nouns ending in **-a**, such as **колле́га**, which may refer to men or women. They have the regular endings of feminine nouns in **-a**, but the form of adjectives and possessives relating to them is masculine if they refer to men, and feminine if they refer to women.

Это **наш но́вый колле́га**. This is our new (male) colleague.
Это **на́ша но́вая колле́га**. This is our new (female) colleague.

There are also a small number of masculine nouns ending in **-a** or **-я** which refer to men, such as **па́па** ('Dad'), **дя́дя** ('uncle'), **мужчи́на** ('man'), and some short forms of names, such as **Ко́ля, Ко́стя**. These also have the regular noun endings of feminine nouns in **-a** or **-я**, but the form of adjectives and possessives relating to them is always masculine.

Мой дя́дя о́чень **ста́рый**. My uncle is very old.
Ко́ля о́чень **бе́дный**. Kolya is very poor.

 Now do activities 3 and 4 on the recording.

Разреши́те предста́виться

🅐 **ACTIVITY 5** is on the recording.

ACTIVITY 6

1 What does Nikolai Konstantinovich's firm do?
2 What countries do they work with?
3 Why are there very few competitors?

DIALOGUE 2

○ Разреши́те предста́виться. Никола́й Константи́нович Булахо́вский, представи́тель фи́рмы «Электроэ́кспорт» в Москве́.

■ Алексе́й Семёнович Гага́рин. О́чень рад с ва́ми познако́миться. А чем и́менно занима́ется ва́ша фи́рма?

○ Мы занима́емся э́кспортом радиотехни́ческого обору́дования на за́падные ры́нки.

■ А с каки́ми стра́нами вы сотру́дничаете?

○ Мы рабо́таем пре́жде всего́ с А́нглией и Фра́нцией.

■ Есть ли у вас конкуре́нция?

○ Конкуре́нтов о́чень ма́ло – на́ша фи́рма специализи́рованная. Есть то́лько три-четы́ре фи́рмы, кото́рые де́йствуют на э́том ры́нке. Мы все друг дру́га зна́ем и да́же помога́ем друг дру́гу. Вот, пожа́луйста, букле́т с информа́цией о на́шей фи́рме. Прими́те, пожа́луйста, э́тот сувени́р. Э́то ру́чка с назва́нием на́шей фи́рмы.

■ Спаси́бо.

VOCABULARY

разреши́ть II *perf.*	to permit, to allow
предста́виться II *perf.*	to introduce oneself
представи́тель (*m*) (+ *gen.*)	representative (of)
радиотехни́ческий	radio engineering [*adjective*]
обору́дование	equipment
за́падный	western
ры́нок	market
сотру́дничать (Ia *imperf.*) **с**	to collaborate with
конкуре́нт	competitor, rival
де́йствовать Ib *imperf.*	to operate, to be active
прими́(те)	take, accept [*imperative*]
ру́чка	pen
назва́ние	name

LANGUAGE BUILDING

✓ ли

The word **ли** may be used to make a question. This is more common in written or formal language; in speech, questions are more often made by intonation only (see Unit 1).

Есть **ли** у вас конкуре́нция? Do you have competitors?
Чита́ете **ли** вы газе́ты? Do you read the newspapers?

ли is also used to form indirect questions, where it is equivalent to English 'if', 'whether'.

Он спроси́л, чита́ю **ли** я газе́ты. He asked me whether I read the newspapers.

✓ друг дру́га

In Unit 8 you met the expression **друг дру́га** 'each other', 'one another'. The first **друг** does not change, but the second changes form as shown below. Prepositions are placed between the two elements.

acc.	**друг дру́га**
gen.	**друг дру́га**
dat.	**друг дру́гу**
instr.	**друг** с **дру́гом**
prep.	**друг** о **дру́ге**

Они́ хорошо́ зна́ют **друг дру́га**. They know each other well.
Мы помога́ем **друг дру́гу**. We help each other.

ACTIVITY 7

Complete the sentences with the correct form of **друг дру́га**.

1 Они́ лю́бят _____ _____ .
2 Мы помога́ем _____ _____ .
3 Вы все зна́ете _____ _____?
4 Они́ забы́ли _____ о _____ .
5 Мы _____ _____ звони́ли.

🎧 Now do activities 8 and 9 on the recording.

13.3 Dear Sir/Madam

Уважа́емые Господа́!

ACTIVITY 10 is on the recording.

ACTIVITY 11

1 What are Roman Aleksandrovich's travel arrangements?
2 What requests does he make regarding the meeting?

27.10.2001

Уважа́емый Серге́й Константи́нович!

Спаси́бо за Ваш факс от 25 октября́. Я с больши́м интере́сом прочита́л Ваш отчёт об усло́виях ры́нка в Ирку́тской о́бласти и о фи́рмах, кото́рые де́йствуют на э́том ры́нке. Ва́ши вы́воды о страте́гии разви́тия би́знеса осо́бенно интере́сны. Я ду́маю, что есть потенциа́л для сотру́дничества ме́жду на́шими организа́циями.

Я прибыва́ю в Ирку́тск в суббо́ту 2 ноября́ на неде́лю. Я бу́ду жить в гости́нице «Байка́л», где я уже́ заказа́л но́мер. Пожа́луйста, позвони́те мне в гости́ницу 2 и́ли 3 октября́ и мы договори́мся о встре́че. Éсли Вам неудо́бно встре́титься со мной в э́ти сро́ки, то, пожа́луйста, свяжи́тесь со мной по фа́ксу и́ли по электро́нной по́чте как мо́жно скоре́е.

С уваже́нием

Мураве́нко Рома́н Алекса́ндрович

VOCABULARY

интере́с	interest
прочита́ть Ia *perf.*	to read
о́бласть (*f*)	province
осо́бенно	particularly
на неде́лю	for a week
но́мер	room [*hotel*]
договори́ться II *perf.* о (+ *instr.*)	to arrange
неудо́бно (+ *dat.*)	inconvenient
срок	time, period
связа́ться Ib *perf.* с (+ *instr.*) (**свяжу́сь**)	to contact
как мо́жно скоре́е	as soon as possible

✅ Business language

Here is a selection of common terms used in business and office contexts.

business	**би́знес**	report	**отчёт**
market	**ры́нок**	conclusion	**вы́вод**
company	**фи́рма**	import	**и́мпорт**
organization	**организа́ция**	export	**э́кспорт**
strategy	**страте́гия**	computer	**компью́тер**
condition	**усло́вие**	printer	**при́нтер**
potential	**потенциа́л**	fax	**факс**
cooperation	**сотру́дничество**	e-mail	**электро́нная по́чта**
development	**разви́тие**	telephone	**телефо́н**

✅ Writing a business letter

Business letters often use a rather formal style. They begin with the word **уважа́емый/уважа́емая** 'respected' + the first name and patronymic (followed by an exclamation mark). The expression **уважа́емые господа́!** is the equivalent of 'dear Sir/Madam'. Letters usually end with **с уваже́нием** ('yours faithfully/yours sincerely'). Notice also that the words for 'you' and 'your' – **Вы, Вас, Вам, Ва́ми, Ваш, Ва́ши**, etc. – are written with a capital letter.

✅ Writing a personal letter

Personal letters use a more informal style. They usually begin **дорого́й/дорога́я** + the first name (followed by an exclamation mark) and may conclude with a phrase such as **всего́ хоро́шего** 'all the best' or **целу́ю** 'I kiss you'.

ACTIVITY 12

Write a business letter incorporating the following:

– *date*
– dear Sir/Madam
– thank you for your letter of …
– I am arriving in Moscow on the …
– I will be staying at the Hotel Cosmos
– please call me on the … and we will arrange meeting
– yours faithfully
– *your name*

🎧 Now do activities 13 and 14 on the recording.

(13.4) Mr Gardiner is arriving …

Господи́н Га́рдинер прибыва́ет…

ACTIVITY 15

Maxim Shuisky's American company is engaged in negotiations with a Russian company over a possible joint project. Read the letter Maxim has written to them and answer the questions below.

1 Who is going to arrive?
2 What date will he arrive, and how long is he staying?
3 What does the letter say about his accommodation?
4 Whom is he meeting in St Petersburg?
5 What does the letter say about his communication needs?
6 In what eventuality should contact be made by telephone or e-mail?

10.05.2000

Уважа́емые господа́!

Спаси́бо за Ва́ше сообще́ние по электро́нной по́чте от 2 ма́я. Президе́нт на́шей фи́рмы господи́н Джон Га́рдинер прибыва́ет в Москву́ в воскресе́нье 16 ию́ня на четы́ре дня и бу́дет жить в гости́нице «Метропо́ль». 20 ию́ня он по́ездом пое́дет в Петербу́рг, где встре́тится с представи́телями организа́ций, кото́рые занима́ются э́кспортом на за́падные ры́нки.

Господи́н Га́рдинер бу́дет пе́рвый раз в Росси́и. Он не говори́т по-ру́сски. Поэ́тому, пожа́луйста, встре́тьте его́ в аэропорту́ Шереме́тьево-2 и предоста́вьте ему́ перево́дчика. Рейс БА506, прилёт в 15.30 по моско́вскому вре́мени. Éсли Вы не смо́жете встре́тить господи́на Га́рдинера в аэропорту́, то, пожа́луйста, свяжи́тесь с на́ми по телефо́ну и́ли по электро́нной по́чте как мо́жно скоре́е.

Наде́юсь на возмо́жность сотру́динчества ме́жду на́шими организа́циями.

С уваже́нием

Макси́м Шу́йский

VOCABULARY

сообще́ние	message
господи́н	Mr
пое́хать Ib *perf.* (пое́ду)	to go [*by transport*]
поэ́тому	therefore
встре́тьте	meet [*imperative*]
аэропо́рт, в аэропорту́	airport
предоста́вьте (+ *dat.* + *acc.*)	provide [*imperative*] (somebody with something)
рейс	flight
прилёт	arrival [*by air*]
возмо́жность (*f*)	possibility

ACTIVITY 16

Fill in the missing verbs in the extract below. Refer back to Maxim Shuisky's letter only if necessary.

Президе́нт на́шей фи́рмы господи́н Джон Га́рдинер (1 is arriving) _____ в Москву́ в воскресе́нье 16 ию́ня и (2 will be staying) _____ _____ в гости́нице «Метропо́ль». 20 ию́ня он по́ездом (3 will go) _____ в Петербу́рг, где (4 will meet) _____ с представи́телями организа́ций, кото́рые (5 are involved in) _____ э́кспортом на за́падные ры́нки. Пожа́луйста, (6 meet) _____ его́ в аэропорту́ и (7 provide) _____ ему́ перево́дчика. Е́сли Вы не (8 will not be able to meet) _____ _____ господи́на Га́рдинера в аэропорту́, то, пожа́луйста, (9 contact) _____ с на́ми по телефо́ну как мо́жно скоре́е.

ACTIVITY 17

You will shortly be travelling to St Petersburg to visit your partner firm there. You have booked your accommodation there already (at the Astoria), but you want to be met at the airport. Write a suitably worded letter to one of your colleagues, including the dates of your stay and flight details.

(13.5) Ла́рины

Письмо́ от Мо́йры
Moira's letter

Back in her hostel, Moira has stayed up all night writing a letter to Oleg.

VOCABULARY

г.	*abbreviation for* **го́род**
молча́ть II *imperf.*	to be silent
невозмо́жно	impossible
испуга́ться Ia *perf.*	to be frightened
я испуга́лась само́й себя́	I was frightened of myself
мгнове́ние	moment, instant
поня́ть Ib *perf.*	to realize, to understand
боя́ться II *imperf.* (бою́сь) (+ *gen.*)	to fear, to be afraid of
влюблён, влюблена́ в (+ *acc.*)	in love with
жени́х	fiancé
реши́ть II *perf.*	to decide
одна́	alone
никто́ … не	no one
проща́й(те)	farewell! goodbye!
навсегда́	for ever

ACTIVITY 18

Listen to the story and answer the following questions.

1 How did Moira feel at the dacha?
2 What did she suddenly realize?
3 Why is this a problem?
4 Who is Graham?
5 What decision has Moira taken?
6 What does Moira ask Oleg to do about contacting her?
7 What final request does she make?

ACTIVITY 19

Complete the sentences below, taken from Moira's letter, with the missing verbs.

1 Снача́ла я (wanted) _____ молча́ть, но я (realized) _____, что э́то невозмо́жно.
2 Когда́ ты мне (told) _____ на да́че, что ты меня́ (love) _____, я о́чень (was frightened) _____ .

3　В Шотла́ндии меня́ (is waiting for) _____ жени́х, Гре́эм.

4　Я (have decided to return) _____ _____ домо́й, к нему́.

5　Я здесь одна́, никто́ меня́ не (understands) _____ .

6　Я (am leaving) _____ за́втра.

7　Ты меня́ бо́льше не (will see) _____ .

STORY TRANSCRIPT

Пя́тница, 5 ию́ля
г. Москва́

Дорого́й Оле́г!

Я тебе́ пишу́ – но как мне тру́дно написа́ть э́ти стра́шные слова́! Снача́ла я хоте́ла молча́ть, но я поняла́, что э́то невозмо́жно.

Когда́ ты мне сказа́л на да́че, что ты меня́ лю́бишь, я о́чень испуга́лась. Но я испуга́лась само́й себя́. В то мгнове́ние я поняла́, что я – да, я не бою́сь э́тих слов – в тебя́ то́же влюблена́! Да, Оле́г, я тебя́ люблю́!

Но я не свобо́дна. В Шотла́ндии меня́ ждёт жени́х, Гре́эм. Я реши́ла верну́ться домо́й, к нему́. Я поняла́, что моё ме́сто не здесь. Я здесь одна́, никто́ меня́ не понима́ет.

Я уезжа́ю за́втра. Ты меня́ бо́льше не уви́дишь. Пожа́луйста, не пиши́ мне, не звони́.

Прости́ меня́, е́сли смо́жешь.

Проща́й навсегда́!

　　　Мо́йра

Before completing the test on pages 192–193 revise job titles for men and women with the activity below.

ACTIVITY 20

Supply the job titles. If there are two forms, use the male or female form as appropriate.

1　Он плохо́й _____ . (translator)

2　Э́то ваш _____ . (driver)

3　Она́ хоро́шая _____ . (businesswoman)

4　Ни́на – _____ . (nurse)

5　Она́ _____ . (school-teacher)

6　Ко́ля – _____ . (consultant)

Test

Now it's time to test your progress in Unit 13.

1 Match 1–8 with the correct English version from a–h.

1	как мо́жно скоре́е	a	dear
2	мы договори́мся о встре́че	b	we will arrange a meeting
3	с уваже́нием	c	meet him at the airport
4	уважа́емые господа́!	d	by fax
5	по фа́ксу	e	contact me
6	свяжи́тесь со мной	f	as soon as possible
7	встре́тьте его́ в аэропорту́	g	dear Sir/Madam
8	дорога́я	h	yours faithfully

8

2 Pair up 1–6 with the correct response from a–f to make six mini-dialogues.

1 Есть ли у вас конкуре́нция?
2 Чем занима́ется ва́ша фи́рма?
3 Вот, пожа́луйста, букле́т с информа́цией о на́шей фи́рме.
4 С каки́ми стра́нами вы сотру́дничаете?
5 Разреши́те предста́виться. Серге́й Ко́сточкин.
6 Ва́ша фи́рма то́же де́йствует на э́том ры́нке?

a Спаси́бо.
b Да, де́йствует. Ка́жется, мы конкуре́нты.
c Мы занима́емся э́кспортом.
d О́льга Бори́сова. О́чень ра́да с ва́ми познако́миться.
e Мы сотру́дничаем то́лько с США.
f Конкуре́нтов о́чень мно́го.

6

3 Translate the following phrases into English.

1 дом, кото́рый нахо́дится здесь
2 дом, в кото́ром я родила́сь
3 челове́к, у кото́рого есть кни́га
4 де́вушка, кото́рая рабо́тает здесь
5 де́вушка, кото́рую вы зна́ете
6 де́вушка, о кото́рой мы говори́м

6

4 Complete the sentences with the correct form of **друг дру́га**.

1 Обы́чно конкуре́нты не помога́ют _____ _____ .
2 Вы забы́ли _____ о _____ ?
3 Мы с бра́том не о́чень лю́бим _____ _____ .
4 Они́ ча́сто звоня́т _____ _____ .
5 Они́ уви́дели _____ _____ в кино́.
6 Мы ре́дко пи́шем _____ _____ .

6

5 Supply the job titles. If there are two forms, use the male or female form as appropriate.

1 Та́ня – _____ (translator)
2 Лари́са – _____ (accountant)
3 О́льга – _____ (guide)
4 И́горь – _____ (policeman)
5 Серге́й – _____ (consultant)
6 Семён – _____ (driver)
7 Рома́н – _____ (businessman)
8 Еле́на – _____ (manager)
9 Бори́с – _____ (lawyer)

9

6 How would you say the following things in Russian?
(2 points if correct, 1 point if only one error)

1 This is my driver, Boris.
2 He's an accountant by profession.
3 This is our new (female) colleague.
4 Elena is our secretary.
5 Our firm is specialized.
6 Please accept this souvenir.
7 Thank you for your fax.
8 Dear Nina

16

TOTAL SCORE **51**

If you scored less than 41, re-read the Language Building sections before completing the Summary on page 194.

Summary 13

 Now try this final test summarizing the main points covered in this unit. You can check your answers on the recording.

How would you:
1 say 'this is our new (male) colleague'?
2 say 'this is our new (female) colleague'?
3 say 'allow me to introduce myself'?
4 ask a business contact what her firm does?
5 say 'there are very few competitors'?
6 say 'here is an information leaflet'?
7 say 'please accept this souvenir'?
8 say '(male) translator'? 'businesswoman'? 'lawyer'?
9 say 'they like each other'?

REVISION

This unit has introduced some key business language and shown you how to write a standard business letter. Once you are confident of this material, you will need to expand your business language to suit your own situation. What sort of business letter might you yourself need to write? How would you describe what your company does, or your own job? Bearing these questions in mind, use the language from this unit and your dictionary to extend your business communication skills.

Health and fitness
Здоро́вье

OBJECTIVES

In this unit you'll learn how to:

- ✓ talk about how often you do something
- ✓ refer to parts of the body
- ✓ describe health complaints
- ✓ give reasons and explanations
- ✓ understand advice and instructions

And cover the following grammar and language:

- ✓ time adverbs
- ✓ double negatives
- ✓ себя́ ('oneself'), свой ('one's own')
- ✓ the conditional
- ✓ conjunctions

LEARNING RUSSIAN 14

This is the last unit in the book, but your learning will continue beyond the final page. There are various ways in which you can put what you have learnt into practice. First, you could of course travel to Russia and enjoy the skills you've worked so hard to achieve. Alternatively, you could try to find a Russian native speaker who wants to improve his or her English. An hour of speaking Russian on a regular basis will improve your listening and speaking skills greatly. Finally, you could join a class and build on the skills you've acquired.

Now start the recording for Unit 14.

14.1 You never go to museums

Ты никогда́ не хо́дишь в музе́и

🎧 **ACTIVITY 1** is on the recording.

ACTIVITY 2

1	Gleb prefers Turgenev to Pushkin.	T / F
2	Svetlana often goes to museums and galleries.	T / F
3	Svetlana is interested in skating.	T / F

DIALOGUE 1

○ Све́та, в после́днее вре́мя ты ка́к-то стра́нно себя́ ведёшь. Скажи́, что случи́лось?

■ Глеб, я поняла́, что мы не о́чень подхо́дим друг дру́гу.

○ Как же э́то так?

■ Ведь я люблю́ чита́ть кни́ги, рома́ны Турге́нева и стихи́ Пу́шкина. А ты предпочита́ешь спорт. Я о́чень ча́сто хожу́ в музе́и, в галере́и, а ты никогда́ не хо́дишь. Ты всегда́ смо́тришь футбо́л по телеви́зору, а я смотрю́ его́ о́чень ре́дко. Че́стно говоря́, я ничего́ не зна́ю о футбо́ле. Футбо́л меня́ совсе́м не интересу́ет.

○ Да что ты говори́шь?!

■ Ведь я интересу́юсь иску́сством, литерату́рой, му́зыкой. Спо́ртом я вообще́ не занима́юсь. Я да́же не уме́ю ката́ться на конька́х. Ты понима́ешь, о чём я говорю́?

○ Я, ка́жется, ничего́ не понима́ю.

■ Глеб, у меня́ свои́ интере́сы, а у тебя́ – свои́. И они́ – совсе́м ра́зные.

○ Зна́чит, ты не пойдёшь со мной на футбо́л в суббо́ту?

■ Не пойду́. Кста́ти, в суббо́ту я занята́. Бори́с пригласи́л меня́ в теа́тр. Твой брат говори́т, что он о́чень лю́бит пье́сы Че́хова.

VOCABULARY

подходи́ть II *imperf.* (+ dat.)	to suit
предпочита́ть Ia *imperf.*	to prefer
телеви́зор	television
че́стно говоря́	to be honest
интересова́ть Ia *imperf.*	to interest
интересова́ться Ia (+ *instr.*)	to be interested in
иску́сство	art
кста́ти	by the way
пригласи́ть II *perf.*	to invite, to ask

LANGUAGE BUILDING

✓ как ча́сто? ('how often?')

ре́дко	rarely	тогда́	then, at that time
иногда́	sometimes	неда́вно	recently
ча́сто	often	сейча́с	now
всегда́	always	пото́м/зате́м	afterwards
давно́	a long time ago, for a long time		

Я **ча́сто** хожу́ в музе́и. I often go to museums.

✓ Double negatives

The following words are always followed by the negative **не**.

никогда́	never	ника́к	in no way
никто́	nobody	нигде́	nowhere
ничего́	nothing		

Я **ничего́ не** зна́ю о футбо́ле. I don't know anything about football.

✓ себя́

The pronoun **себя́** means 'oneself', 'myself', 'yourself' (and so on), but where it is part of the verb it is sometimes not translated, e.g. **вести́ себя́** 'to behave'. It has the following forms: **себя́** (*acc./gen.*), **себе́** (*dat.*), **собо́й/собо́ю** (*instr.*), **себе́** (*prep.*).

Он то́лько ду́мает о **себе́**. He only thinks of himself.

Ты стра́нно **себя́** ведёшь. You're behaving oddly.

✓ свой

The reflexive possessive form **свой** means 'one's own', 'my', 'your' etc. It has the same pattern of endings as **мой** (see Grammar Summary).

У меня́ **свои́** интере́сы, а у тебя́ – **свои́**. I have my interests, you have yours.

Ива́н взял **свою́** кни́гу. Ivan took his book. [*his own*]

ACTIVITY 3

Complete the sentences with the correct 'double negative' forms.

1 Почему́ _____ __ хо́чет смотре́ть фильм? (nobody)
2 Я _____ __ нашла́ по́чту. (nowhere)
3 Он _____ __ занима́ется спо́ртом. (never)
4 Когда́ он говори́л, я _____ __ понима́л. (nothing)

🎧 Now do activities 4 and 5 on the recording.

I've caught a chill

Я простуди́лся

ACTIVITY 6 is on the recording.

ACTIVITY 7

Kolya's mother thinks he has a chill because he never wears
(1) _____ . She tells him to go to bed – she will make
him some (2) _____ . Kolya is worried that he might
have (3) _____ , and thinks he should maybe go to the
(4) _____ in St Petersburg. Kolya's mother doesn't
agree; she is going to treat him herself with (5) _____ .

DIALOGUE 2

○ Ма́ма, я себя́ о́чень пло́хо чу́вствую. У меня́ боли́т голова́
и го́рло. Все ко́сти боля́т. У меня́, наве́рное, температу́ра.
Ка́жется, я простуди́лся.

■ А чего́ же ты хо́чешь? Хо́дишь без та́почек, почти́ го́лый!
Сто́лько раз я тебе́ говори́ла, не ходи́ босо́й, одева́йся
тепло́!

○ Да, ма́ма. Ты права́.

■ Бе́дный мой Ко́ленька! Тебе́ на́до лежа́ть в крова́ти. Я
сейча́с сварю́ суп, накормлю́ тебя́.

○ Ма́ма, мо́жет быть, мне лу́чше верну́ться в Петербу́рг и
за́втра пойти́ к врачу́. Мо́жет быть, у меня́ грипп.

■ Како́й же у тебя́ грипп?! Тьфу-тьфу-тьфу! Э́то то́лько
просту́да и бо́льше ничего́. Сейча́с же ложи́сь в крова́ть, а
я тебе́ принесу́ суп и поста́влю на спи́ну горчи́чники.

○ Хорошо́, ма́ма.

VOCABULARY

чу́вствовать Ib *imperf.* себя́	to feel
го́лый	naked
босо́й	barefoot
одева́ться Ia *imperf.*	to dress
прав, права́, пра́вы	right
бе́дный	poor
крова́ть (f)	bed
свари́ть II *perf.*	to boil, to cook
накорми́ть II *perf.* (накормлю́)	to feed
како́й же у тебя́ грипп?!	flu? what nonsense!
тьфу-тьфу-тьфу!	*said to ward off bad luck*
поста́вить II *perf.*	to put, to place
горчи́чник	mustard-poultice

✅ Parts of the body

arm/hand	**рука́**	head	**голова́**
back	**спина́**	heart	**се́рдце**
blood	**кровь** (*f*)	leg/foot	**нога́**
bone	**кость** (*f*)	nose	**нос**
breast, chest	**грудь** (*f*)	mouth	**рот**
ear	**у́хо** (*pl.* **у́ши**)	throat	**го́рло**
eye	**глаз** (*pl.* **глаза́**)	tooth	**зуб**
finger/toe	**па́лец** (*pl.* **па́льцы**)	skin	**ко́жа**
hair	**во́лосы**	stomach	**желу́док**

✅ У меня́ боли́т, боля́т …

Notice how you say something hurts or aches in Russian: **у меня́ боли́т** …, literally 'by me (*genitive after* **y**) hurts …'. The thing that hurts is in the nominative. If it is plural, the verb must also be plural – **боля́т.**

> У меня́ **боли́т** голова́. I have a headache.
> У него́ **боля́т** глаза́. His eyes are hurting him.

✅ Common illnesses and medical procedures

flu	**грипп**	I have diarrhoea	**у меня́ поно́с**
inflammation	**воспале́ние**	to be treated	**лечи́ться**
temperature	**температу́ра**	X-ray	**рентге́н**
wound	**ра́на**	blood-test	**ана́лиз кро́ви**
to catch a chill/cold	**простуди́ться**	urine analysis	**ана́лиз мочи́**
I have a cold	**у меня́ просту́да**	plaster	**пла́стырь** (*m*)
I am ill	**я бо́лен/больна́**	medicine	**лека́рство**
I feel nauseous	**меня́ тошни́т**	prescription	**реце́пт**
I am allergic to	**у меня́ аллерги́я к**	clinic	**поликли́ника**
I am constipated	**у меня́ запо́р**	hospital	**больни́ца**

ACTIVITY 8

Translate the sentences below into Russian.

1 My legs hurt.
2 I have a toothache.
3 My throat hurts.
4 My eyes hurts.
5 I have a headache.
6 My back aches.

ACTIVITY 9

Match the following sentences.

1 У него́ грипп.
2 Меня́ тошни́т.
3 Он бо́лен.
4 Она́ простуди́лась.

a She's caught a chill.
b I feel nauseous.
c He has flu.
d He's sick.

🎧 Now do activities 10 and 11 on the recording.

At the doctor's
У врача́

(14) **ACTIVITY 12** is on the recording.

ACTIVITY 13

1 What are Kolya's symptoms?
2 What is the doctor's diagnosis?
3 What does she prescribe?
4 What other advice does she give?

DIALOGUE 3

○ В чём пробле́ма?

■ Я пришёл к вам, потому́ что я себя́ о́чень пло́хо чу́вствую. У меня́ боли́т голова́ и го́рло. Я пло́хо сплю. Мне ка́жется, что у меня́ температу́ра.

○ Температу́ру мы сейча́с изме́рим. Вы давно́ себя́ так чу́вствуете?

■ Уже́ четвёртый день.

○ Пожа́луйста, раздева́йтесь. Дыши́те. Ещё раз. Дыши́те глубоко́. Мо́жете одева́ться.

■ Что у меня́? Грипп и́ли воспале́ние лёгких?

○ Вы простуди́лись. Я вам вы́пишу реце́пт.

■ Что э́то за лека́рство?

○ Э́то болеутоля́ющее. Принима́йте его́ три ра́за в день по две табле́тки по́сле еды́. А вот э́то витами́ны. Их на́до принима́ть три ра́за в день по одно́й табле́тке. Я бы вам сове́товала отлежа́ться три-четы́ре дня. Е́сли вы не попра́витесь че́рез неде́лю, то приходи́те ко мне ещё раз.

■ Спаси́бо. До свида́ния.

○ До свида́ния. Сле́дующий!

VOCABULARY	
в чём пробле́ма?	what's the problem?
спа́ть II *imperf.* **(сплю, спишь)**	to sleep
изме́рить II *perf.* **(температу́ру)**	to take s.o.'s temperature
дыша́ть II *imperf.*	to breathe
глубоко́	deeply
воспале́ние лёгких	pneumonia
болеутоля́ющее	painkiller
сове́товать Ia *imperf.* (+ *dat.*)	to advise
отлежа́ться II *perf.*	to rest [*in bed*]
попра́виться II *perf.*	to get better

✅ The conditional

The conditional form is made up of the word **бы** + an imperfective or perfective past. **бы** usually appears either as second word in the sentence or immediately after the verb. This form is used with **если** ('if') in conditional sentences such as 'if I were … ', 'if I had … ', as in the first example below. It is also used idiomatically to make polite requests or suggestions, in sentences such as 'I would like … ', 'I would advise you … '.

Éсли **бы** я **был** свобóден, я **бы поéхал** с вáми. I would go with you if I were free.

Я **бы хотéл** пойти с тобóй. I would like to go with you.

Что вы **хотéли бы** дéлать зáвтра? What would you like to do tomorrow?

Я **бы** вам **совéтовала** … I would advise you …

Я **бы сказáл**, что … I would say that …

✅ Conjunctions

Here are some useful conjunctions, some of which you have met already:

и	and	**éсли … не**	unless
а	but, and	**когдá**	when(ever)
но	but	**чтóбы**	(in order) to
и́ли	or	**хотя́**	although
потому́ что	because	**пока́**	while
поэ́тому	therefore	**пока́ … не**	until
éсли	if	**однáко**	however

Я пришёл, **потому́ что** вы здесь. I have come because you are here.
Чтóбы хорошó говори́ть по-ру́сски, нáдо учи́ться кáждый день.
In order to speak Russian well, you need to study every day.

ACTIVITY 14

Complete the sentences by inserting the verb in brackets in the conditional.

1 Éсли ___ он _____ свобóден, то он (быть)
___ _____ в футбóл с тобóй. (игрáть)
2 Éсли ___ онá _____ дóма, то онá (быть)
___ всё вам _____ . (рассказáть)
3 Я ___ вам _____ пойти домóй. (совéтовать)
4 Я ___ _____, что лу́чше снача́ла позвони́ть. (сказáть)
5 Что ___ вы _____ дéлать в четвéрг? (хотéть)

🎧 Now do activities 15 and 16 on the recording.

14.4 The clinic

Поликли́ника

ACTIVITY 17

Match the following words with their English translations.

1	специали́ст	a	registration
2	хирурги́я	b	plastic [*adjective*]
3	опера́ция	c	private
4	регистрату́ра	d	operation
5	ча́стный	e	specialist
6	пласти́ческий	f	surgery

ACTIVITY 18

Read the following advertisement for a private clinic and hospital in Moscow offering a range of services.

1 Where is the clinic located?
2 What time are home calls made?
3 What time is the clinic open normally?
4 What time is the clinic open on Saturdays?
5 What time are hospital services available?

ЧА́СТНАЯ ПОЛИКЛИ́НИКА И БОЛЬНИ́ЦА «ВЛАДПОЛ»

(о́коло ста́нции метро́ Влады́кино)
Регистрату́ра: тел. 250-33-10
Визи́ты на дому́ с 13.00 до 20.00: тел. 250-33-83
email: info@vladpol.com.ru

Приглаша́ем с 7.00 до 20.00, суббо́та с 8.00 до 13.00

Большо́й вы́бор враче́й-
специали́стов
Врачи́ всех специа́льностей
Специализиро́ванные
    поликли́ники:
– дерматоло́гия (аллерги́и
    ко́жи)
– кардиоло́гия
– лече́ние диабе́та
– лече́ние повы́шенного
    давле́ния
– педиатри́я
– хирурги́я

По́лная диагно́стика
EEG, EKG, RTG, USG
Лабора́торные ана́лизы
    кро́ви, мочи́

Больни́чное обслу́живание –
24 часа́ в су́тки
Класси́ческая хирурги́я
Операцио́нное лече́ние
    ра́ка груди́
Пласти́ческие опера́ции
Ро́ды

визи́т на дому́	home call
приглаша́ем	we are open
дерматоло́гия	dermatology
кардиоло́гия	cardiology
диабе́т	diabetes
повы́шенное давле́ние	high blood pressure
педиатри́я	pediatrics
диагно́стика	diagnostics
лаборато́рный	laboratory [*adjective*]
больни́чный	hospital [*adjective*]
обслу́живание	service
24 часа́ в су́тки	24 hours a day
операцио́нный	operation [*adjective*]
класси́ческий	classical
рак	cancer
ро́ды	labour, childbirth

ACTIVITY 19

Read the advertisement aloud. Where necessary, make use of the techniques you have learned for pronouncing long words correctly – breaking words down into smaller sections, into syllables, noting the position of stress, etc.

Сно́ва на Тверско́м бульва́ре
Back on the Tverskoi Boulevard

Evgeniya Pavlovna, Mariya Ivanovna, and Lena are out again for an afternoon stroll on Moscow's Tverskoi Boulevard.

VOCABULARY	
грусти́ть II *imperf.*	to be sad, to grieve
легко́	it is easy
сквозня́к	draught
вообще́	in general
пригото́вить II *perf.*	to prepare
пра́здничный	festive
вку́сно	tastily
не забу́дь(те)	don't forget
испе́чь Ib *perf.*	to bake

ACTIVITY 20

Listen to the story and answer the following questions.

1 Why was Mariya worried at the dacha?
2 How in fact does Evgeniya say she felt?
3 How does Evgeniya feel about birthdays generally?
4 When is Ivan's birthday?
5 How old will he be?
6 What does Evgeniya say they will have to do?
7 When is Auntie Tanya's birthday?
8 How old will she be?

ACTIVITY 21

Add the correct endings to the nouns, adjectives, and verbs in the extracts from the story below.

1 В холо́дн__ ко́мнат__ о́чень легко́ простуди́ться.
2 А вообще́ я люблю́ дн__ рожде́ния.
3 Ма́ша, ты не забы́л__, что у Ива́н__ бу́дет день рожде́ния че́рез ме́сяц.
4 На́до бу́дет купи́ть пода́рк__, пригласи́ть гост__.
5 А в сентябр__ у тёт__ Та́ни бу́дет день рожде́ния.
6 Дава́й пойд__ домо́й!

STORY TRANSCRIPT

Mariya Ivanovna	Ма́ма, как ты сейча́с себя́ чу́вствуешь? В свой день рожде́ния ты о́чень грусти́ла. Я да́же немно́го волнова́лась. У тебя́ сейча́с всё в поря́дке?
Evgeniya Pavlovna	Да, коне́чно. Мне бы́ло не гру́стно, а про́сто хо́лодно. В холо́дной ко́мнате о́чень легко́ простуди́ться. Ведь на да́че таки́е сквозняки́! А вообще́ я люблю́ дни рожде́ния.
Mariya Ivanovna	Пра́вда, ма́ма?
Evgeniya Pavlovna	Да, коне́чно. Кста́ти, Ма́ша, ты не забы́ла, что у Ива́на бу́дет день рожде́ния че́рез ме́сяц – восемна́дцатого а́вгуста? Ему́ испо́лнится се́мьдесят лет. На́до бу́дет купи́ть пода́рки, пригласи́ть госте́й, пригото́вить пра́здничные блю́да ... Ведь ты так вку́сно гото́вишь!
Mariya Ivanovna	Но, ма́ма ...
Evgeniya Pavlovna	А в сентябре́ у тёти Та́ни бу́дет день рожде́ния. Не забу́дь, что ей испо́лнится се́мьдесят пять лет. На́до бу́дет опя́ть пригласи́ть госте́й, купи́ть пода́рки, ты испечёшь торт ...
Mariya Ivanovna	Ма́ма, извини́, пожа́луйста, но я пло́хо себя́ чу́вствую. Дава́й пойдём домо́й!

Before completing the test on pages 206–207 revise conjunctions with the activity below.

ACTIVITY 22

Complete the sentences with the appropriate conjunctions.

1 Он не придёт, _____ ___ не лю́бит бра́та. (because)
2 _____ он бо́лен, он бу́дет рабо́тать. (although)
3 Принима́йте э́то лека́рство три _____ четы́ре ра́за в день. (or)
4 Она́ мо́жет, _____ она́ не о́чень хо́чет помо́чь. (however)
5 На́до путеше́ствовать, _____ ты молодо́й. (while)
6 Я бу́ду писа́ть, _____ она́ ___ придёт. (until)

Test

Now it's time to test your progress in Unit 14.

1 Match 1–8 with the correct English version from a–h.

1	у меня́ боли́т нос	a I've got a cold / chill
2	у него́ боля́т глаза́	b I've got diarrhoea
3	у неё температу́ра	c his eyes hurt
4	у меня́ поно́с	d his toe hurts
5	я бо́лен	e my nose hurts
6	у меня́ просту́да	f he's nauseous
7	его́ тошни́т	g I'm sick
8	у него́ боли́т па́лец	h she's got a temperature

8

2 Pair up 1–6 with the correct response from a-f to make six mini-dialogues.

1 Как вы себя́ чу́вствуете?
2 Почему́ вы пришли́?
3 Что у меня́?
4 Вы давно́ себя́ так чу́вствуете?
5 Он ча́сто игра́ет в волейбо́л?
6 Как ча́сто вы смо́трите телеви́зор?

a У вас грипп.
b Уже́ пя́тый день.
c Я ре́дко смотрю́.
d Потому́ что я бо́лен.
e Пло́хо. Я, наве́рное, простуди́лась.
f Нет, о́чень ре́дко.

6

3 Complete the sentences with the appropriate time adverb.

1 _____ мы смо́трим телеви́зор. (sometimes)
2 Я _____ ду́маю о тебе́. (often)
3 Он _____ е́здит на такси́. (rarely)
4 Вы _____ живёте в Москве́? (for a long time)
5 Нет, я _____ прие́хал сюда́. (recently)
6 _____ она́ живёт в Пра́ге. (now)

6

4 Complete the sentences with the correct 'double
negative' forms.

1 Он _____ __ понима́ет. (nothing)
2 Па́па _____ __ гото́вит ужи́н. (never)
3 Я _____ __ нашла́ бана́ны. (nowhere)
4 Сего́дня _____ __ могу́. Я о́чень за́нят. (in no way)
5 Она́ _____ __ зна́ет об о́пере. (nothing)
6 _____ туда́ __ хо́дит. (nobody)

| | 6 |

5 Complete each phrase by inserting the verb in brackets in
the conditional.

1 е́сли ___ она́ _____ свобо́дна (быть)
2 е́сли ___ вы _____ (знать)
3 я ___ вам _____ (сове́товать)
4 я ___ _____ (хоте́ть)
5 она́ ___ _____ (верну́ться)
6 мы ___ _____ (чита́ть)
7 вы ___ _____ (сказа́ть)
8 е́сли ___ она́ _____ в Аме́рике (жить)
9 е́сли ___ я _____ на фа́брике (рабо́тать)

| | 9 |

6 How would you do the following in Russian?
(2 points if correct, 1 point if only one error)

1 Say he's behaving oddly.
2 Say he only thinks about himself.
3 Say you never go to museums.
4 Complain you feel really ill.
5 Say you have a headache.
6 Say you have a sore throat.
7 Ask 'what medicine is this?'
8 Say 'three tablets, twice a day'.

| | 16 |

TOTAL SCORE | 51 |

If you scored less than 41, re-read the Language Building
sections before completing the Summary on page 208.

Summary 14

Now try this final test summarizing the main points covered in this unit. You can check your answers on the recording.

How would you:
1 say you rarely go to restaurants?
2 say your leg hurts?
3 say you're nauseous?
4 say 'because I've got flu'?
5 say you saw nothing?
6 say 'nobody wants to watch television'?
7 say 'I would advise you …'?
8 say 'I would like …'?

REVISION

You have now almost completed the course and there is just the final Review to do. Once you have tried this, have a look at the first and last pages of each unit to show yourself how much you have achieved and see whether you can remember the points listed. Use the revision sections at the end of the units to check your memory skills and look for any weaknesses in your knowledge. Concentrate on the areas you have most problems with and revise those units.

Learning and relearning your endings will always require a bit of effort. You will probably find that when you first start talking to Russians in real situations, you confuse most of your endings! Don't despair – communication is the main thing, and in time they will come back to you. Eventually they will become automatic, and you may even begin to wonder how English manages without an instrumental or a prepositional plural.

We wish you luck in your future study of the Russian language, or, as we say in Russian, **ни пу́ха, ни пера́!**, literally 'neither down, nor feather' – to which the traditional reply is **к чёрту!** – 'to hell with it!'

Review 4

VOCABULARY

1 Which is the odd one out in each group?

1 рассо́льник / соля́нка / беспоря́дки / щи
2 бухга́лтер / горчи́чник / консульта́нт / води́тель
3 ры́нок / бли́нчик / фи́рма / би́знес
4 грудь / спина́ / ло́зунг / нога́
5 лека́рство / реце́пт / больни́ца / переу́лок

2 Match 1–5 with the appropriate English version from a–e.

1 с уваже́нием   a contact them
2 как мо́жно скоре́е   b we will arrange a meeting
3 свяжи́тесь с ни́ми   c yours sincerely
4 уважа́емые господа́!   d dear Sir/Madam
5 мы договори́мся о   e as soon as possible
   встре́че

GRAMMAR AND USAGE

3 Complete the sentences with the imperfective or perfective past of the verbs.

1 Она́ _____ спо́ртом. (занима́ться, *imperf.*)
2 Ма́ма _____ на фа́брике. (рабо́тать, *imperf.*)
3 Он ча́сто _____ в футбо́л. (игра́ть, *imperf.*)
4 Где вы _____? (роди́ться, *perf.*)
5 Мы _____ поку́пки. (сде́лать, *perf.*)

4 Complete the sentences with the correct form of the adjectives.

1 Да́йте _____ буты́лку воды́. (большо́й)
2 Вот ко́мната _____ учи́теля. (но́вый)
3 Э́то недалеко́ от _____ пло́щади. (Кра́сный)
4 Я написа́л письмо́ _____ дру́гу. (ста́рый)
5 Трина́дцать _____ америка́нцев. (молодо́й)

5 Complete the sentences with the correct form of the possessives.

  1 Вы лю́бите _____ тётю? (мой)
  2 Дом _____ отца́. (наш)
  3 Она́ пошла́ к _____ ба́бушке. (твой)
  4 Вме́сте с _____ бра́том. (мой)
  5 Письмо́ от _____ друзе́й. (ваш)

6 Complete the sentences with the appropriate 'double negative' form.

  1 Я _____ __ была́ в Кана́де. (never)
  2 _____ __ зна́ет, где он. (nobody)
  3 Э́то _____ __ зна́чит. (nothing)
  4 Я _____ __ нашёл его́. (nowhere)
  5 Где он? _____ __ найду́ его́. (in no way / I just can't)

7 Fill the blanks with the correct form of **есть** (present) or **дать** (perfective future).

  1 Ты _____ моро́женое? (есть)
  2 Мы _____ борщ. (есть)
  3 Вы _____ ему́ хлеб? (дать)
  4 Я _____ тебе́ де́ньги. (дать)
  5 Они́ _____ ему́ су́мку. (дать)

8 Complete the sentences with the correct form of **друг дру́га**.

  1 Что вы хоти́те знать _____ о _____?
  2 Вы лю́бите _____ _____?
  3 Вы помога́ли _____ _____?
  4 Мы уви́дели _____ _____ .
  5 Они́ не подхо́дят _____ _____ .

9 Complete the following with the conditional of the verbs in brackets.

  1 е́сли ___ он _____ здесь (быть)
  2 он ___ _____ (сказа́ть)
  3 она́ ___ _____ (хоте́ть)
  4 е́сли ___ вы _____ (рабо́тать)
  5 они́ ___ _____ спо́ртом (занима́ться)

10 Gleb is sitting on his own in a café. Listen to his conversation with the waitress and answer the questions below.

1 What starter does Gleb order?
2 What main course does he want?
3 What main courses are available?
4 What fish is available?
5 What main course does he ultimately order?
6 What dessert does he order?
7 What drink does he order?

11 There's been a change of travel plans, and Aleksei Semyonovich Gagarin is calling Maxim Shuisky in America to make sure he has the details correct. Listen to their conversation and complete the notes below.

President coming (date): _____
Flight: _____
Arriving: _____
Will be met by: _____
Staying in: _____

🎧 **SPEAKING**

12 You're feeling unwell and you've decided to go the doctor's. Answer her questions as prompted.

Doctor   1 В чём проблéма?
You   Say you're feeling really ill – you have a temperature.

Doctor   2 У вас болúт головá úли гóрло?
You   Say you have a headache.

Doctor   3 И давнó вы себя́ так чýвствуете?
You   Say it's already the fourth day.

Doctor   4 Вы простудúлись. Я вам вы́пишу рецéпт.
You   Ask what medicine it is.

Doctor   5 Э́то болеутоля́ющее и витамúны.
You   Say thank you, and goodbye.

13 How you would say the following things? First of all
write down the Russian, then try to do the activity using
only the recording, without looking at your notes. Use
polite forms (**вы**) wherever possible.

1 Did you get there alright?
2 Have you always lived in Moscow?
3 When did you move to Kazan?
4 I'd like to book a table for three people.
5 What do you have that doesn't have meat in it?
6 The bill, please.
7 Do you take credit cards?
8 Do you agree?
9 Please accept this souvenir.
10 I have a headache.

14 Now it's time for you to answer some questions. Listen to
the questions on the recording and give an appropriate
answer. You will be asked about the following, though
not necessarily in this order:

– why you are learning Russian
– where you were born
– whether you go to museums often
– how you are
– what the date is
– whether you eat meat
– what your parents did
– what you would like to do tomorrow

Answers

Unit 1

1 1 bortsch [*beetroot soup*], 2 forum, 3 era, 4 garage, 5 visa, 6 mayonnaise, 7 chauffeur, 8 interior [*art*], 9 cyclone, 10 Yankee, 11 hobby, 12 London, 13 Chicago, 14 New York, 15 America, 16 Saint Petersburg

7 A: 2, 3; B: a 3, b 2, c 1

9 1 bar, 2 fax, 3 (*political*) summit, 4 (*computer*) printer, 5 whisky, 6 football, 7 nylon, 8 anorak, 9 hooligan, 10 Parliament,11 pizza, 12 yoga, 13 optimist, 14 culture, 15 embargo, 16 feminism, 17 avocado, 18 gymnastics, 19 literature, 20 revolution, 21 organization

13 1 both students, 2 both Muscovites, 3 both love St Petersburg

14 A 1 b, 2 c, 3 a, B 1 b, 2 c, 3 a

19 (to host) Это Алексе́й Семёнович? (to Aleksei Semyonovich) Здра́вствуйте, Алексе́й Семёнович.

20 1 э́то вы?; 2 ма́ма; 3 здра́вствуйте; 4 кто; 5 э́то; 6 приве́т

21 1 Boris Mikhailovich; 2 her mother, Evgeniya Pavlovna; 3 He asks 'And who is this?' 4 She says, 'This is my daughter, Lena.' 5 He is a journalist.

Unit 2

2 1 yes, 2 no, 3 no

6 1 T; 2 F: She doesn't drink tea at all. 3 T; 4 F: She has ordered it for Kolya.

7 1 смета́ну, 2 Ло́ндон, 3 це́рковь, 4 у́лицу, 5 молоко́, 6 день

11 1 *Nezavisimaya Gazeta*, 2 it's old, Tuesday's edition, 3 a little calendar, 4 the little calendar, *Pravda*, and the matches

12 1 b, 2 d, 3 a, 4 c

15 1 post-office, 2 ice-cream, 3 entrance, 4 trolleybus, 5 bus, 6 toilets, 7 books, 8 railway station, 9 kiosk, 10 cinema, 11 restaurant, 12 kvass, 13 metro, 14 beer, 15 ticket-office/box-office/cash-desk, 16 taxi, 17 chemist's, 18 telephone

16 1 Copacabana Café, 2 Museum of Ceramics, 3 Tverskoi Boulevard, 4 House-Museum of K. S. Stanislavsky, 5 New Square, 6 House-Museum of A. P. Chekhov 7 University, 8 Revolution Square, 9 Restaurant 'At Granny's House', 10 the Kremlin, 11 Museum of the Revolution, 12 Red Square

17 1, 4 Mariya Ivanovna; 2, 3, 6 Lena; 5 the ice-cream man.

18 1 F: She is delighted at the prospect. 2 T, 3 T, 4 F: Evgenia Pavlovna doesn't like ice-cream. 5 T

19 1 смотри́ look, 2 скажи́ tell me, 3 да́йте give me/could I have, 4 извини́ excuse me/sorry

Unit 3

2 1 everything, 2 Turgenev and Pushkin, 3 by the Revolution Square metro station, 4 a long way from the centre, near the University metro station

6 The map on the right.

7 1 ма́мы, 2 Оле́га, 3 Ни́ны, 4 меня́, 5 неё, 6 него́

11 1 straight on, 2 end of the street, 3 left, 4 right, 5 left, 6 park, 7 by the park

12 1 f, 2 b, 3 e, 4 d, 5 a, 6 c

13 1 бы́стро, 2 гро́мко, 3 напра́во,

4 ме́дленно, 5 хорошо́

18 1 T, 2 F: He says it's near. 3 T, 4 T, 5 F: She says she's going there. 6 T

19 1 вы не ска́жете, 2 далеко́, 3 как туда́ пройти́, 4 скажи́те, нахо́дится, 5 ищу́

20 1 Москвы́, 2 Пу́шкина, 3 молока́, 4 Кремля́, 5 кино́ (neuter indeclinable)

Test

1 1 d, 2 e, 3 h, 4 f, 5 g, 6 b, 7 c, 8 a

2 1 c, 2 e, 3 b, 4 d, 5 f, 6 a

3 1 c, 2 d, 3 a, 4 b

4 1 Ле́рмонтова, 2 молока́, 3 по́чты, 4 го́стя, 5 револю́ции, 6 вина́

5 1 есть 2 туда́, 3 пешко́м, 4 иди́те, 5 поверни́те, 6 нахо́дится, 7 ищу́, 8 побли́зости, 9 до

6 1 где нахо́дится гости́ница? 2 э́то далеко́? 3 как туда́ пройти́? 4 где тут побли́зости по́чта? 5 у вас есть план го́рода? 6 я ищу́ рестора́н «Ара́гви», 7 большо́е спаси́бо, 8 я люблю́ Пу́шкина

Review 1

1 1 хлеб (not a drink), 2 приве́т (not a farewell), 3 ры́ба (not a building), 4 то́лько (not a direction), 5 спи́чки (not human beings)

2 1 d, 2 c, 3 a, 4 e, 5 b

3 1 они́, 2 он, 3 она́, 4 она́, 5 он

4 1 лю́бишь 2 иду́т, 3 рабо́таем, 4 говори́те, 5 понима́ю

5 1 газе́ту, 2 тётю, 3 язы́к, 4 молоко́, 5 Ива́на (masculine animate)

6 1 её, 2 нас, 3 вас, 4 тебя́, 5 меня́

7 1 сигаре́ты, 2 о́кна, 3 откры́тки (Spelling Rule 1), 4 студе́нты, 5 языки́ (Spelling Rule 1)

8 1 вина́, 2 хле́ба, 3 смета́ны, 4 Пу́шкина, 5 ста́нции метро́

9 1 on foot, 2 straight on, 3 end of the street, 4 turn left, 5 you will see, 6 opposite, 7 not far from

10 1 *Izvestiya*, 2 *Pravda* and *Nezavisimaya Gazeta*, 3 *Pravda*, 4 a city map, 5 they don't have one, 6 у́лица Петро́вка – Petrovka Street, 7 he's not a Muscovite

11 1 вы студе́нтка? 2 где нахо́дится гости́ница? 3 э́то Ни́на и́ли Мари́я? 4 вы лю́бите Москву́?, 5 вы сего́дня рабо́таете?, 6 что он де́лает?, 7 вы не ска́жете (ог скажи́те, пожа́луйста), где по́чта? 8 э́то далеко́? 9 у вас есть план го́рода?, 10 где тут побли́зости телефо́н-автома́т?

Unit 4

2 1 she doesn't like twentieth-century writers very much; 2 it doesn't have them separately (although it does have

214

Lermontov's complete works); 3 300 roubles; 4 it's not the *complete* works

3 1 книг; 2 кио́сков; 3 гости́ниц; 4 пи́сем; 5 госте́й

7 bananas: 22 roubles; apples: 35 roubles; oranges: 21 roubles; red cherries: 28 roubles

8 6 шесть; 16 шестна́дцать; 40 со́рок; 15 пятна́дцать; 76 се́мьдесят шесть; 606 шестьсо́т шесть; 4 четы́ре; 14 четы́рнадцать; 5 пять; 67 шестьдеся́т семь

12 airmail letter to England: 8 roubles; postcard to America: 7 roubles 50 kopecks; postcard to Canada: 7 roubles 50 kopecks; postcard to Armenia: 5 roubles 50 kopecks

13 1 хо́чет; 2 хотя́т; 3 хо́чешь; 4 хоти́те; 5 хоти́м; 6 хочу́

14 1 Кана́ду; 2 Аме́рику; 3 А́нглию; 4 Москву́; 5 вокза́л

17 украи́нская гри́вна; англи́йский фунт; до́ллар США; австри́йский ши́ллинг; да́тская кро́на; италья́нская ли́ра

19 first teapot: 331 roubles; second teapot: 123 roubles; third teapot: 65 roubles; china cup and saucer: 25 roubles; tea-service: 254 roubles

20 1, 4, 6 Mariya Ivanovna; 2, 3, 5 shop assistant

Test

1 1 h; 2 a; 3 e; 4 c; 5 b; 6 g; 7 f; 8 d

2 1 e; 2 a; 3 c; 4 b; 5 f; 6 d

3 1 госте́й; 2 виз; 3 апте́к; 4 буты́лок; 5 пи́сем; 6 домо́в

4 1 b; 2 d; 3 a; 4 c

5 1 хо́чет; 2 хочу́; 3 хоти́те; 4 хо́чет; 5 хоти́м; 6 хо́чешь; 7 хо́чет; 8 хотя́т; 9 хотя́т

6 1 рубль, nominative singular; 2 копе́йка, nominative singular; 3 апельси́на, genitive singular; 4 рубля́, genitive singular; 5 магази́нов, genitive plural; 6 рубле́й, genitive plural

7 1 покажи́те, пожа́луйста, ча́йник; 2 ско́лько э́то/он сто́ит? 3 э́то о́чень до́рого/он о́чень дорого́й, 4 где мо́жно купи́ть откры́тки? 5 ско́лько сто́ит (одна́) ма́рка на письмо́ в Аме́рику? 6 да́йте, пожа́луйста, (одну́) ма́рку по де́сять рубле́й

Unit 5

2 1 nine o'clock; 2 ten past eleven; 3 nearly two o'clock; 4 twenty past four; 5 seven-thirty; 6 sometime between ten and eleven

6 day-train: departs 9.20 a.m., arrives 5.03 p.m. (17.03); night-train: departs 10.45 p.m. (22.45), arrives 11.45 a.m.; price: 162 roubles

10 1 Tuesday–Saturday: 10 a.m. to 6 p.m. (18.00); Sunday: 12 noon to 6 p.m. (18.00); Monday: closed; 2 200 roubles; 3 7 p.m. (19.00)

11 1 d; 2 e; 3 b; 4 a; 5 c

14 Bolshoi – Tuesday & Thursday at 19.30 (*Queen of Spades*), Wednesday at 19.00 (*Ruslan and Ludmilla*), Saturday at 19.00 (*Prince Igor*). Kremlin – 10.00-17.00, closed on Thursday

15 Sunday evening: V Moscow Jazz Rally Festival, Moscow Conservatoire, Large Hall, 19.00; *Metro*, Operetta Theatre, 20.00; *Petrushka*, Central Puppet Theatre, 19.00. Monday morning: Kremlin, open from 10.00.

16 1 T; 2 F: It finishes about 11 p.m. 3 F: She doesn't like them at all. 4 T; 5 T; 6 T

17 1 Wednesday; 2 Thursday; 3 Friday; 4 Thursday; 5 Sunday

18 3.00 три часа́; 3.05 пять мину́т четвёртого; 4.15 че́тверть пя́того; 6.45 без пятна́дцати семь; 8.30 полови́на девя́того; 9.25 два́дцать пять мину́т деся́того

19 1 понеде́льник; 2 вто́рник; 3 сре́ду; 4 четве́рг; 5 пя́тницу; 6 суббо́ту; 7 воскресе́нье

Test

1 1 e; 2 c; 3 b; 4 g; 5 a; 6 d; 7 f

2 1 d; 2 c; 3 a; 4 f; 5 b; 6 e

3 1 6.20; 2 3.15; 3 10.00; 4 1.35; 5 19.30/7.30 p.m.; 6 15.40/3.40 p.m.

4 1 до; 2 зака́нчивается; 3 понеде́льник; 4 пя́тницы; 5 наде́юсь; 6 утра́; 7 дли́тся; 8 волну́йтесь; 9 без

5 1 но́чи; 2 дня; 3 ве́чера; 4 утра́; 5 ве́чера; 6 утра́

6 1 кото́рый час/ско́лько (сейча́с) вре́мени? 2 во́семь утра́; 3 полови́на /пол-седьмо́го ве́чера; 4 во ско́лько/когда́ отхо́дит по́езд в Каза́нь? 5 да́йте, пожа́луйста, оди́н биле́т на де́сять часо́в; 6 во ско́лько/когда́ открыва́ется ка́сса? 7 во ско́лько/когда́ начина́ется спекта́кль? 8 ско́лько вре́мени дли́тся о́пера?

Unit 6

2 1 T; 2 F: He is from New York. 3 T; 4 F: He speaks it so well because his family is Russian. 5 F: They are originally from Tomsk, but they live in the USA, in Chicago.

3 1 ва́ша; 2 мой; 3 на́ше; 4 твоя́; 5 моя́; 6 на́ши

7 1 Hungarian, Russian; 2 a gypsy orchestra/band; 3 red, Hungary; 4 very high

8 1 больша́я; 2 но́вые; 3 друга́я; 4 венге́рское; 5 сего́дняшняя

12 1 as a very beautiful flat; 2 as very small; 3 they are Gleb's brother's slippers; 4 it's Gleb's brother's seat

13 1 его́; 2 его́; 3 её; 4 его́; 5 её; 6 их

14 1 e; 2 d; 3 b; 4 a; 5 c

17 1 Евге́ния Па́вловна Ла́рина; 2 Мари́я Ива́новна Жа́рова; 3 Еле́на Миха́йловна Жа́рова; 4 Пётр Ива́нович Ла́рин

18 (left to right) Влади́мир; Бори́с; Па́вел; Ива́н

19 Ю́рий Григо́рьевич – Григо́рий Влади́мирович; Еле́на Миха́йловна – Михаи́л Алексе́евич; Оле́г Ива́нович – Ива́н Григо́рьевич; Евге́ния Па́вловна – Па́вел Па́влович

20 1 T; 2 F: They do live there, but they are not in at the moment. 3 T; 4 T; 5 F: It is delicious – home-made. 6 T

21 1 Ivan; 2 Moira; 3 Evgeniya; 4 Oleg; 5 Moira; 6 Evgeniya; 7 Moira; 8 Evgeniya

22 1 больша́я; 2 ста́рая; 3 вку́сный; 4 дома́шний; 5 отде́льная

Test

1 1 e; 2 g; 3 a; 4 c; 5 d; 6 b; 7 h; 8 f

2 1 e; 2 f; 3 b; 4 d; 5 a; 6 c

3 1 Кра́сная; 2 ма́ленький; 3 люби́мые; 4 хоро́шие (Spelling Rule 1); 5 друго́е; 6 вчера́шняя (soft)

4 1 b; 2 d; 3 e; 4 c; 5 f; 6 a

5 1 моя́; 2 моё; 3 твой; 4 твои́; 5 на́ше; 6 на́ша; 7 ваш; 8 ва́ши; 9 их (indeclinable)

6 1 как ва́ше о́тчество? 2 це́ны высо́кие? 3 кварти́ра больша́я? 4 да, с удово́льствием; 5 вот, пожа́луйста, моя́ визи́тная ка́рточка; 6 о́чень рад/ра́да с ва́ми познако́миться; 7 како́й дорого́й рестора́н! 8 он о́чень вку́сный (торт is masculine)

Unit 7

2 1 he says 'what a beautiful name'; 2 he says they're such beauties; 3 no, she's Russian; 4 she's at a conference at the Institute of Sociology at the Academy of Sciences; 5 feminism and male chauvinism

6 Ukrainian; Kazan; flat; small; Pushkin; America (New York or Washington, he can't remember which)

7 1 большо́й; 2 мужско́м; 3 Кра́сной; 4 тебе́; 5 на́шей; 6 ва́шей; 7 нём; 8 твоём; 9 вчера́шней; 10 моём

11 1 T; 2 F: He says Pushkin is better – the greatest poet ever. 3 T; 4 T; 5 F: He asks her what the English is for футбо́л.

12 1 e; 2 d; 3 b; 4 c; 5 a

16 Numbers refer to questions on visa-application form: 1 США; 2 Шу́йский; 3 Макси́м Бори́сович; 6 M; 7 делова́я; 8 Москва́; 12 Нью-Йо́рк …; 13 Нью-Йо́рк …; 14 Чика́го; 15 4, 1998

17 1 Peters; 2 Petrov (given in the plural in the dialogue: Петро́вы); 3 Russian; 4 Glasgow; 5 big house; 6 Canada (British Columbia); 7 Vancouver; 8 third; 9 two; 10 Moscow.

18 1 Russian; 2 English; 3 Canadian; 4 Ukrainian

19 1 краси́вее; ста́рше; бо́льше; интере́снее; 2 са́мый тру́дный; са́мый краси́вый

20 1 Москве́; 2 Пу́шкине; 3 рабо́те; 4 письме́; 5 Ванку́вере; 6 у́лице

Test

1 1 e; 2 g; 3 a; 4 f; 5 d; 6 b; 7 c

2 1 c; 2 f; 3 b; 4 e; 5 a; 6 d

3 1 вокза́ле; 2 Нью-Йо́рке; 3 у́лице; 4 пло́щади; 5 А́нглии; 6 пи́ве

4 1 кана́дка; 2 америка́нец; 3 англича́не; 4 ирла́ндская; 5 ру́сская

5 1 тебе́; 2 вас; 3 ней; 4 них; 5 мне

6 1 краси́вой; 2 Большо́м; 3 вчера́шней (a soft adjective); 4 твоём; 5 ва́шем; 6 на́шей; 7 тебе́; 8 ней

7 1 я живу́ в Москве́; 2 я америка́нец/америка́нка; 3 я живу́ в ма́ленькой кварти́ре; 4 Санкт-Петербу́рг краси́вее, чем Москва́; 5 я хочу́ чита́ть рома́ны по-ру́сски; 6 я не по́мню; 7 у вас/тебя́ есть брат и́ли сестра́?

Review 2

1 1 украи́нец (not a woman); 2 семья́ (not part of a name); 3 вре́мя (not a day of the week); 4 та́почки (not usually a form of entertainment); 5 вку́сный (not a colour)

2 1 b; 2 d; 3 e; 4 a; 5 c

3 1 рестора́нов; 2 у́лиц; 3 пи́сем; 4 кни́г; 5 госте́й (animate accusative plural)

4 1 мой; 2 твоя́; 3 на́ше; 4 ваш; 5 его́ (indeclinable)

5 1 но́вые; 2 молода́я; 3 ру́сские (Spelling Rule 1); 4 люби́мая; 5 после́днее (a soft adjective)

6 1 Санкт-Петербу́рге; 2 рабо́те; 3 письме́; 4 пло́щади; 5 Австра́лии

7 1 мое́й; 2 ва́шем; 3 ма́леньком; 4 большо́й; 5 вече́рней (a soft adjective)

8 1 мне; 2 тебе́; 3 ней; 4 нас; 5 них

9 1 сло́во (nom. sing.); 2 сло́ва (gen. sing.); 3 слов (gen. pl.); 4 сло́ва (gen. sing.); 5 сло́во (nom. sing.)

10 1 21 roubles; 2 30 roubles; 3 19 roubles; 4 25 roubles; 5 24 roubles

11 Monday: at work, meeting; Tuesday: at work, meeting with Shuisky at 15.30; Wednesday: at work; Thursday: in St Petersburg; Friday; day off

12 1 ско́лько э́то сто́ит? 2 (a) есть подеше́вле? 3 ско́лько сто́ит ма́рка на письмо́ в А́нлгию; 4 кото́рый час? or ско́лько (сейча́с) вре́мени? 5 во ско́лько отхо́дит по́езд в Москву́? 6 во ско́лько/когда́ открыва́ется ка́сса? 7 ско́лько вре́мени дли́тся спекта́кль? 8 как вас зову́т? 10 как по-ру́сски «salmon»?

Unit 8

2 *Tuesday* shopping, opera; *Wednesday* Petrodvorets; *Thursday* The Russian Museum; *Friday* The Hermitage; *Saturday* Kolya's mother goes home

6 1 (here) by the metro at 3 p.m. (1500 hours); 2 go skating; 3 she says that unfortunately she can't skate; 4 that they go to a gallery (the 'Central House of Artists'); 5 she says there's a very good café there

7 1 c; 2 d; 3 a; 4 b

11 1 lying; 2 books; 3 looking at; 4 restaurants; 5 souvenirs

12 1 бу́дут; 2 бу́ду; 3 бу́дет; 4 бу́дем; 5 бу́дешь; 6 бу́дете

16 (095) 209-55-65; (095) 288-39-52

17 259-14-90; 250-27-04; 8-10-420604433859

18 1 F (she will probably stay three more months); 2 T; 3 F (Moira makes this suggestion); 4 T; 5 T; 6 F (they arrange to meet at 9 a.m.)

19 1 верну́сь, perfective future; 2 прие́дете, perfective future; 3 бу́ду учи́ться, imperfective future; 4 пое́дем, perfective future; 5 встре́тимся, perfective future

20 1 In September I'll return home to Scotland. 2 And when will you come back to Russia again? 3 From September I'll be studying in Glasgow. 4 It's a long way away – we'll go together. 5 OK. Where shall we meet?

Test

1 1 f; 2 c; 3 g; 4 a; 5 d; 6 b; 7 h; 8 e

2 1 e; 2 a; 3 d; 4 b; 5 f; 6 c

3 1 занята́; 2 за́няты; 3 свобо́ден;
4 свобо́дна; 5 свобо́дны

4 1 феврале́; 2 апре́ль; 3 ию́не; 4 а́вгуста;
5 октябре́; 6 декабря́

5 1 сде́лаем; 2 пое́дет; 3 возьму́;
4 прочита́ете; 5 уе́дет; 6 позвони́шь

6 1 бу́дете; 2 бу́дешь; 3 бу́ду; 4 бу́дут;
5 бу́дем; 6 бу́дет

7 1 дава́й(те) пойдём на прогу́лку;
2 дава́й(те) встре́тимся в четве́рг; 3 в
сре́ду я не могу́; 4 я о́чень
за́нят/занята́; 5 я бу́ду жить в
гости́нице; 6 в сентябре́

Unit 9

2 1 in July; 2 he likes everyone to get
together at the dacha; 3 she says he is
an old man already; 4 something for
the dacha, but he's not sure exactly
what yet; 5 on Monday or Tuesday

3 1 го́роду; 2 ба́бушке; 3 нему́; 4 Бори́су;
5 вам

7 1 three or four; 2 one bottle of vodka;
3 because it is not permitted to export
old things; 4 the computer

8 1 нельзя́; 2 мо́жно; 3 нельзя́;
4 на́до/ну́жно; 5 мо́жно; 6 не на́до

12 1 Easter and Christmas; 2 at her
grandmother's; 3 the May Day holiday
('holiday of the first of May') and the
Anniversary of the October Revolution
('holiday of the October Revolution');
4 fifty-five; 5 men give women flowers
and small presents

13 1 жа́рко; 2 ску́чно; 3 хо́лодно; 4 гру́стно

14 1 c (Ива́ну); 2 b (вам); 3 e (мне); 4 d
(ему́); 5 a (ей)

17 1 нового́дний; 2 суверените́т;
3 федера́ция; 4 конститу́ция;
5 неофициа́льный; 6 славя́нский

18 1 Russia's Pushkin Day; 2 Constitution
of the Russian Federation Day; 3 Spring
Festival/Labour Day; 4 Day of Accord
and Reconciliation (formerly the
Anniversary of the October Revolution);
5 Day of Slav Culture

19 1 9th May; 2 30th April; 3 23rd
February; 4 7th January; 5 14th January

20 1 very cold; 2 that they open another
window; 3 in the other room; 4 she says
she's bored (she doesn't like it at the
dacha at all); 5 in the kitchen;
6 working — cleaning and cooking

21 1 T; 2 T; 3 F: He says he feels great
when they are together, but very bored
without her. 4 F: He says this about
Moira. 5 T; 6 F: She tells him to stop,
and then she leaves.

Test

1 1 g; 2 e; 3 h; 4 a; 5 d; 6 b; 7 f; 8 c

2 1 d; 2 e; 3 b; 4 a; 5 f; 6 c

3 1 ма́ме; 2 Санкт-Петербу́ргу; 3 го́стю;
4 Ива́ну; 5 Мари́и; 6 ба́бушке

4 1 нам; 2 тебе́; 3 ему́; 4 мне; 5 вам; 6 им;
7 мне; 8 ей; 9 вам

5 1 мо́жно его́ вывози́ть?; 2 мне мо́жно
идти́?; 3 ско́лько ему́ лет?; 4 я скуча́ю
по тебе́; 5 я тебе́/вам позвоню́ за́втра;
6 нам на́до/ну́жно отдыха́ть; 7 мне
хо́лодно; 8 мне нра́вится э́та му́зыка

6 1 (У меня́) оди́н чемода́н. 2 Нет, мне
жа́рко. 3 Ей со́рок три го́да. 4 Нет,
нельзя́. 5 Э́то пода́рок для ма́мы.

Unit 10

2 1 metro; 2 (opposite the hotel), behind
the kiosks; 3 at the ticket-office or from
a machine; 4 it is quite far (and can be
reached by bus)

3 1 преподава́телем; 2 гости́ницей
(Spelling Rule 2); 3 у́тром; 4 авто́бусом;
5 смета́ной

4 1 пе́ред теа́тром; 2 над две́рью; 3 за
це́рковью; 4 над го́родом; 5 ко́фе с
молоко́м; 6 под до́мом

8 1 F: All buses go there – she can take
any one. 2 T; 3 F: They are sold by the
driver. 4 T; 5 T

9 1 ва́ми; 2 мной; 3 ним; 4 ни́ми; 5 тобо́й;
6 ней/не́ю

13 1 direct; 2 St Petersburg; 3 18.35; 4 1; 5 2

14 1 шу́мными; 2 молоды́ми; 3 откры́тыми;
4 тру́дными; 5 вку́сных; 6 сего́дняшних

15 1 b; 2 a; 3 c

18 1 10 a.m. and 3 p.m. (1500 hours);
2 Saturdays and Sundays; 3 two hours;
4 seventy-five roubles; 5 the station
Пло́щадь Револю́ции (Revolution Square)
on the Zamoskvoretskaya line, in the
centre of the station concourse

19 Новокузне́цкая, Пло́щадь Револю́ции,
Белору́сская, Мая́ковская,
Комсомо́льская, Парк Культу́ры

20 1 экску́рсию; 2 ста́нцию; 3 две
остано́вки; 4 сле́дующая; 5 перейдём;
6 вернёмся

21 1 F: It's coming *from* Moscow. 2 T; 3 T;
4 F: It's between the kiosks and the
shop 'Молоко́' ('milk'). 5 T; 6 F: He says
she can take a bus or the metro. 7 T

22 1 идёт; 2 де́лать; 3 ждать; 4 е́дет;
5 нахо́дится; 6 пройти́; 7 е́хать;
8 возьму́

23 1 города́м; 2 роди́телям; 3 кио́сками;
4 гостя́ми; 5 дома́х; 6 ре́ках

Test

1 1 b; 2 c; 3 d; 4 a

2 1 d; 2 f; 3 e; 4 c; 5 a; 6 b

3 1 тобо́й; 2 на́ми; 3 ним; 4 мной; 5 ней/не́ю; 6 ни́ми

4 1 ве́чером; 2 ба́бушкой; 3 вокза́лом; 4 преподава́телем; 5 молоко́м; 6 по́ездом; 7 тролле́йбусом; 8 кни́гой; 9 у́тром

5 1 Мо́жно дое́хать авто́бусом? 2 Где мо́жно купи́ть тало́ны? 3 Где тут авто́бусная остано́вка? 4 На како́м авто́бусе мо́жно дое́хать до Кремля́? 5 Тролле́йбус е́дет до Кремля́? 6 Э́то прямо́й по́езд? 7 Мне ну́жно/на́до де́лать переса́дку? 8 Вы свобо́дны?

6 1 Она́ за кио́сками. 2 За́втра у́тром. 3 Мне на́до дое́хать до университе́та. 4 У меня́ уже́ есть биле́ты. 5 Я не зна́ю.

Review 3

1 1 Пари́ж (not a country); 2 па́па (not a female relative); 3 Кра́сная пло́щадь (not a holiday or festival); 4 автома́т (not a means of transport); 5 календа́рь (not a month)

2 1 d; 2 b; 3 a; 4 e; 5 c

3 1 возьмёшь; 2 пойдёшь; 3 уе́дут; 4 сде́лает; 5 прочита́ю

4 1 бу́дете; 2 бу́дут; 3 бу́ду; 4 бу́дет; 5 бу́дем

5 1 го́роду; 2 ма́ме; 3 го́стю; 4 Москве́; 5 Бори́су

6 1 ему́; 2 мне; 3 тебе́; 4 вам; 5 ей

7 1 мо́жно; 2 не на́до; 3 нельзя́; 4 нельзя́; 5 мо́жно

8 1 по́ездом; 2 ма́мой; 3 ве́чером; 4 по́чтой; 5 молоко́м

9 1 ва́ми; 2 тобо́й; 3 ней/не́ю (forms in н- after a preposition); 4 мной; 5 на́ми

10 1 at 9 a.m. here in the hotel; 2 buy souvenirs; 3 a trip to the Kremlin and, in the evening, a ballet at the Bolshoi Theatre; 4 an excursion on the metro; 5 we meet here at the hotel and go to the Leningrad Station (Ленингра́дский вокза́л); 6 10.30 p.m. (2230 hours); 7 four days; 8 excursions to Petrodvorets and to the Hermitage Museum; 9 on whether there are tickets

11 1 F: It's quicker by metro. 2 T; 3 F: You need to take the metro to Чи́стые Пруды́ and then cross on foot. 4 T; 5 T; 6 F: You can – it's not far at all.

12 1 Когда́ мы вернёмся в гости́ницу? 2 Каки́е пла́ны у нас на вто́рник и сре́ду? 3 Вам нра́вится гости́ница? 4 Где вы бу́дете жить? 5 Мо́жно его́ вывози́ть? 6 Как мне добра́ться до Кремля́? 7 Где мо́жно купи́ть тало́ны? 8 Ско́лько остано́вок до Кремля́? 9 Мне ну́жно/на́до де́лать переса́дку?

Unit 11

2 1 T; 2 F: She worked in a grocer's. 3 F: They would go in summer. 4 T

3 1 жила́; 2 занима́лся; 3 де́лали; 4 сде́лали; 5 родила́сь; 6 перее́хал

7 1 she met a very interesting woman; 2 he's glad that Kolya is coming for his birthday; 3 a large, warm rug; 4 two new rugs

8 1 большу́ю; 2 пе́рвого; 3 тёплых; 4 но́вых; 5 мою́; 6 твоего́

12 1 Gleb's brother, Boris; 2 the stadium; 3 Gleb; 4 Saturday 12th June

13 1 e; 2 c; 3 d; 4 a; 5 b

14 1 e; 2 d; 3 b; 4 a; 5 c

17 1 e; 2 f; 3 d; 4 b; 5 g; 6 a; 7 c

18 1 in Moscow, before the Revolution, under the tsar; 2 the Bolsheviks came to power; 3 they were closed; 4 there were a lot of horses and carriages, and few cars; 5 she remembers when Lenin died; 6 they liked him very much; 7 'Stalin is Lenin today', 'Stalin is our Father and Teacher'; 8 1937 and '38

19 1 in the metro; 2 in a hospital; 3 the shops were empty, or when you wanted to buy sour-cream there was only kefir, and vice versa; 4 (he asks what you can buy with them and) he says they're not enough to live on; 5 he was imprisoned in a GULAG; 6 they travel, meet interesting people (Moira, for example), and they have interesting lives

20 1 измени́лось; 2 познако́мились; 3 зараба́тывали; 4 бы́ло; 5 голода́ли; 6 боя́лись; 7 прошли́

Test

1 1 e; 2 d; 3 b; 4 c; 5 a; 6 f

2 1 a; 2 e; 3 f; 4 d; 5 b; 6 c

3 1 сего́дняшнюю; 2 большу́ю; 3 но́вого; 4 Кра́сной; 5 но́вых; 6 ста́рых

4 1 мою́; 2 на́шу; 3 твоего́; 4 ва́шей; 5 ва́ших; 6 мои́х

5 1 жи́ли; 2 занима́лись; 3 рабо́тала; 4 ката́лся; 5 пи́ли; 6 получи́ли; 7 роди́лись; 8 сде́лала; 9 перее́хала

6 1 вы всегда́ жи́ли в Москве́?; 2 когда́ вы перее́хали в Санкт-Петербу́рг?; 3 мо́жно Гле́ба?/мо́жно попроси́ть Гле́ба?; 4 как ты пожива́ешь?; 5 моя́ ма́ма рабо́тала в больни́це; 6 э́то была́ хоро́шая рабо́та; 7 я позвоню́ попо́зже; 8 вы не туда́ попа́ли

Unit 12

2 1 Tuesday 15th June; 2 7 p.m. (1900 hours); 3 four people; 4 in dining area number 2 (the second)

3 1 но́вому; 2 ста́рой; 3 сего́дняшней; 4 моему́; 5 ва́шей; 6 твои́м

7 mushrooms in sour cream, cutlets, fish, noodle-soup, cabbage soup, omelette, fried eggs, compote (plum or pear)

8 1 e; 2 a; 3 d; 4 c; 5 b

9 1 ест; 2 ем; 3 еди́те; 4 едя́т; 5 даду́т; 6 дам; 7 даст

13 1T; 2 F: The waiter suggests them, but Aleksei Semyonovich asks for the bill. 3 T; 4 F: He says that there are taxis by the entrance to the restaurant.

14 1 c; 2 d; 3 b; 4 a; 5 f; 6 e

15 1 согла́сен; 2 согла́сна; 3 согла́сны; 4 согла́сен; 5 согла́сны; 6 согла́сна

18 1 d; 2 f; 3 h; 4 c; 5 a; 6 b; 7 e; 8 g

20 Russian salad, 'Capital salad', salad of fresh vegetables, tomato salad, mushrooms in sour-cream

21 1 T; 2 F: She says she can't meet him any more. 3 F: He hopes that he and Rustam will carry on seeing her. 4 T; 5 T; 6 F: He says the passion is just like in an opera.

22 salad of fresh vegetables, turkey, ice-cream, rassolnik (twice), beef Stroganoff, meat pancakes, a large bottle of mineral water, two beers

24 1 мы; 2 ва́ми; 3 вас; 4 нас; 5 мне; 6 ты; 7 тобо́й

Test

1 1d; 2g; 3a; 4h; 5c; 6f; 7b; 8e

2 1f; 2a; 3e; 4d; 5b; 6c

3 1 ест; 2 еди́м; 3 едя́т; 4 даду́т 5 дам; 6 даст

4 1 Большо́му; 2 молодо́й; 3 Кра́сной; 4 но́вым; 5 ста́рой; 6 моему́; 7 твое́й; 8 на́шим; 9 ва́шей

5 1 Здра́вствуйте. Это рестора́н «Ара́гви»? 2 Я хочу́ заказа́ть сто́лик. 3 На суббо́ту. 4 На восемна́дцать три́дцать. 5 На трёх челове́к. 6 *your surname*; 7 До свида́ния!

6 1 Я не ем мясно́е. 2 Что ты бу́дешь пить? 3 Что здесь вку́сное? 4 Счёт, пожа́луйста. 5 Это для вас.

Unit 13

2 1 consultant; 2 president of the firm; 3 translator; 4 accountant; 5 driver; 6 secretaries

6 1 it is involved in the export of radio-engineering equipment to Western markets; 2 England and France; 3 because the firm is very specialized.

7 1 друг дру́га; 2 друг дру́гу; 3 друг дру́га; 4 друг о дру́ге; 5 друг дру́гу

11 1 He is arriving in Irkutsk on Saturday, 2nd November, for a week, and will be staying in the Baikal Hotel, where he has already booked a room. 2 He asks Sergei Konstantinovich to call him at the hotel on 2nd or 3rd October to arrange a meeting, or to contact him as soon as possible by fax or e-mail if it will be inconvenient to meet him during this time.

12 *Sample answer*: [date] Уважа́емые господа́! Спаси́бо за Ва́ше письмо́ от [date]. Я прибыва́ю в Москву́ [date]. Я бу́ду жить в гости́нице «Ко́смос». Пожа́луйста, позвони́те мне [date] и мы договори́мся о встре́че. С уваже́нием [name]

15 1 the president of the company, Mr John Gardiner; 2 16th June, for four days; 3 he will be staying in the Metropole Hotel; 4 representatives of organisations involved in export to Western markets; 5 it states that he doesn't speak Russian and requests that he be provided with an interpreter; 6 if he cannot be met at the airport

16 1 прибыва́ет; 2 бу́дет жить; 3 пое́дет; 4 встре́тится; 5 занима́ются; 6 встре́тьте; 7 предоста́вьте; 8 смо́жете встре́тить; 9 свяжи́тесь

17 *Sample answer*: [date] Уважа́емые господа́! Я прибыва́ю в Санкт-Петербу́рг [date]. Я бу́ду жить в гости́нице «Асто́рия», где я уже́ заказа́л/заказа́ла но́мер. Пожа́луйста, встре́тьте меня́ в аэропорту́ [flight details] С уваже́нием [name]

18 1 very frightened; 2 that she was in love with Oleg; 3 she is not free; 4 her fiancé is in Scotland; 5 to return home to Graham; 6 she asks Oleg not to write or phone her; 7 that he forgive her, if he is able to

19 1 хоте́ла, поняла́; 2 сказа́л, лю́бишь, испуга́лась; 3 ждёт; 4 реши́ла верну́ться; 5 понима́ет; 6 уезжа́ю; 7 уви́дишь

20 1 перево́дчик; 2 води́тель; 3 бизнесме́нка; 4 медсестра́; 5 учи́тельница; 6 консульта́нт

Test

1 1 f; 2 b; 3 h; 4 g; 5 d; 6 e; 7 c; 8 a

2 1 f; 2 c; 3 a; 4 e; 5 d; 6 b

3 1 the house which is located here; 2 the house in which I was born; 3 the person who has a/the book; 4 the girl who works here; 5 the girl whom you know; 6 the girl we're talking about

4 1 друг дру́гу; 2 друг о дру́ге; 3 друг дру́га; 4 друг дру́гу; 5 друг дру́га; 6 друг дру́гу

5 1 перево́дчица; 2 бухга́лтер; 3 гид; 4 милиционе́р; 5 консульта́нт; 6 води́тель; 7 бизнесме́н; 8 нача́льник; 9 адвока́т

6 1 э́то мой води́тель, Бори́с; 2 он бухга́лтер по специа́льности; 3 э́то на́ша но́вая колле́га; 4 Еле́на на́ша секрета́рша; 5 на́ша фи́рма специализи́рованная; 6 прими́те, пожа́луйста, э́тот сувени́р; 7 Спаси́бо за Ваш факс. 8 дорога́я Ни́на

Unit 14

2 1 F: He prefers sport. 2 T; 3 F: She is interested in art, literature, and music – she can't even skate.

3 1 никто́ не; 2 нигде́ не; 3 никогда́ не; 4 ничего́ не

7 1 slippers; 2 soup; 3 flu; 4 doctor's; 5 mustard-poultices

8 1 У меня́ боля́т но́ги. 2 У меня́ боли́т зуб. 3 У меня́ боли́т го́рло. 4 У меня́ боля́т глаза́. 5 У меня́ боли́т голова́. 6 У меня́ боли́т спина́.

9 1 c; 2 b; 3 d; 4 a

13 1 (he feels very ill), he has a headache and a sore throat, he is sleeping badly and he thinks he may have a temperature; 2 he has caught a chill/cold; 3 pain-killers and vitamins; 4 to stay in bed for three or four days (and if he doesn't improve in week's time, to come and see her again)

14 1 бы, был; бы игра́л; 2 бы, была́; бы, рассказа́ла; 3 бы, сове́товал/сове́товала; 4 бы сказа́л/сказа́ла; 5 бы, хоте́ли

17 1 e; 2 f; 3 d; 4 a; 5 c; 6 b

18 1 near to the Vladykino metro station; 2 1 p.m. to 8 p.m.; 3 7 a.m. to 8 p.m.; 4 8 a.m. to 1p.m.; 5 24 hours a day

20 1 because Evgeniya appeared to be very sad; 2 not sad, but simply cold; 3 she likes them; 4 in a month's time, the 18th August; 5 70; 6 buy presents, invite guests, prepare festive dishes; 7 in September; 8 75

21 1 -ой, -е; 2 -и; 3 -а, -а; 4 -и, -ей (animate plural object); 5 -é, -и; 6 -ём

22 1 потому́ что; 2 хотя́; 3 и́ли; 4 одна́ко/но; 5 пока́; 6 пока́, не

Test

1 1 e; 2 c; 3 h; 4 b; 5 g; 6 a; 7 f; 8 d

2 1 e; 2 d; 3 a; 4 b; 5 f; 6 c

3 1 иногда́; 2 ча́сто; 3 ре́дко; 4 давно́; 5 неда́вно; 6 сейча́с

4 1 ничего́ не; 2 никогда́ не; 3 нигде́ не; 4 ника́к не; 5 ничего́ не; 6 никто́, не

5 1 бы, была́; 2 бы, зна́ли; 3 бы, сове́товал/сове́товала; 4 бы хоте́л/хоте́ла; 5 бы верну́лась; 6 бы чита́ли; 7 бы сказа́ли; 8 бы, жила́; 9 бы, рабо́тал/рабо́тала

6 1 он стра́нно себя́ ведёт; 2 он то́лько ду́мает о себе́; 3 я никогда́ не хожу́ в музе́и; 4 я себя́ о́чень пло́хо чу́вствую; 5 у меня́ боли́т голова́; 6 у меня́ боли́т го́рло; 7 что э́то за лека́рство? 8 два ра́за в день по три табле́тки

Review 4

1 1 беспоря́дки (not a variety of soup/food); 2 горчи́чник (not a job title); 3 бли́нчик (not a business term); 4 ло́зунг (not a part of the body); 5 переу́лок (not related to medicine)

2 1 c; 2 e; 3 a; 4 d; 5 b

3 1 занима́лась; 2 рабо́тала; 3 игра́л; 4 родили́сь; 5 сде́лали

4 1 большу́ю; 2 но́вого; 3 Кра́сной; 4 ста́рому; 5 молоды́х

5 1 мою́; 2 на́шего; 3 твое́й; 4 мои́м; 5 ва́ших

6 1 никогда́ не; 2 никто́ не; 3 ничего́ не; 4 нигде́ не; 5 ника́к не

7 1 ешь; 2 еди́м; 3 да́йте; 4 дам; 5 даду́т

8 1 друг о дру́ге; 2 друг дру́га; 3 друг дру́гу; 4 друг дру́га; 5 друг дру́гу

9 1 бы, был; 2 бы сказа́л; 3 бы хоте́ла; 4 бы, рабо́тали; 5 бы занима́лись

10 1 rassolnik; 2 beef Stroganoff; 3 meat pancakes, kebabs and fish; 4 trout; 5 a kebab; 6 ice-cream; 7 a large glass of kvass

11 *President coming*: 17th of June; *Flight*: BA122; *Arriving*: 9.45, Moscow time; *Will be met by*: Aleksei Semyonovich and interpreter; *Staying in*: Metropole Hotel

12 1 Я чу́вствую себя́ о́чень пло́хо. У меня́ температу́ра. 2 У меня́ боли́т голова́. 3 Уже́ четвёртый день. 4 Что э́то за лека́рство? 5 Спаси́бо. До свида́ния!

13 1 Как вы добрали́сь? 2 Вы всегда́ жи́ли в Москве́? 3 Когда́ вы перее́хали в Каза́нь? 4 Я хочу́ заказа́ть сто́лик на трёх челове́к. 5 Что у вас есть без мя́са? 6 Счёт, пожа́луйста. 7 Вы креди́тные ка́рточки принима́ете? 8 Вы согла́сны? 9 Прими́те, пожа́луйста, э́тот сувени́р. 10 У меня́ боли́т голова́.

Grammar summary

Spelling Rule 1: after **г, к, х, ж, ч, ш**, or **щ**:
- **ы** must be replaced by **и**
- **я** must be replaced by **а**
- **ю** must be replaced by **у**

This affects, for example: nominative plural of nouns: **спи́чки, откры́тки, языки́, ба́бушки**; many adjectives: **ру́сский, америка́нский**.

Spelling Rule 2: after **ж, ч, ш**, or **щ**:
- **о** must be replaced by **е** (unless stressed)

This affects, for example, the instrumental singular of many nouns: **у́лицей, гости́ницей, ме́сяцем**. It also affects adjectives: neuter nominative singular **хоро́шее**.

Cases

Nominative
The nominative is used for the grammatical subject of a sentence. It is the form used in the dictionary.

    Гость отдыха́ет. The guest is resting.

Accusative
The accusative is used for the direct object of a verb.

    Я ищу́ **гости́ницу**. I am looking for the hotel.

It is also used after the prepositions **в** 'in, into', and **на** 'on, onto' to express movement, in answer to the question **куда́** 'where to?'.

    Куда́ ты идёшь? В **апте́ку**. Where are you going? To the chemist's.

Genitive
The genitive is used to express possession, the equivalent of the English ''s' or 'of'.

    стихи́ **Пу́шкина** Pushkin's poetry
    стака́н **молока́** a glass of milk

It is also used:
- after words such as **мно́го** 'a lot of', **ско́лько** 'how much?'
    Ско́лько **во́дки**? How much vodka?

- after a number of prepositions, including: **без** ('without'), **для** ('for'), **до** ('up to, as far as, until'), **из** ('from, out of'), **о́коло** ('near, by'), **от** ('from'), **по́сле** ('after'), **у** ('by'), **напро́тив** ('opposite'), **бли́зко от** ('near'), **далеко́ от** ('far away from'), **недалеко́ от** ('not far from').
    ко́фе без **молока́** coffee without milk
    Я живу́ далеко́ от **Ло́ндона**. I live a long way from London.

– in the Russian equivalent of 'to have' (after the preposition **y**)
   У **Ива́на** есть откры́тка. Ivan has a postcard.

– after **нет** 'there is no', 'there are no'
   Нет **молока́**. There is no milk.

Dative
The dative is used to express the indirect object, the person or thing to whom something is given, said, etc. Thus it used, for example, after the verbs **дать** ('to give'), **звони́ть** ('to phone'), **говори́ть** ('to speak'), **подари́ть** ('to give [a present]').
   Она́ пото́м **нам** ска́жет. She will tell us later.
   Я **ей** позвоню́. I'll call her.

It is also used:
– after the prepositions **к** 'to, towards' and **по** 'along'.
   Я прие́ду к **вам** в феврале́. I'll come to see you in February.

– with a number of invariable forms in **-о**:
   Мне ску́чно. I am bored.
   Вам хо́лодно? Are you cold?

– to give ages: **Ему́** два́дцать два го́да. He is twenty-two.

– in modal expressions: **Мне** нельзя́ рабо́тать. I'm not allowed to work.

Instrumental
The instrumental is used:
– to give means of transport: **авто́бусом** ('by bus'), **по́ездом** ('by train').
– to express times of the day: **у́тром** ('in the morning'), **ве́чером** ('in the evening').
– after the prepositions **с/со** ('with'), **над** ('above, over'), **ме́жду** ('between'), **пе́ред** ('in front of, before'), **под** ('underneath, under' [*location*]), **за** ('behind' [*location*]).
   Англича́не пьют чай с **молоко́м**. The English drink tea with milk.
   Э́то ме́жду **гости́ницей** и **магази́ном**. It's between the hotel and the shop.

– to say 'in' a season: **ле́том** ('in summer'), **зимо́й** ('in winter').

Prepositional
The prepositional is used after the prepositions **в** ('in') and **на** ('on, at') to express location. It is also used after the prepositions **о** ('about') and **при** ('by', 'at', 'attached to').
   Я живу́ в **Москве́**. I live in Moscow.
   докла́д о **фемини́зме** a paper on feminism

Nouns

Gender

All Russian nouns have a gender. Nouns ending in a consonant in the nominative singular are masculine (**вокзал** 'railway station', **хлеб** 'bread'). Most nouns ending in **-а** or **-ия** are feminine (**виза** 'visa', **революция** 'revolution'). Nouns ending in **-о**, **-е**, or **-ие** are neuter (**слово** 'word', **свидание** 'meeting'). Nouns ending in a soft sign (**-ь**) may be either masculine or feminine (**день** 'day' m, **площадь** 'square' f).

Masculine nouns ending in a consonant: **вокзал** 'station'

	singular	plural
nominative	вокзал	вокзал**ы**
accusative	вокзал	вокзал**ы**
genitive	вокзал**а**	вокзал**ов**
dative	вокзал**у**	вокзал**ам**
instrumental	вокзал**ом**	вокзал**ами**
prepositional	вокзал**е**	вокзал**ах**

Masculine nouns ending in a soft sign (**-ь**): **рубль** 'rouble'

	singular	plural
nominative	рубль	рубл**и**
accusative	рубль	рубл**и**
genitive	рубл**я**	рубл**ей**
dative	рубл**ю**	рубл**ям**
instrumental	рубл**ём**	рубл**ями**
prepositional	рубл**е**	рубл**ях**

Note: The instrumental singular ending is **-ём** if stressed (**рублём**) and **-ем** if unstressed (**гостем**).

Feminine nouns ending in **-а**: **виза** 'visa'

	singular	plural
nominative	виз**а**	виз**ы**
accusative	виз**у**	виз**ы**
genitive	виз**ы**	виз
dative	виз**е**	виз**ам**
instrumental	виз**ой**	виз**ами**
prepositional	виз**е**	виз**ах**

Note: Sometimes an extra vowel (**-о-** or **-е-**) appears in the genitive plural, especially where the stem ends in more than one consonant: **бутылка**, *gen. pl.* **бутыл**о**к**; **бабушка**, *gen. pl.* **бабуш**е**к.**

Feminine nouns ending in **-ия**: **револю́ция** 'revolution'

	singular	plural
nominative	**револю́ция**	**револю́ции**
accusative	**револю́цию**	**револю́ции**
genitive	**револю́ции**	**револю́ций**
dative	**револю́ции**	**револю́циям**
instrumental	**револю́цией**	**револю́циями**
prepositional	**револю́ции**	**револю́циях**

Feminine nouns ending in a soft sign (**-ь**): **пло́щадь** 'square'

	singular	plural
nominative	**пло́щадь**	**пло́щади**
accusative	**пло́щадь**	**пло́щади**
genitive	**пло́щади**	**площаде́й**
dative	**пло́щади**	**площадя́м**
instrumental	**пло́щадью**	**площадя́ми**
prepositional	**пло́щади**	**площадя́х**

Neuter nouns ending in **-о**: **сло́во** 'word'

	singular	plural
nominative	**сло́во**	**слова́**
accusative	**сло́во**	**слова́**
genitive	**сло́ва**	**слов**
dative	**сло́ву**	**слова́м**
instrumental	**сло́вом**	**слова́ми**
prepositional	**сло́ве**	**слова́х**

Notes:

1 Some neuter nouns are indeclinable (that is, they only have a single form, whatever their case or number): **авока́до, метро́, кино́**.

2 Sometimes an extra vowel (**-о-** or **-е-**) appears in the genitive plural, especially where the stem ends in more than one consonant: **окно́**, *gen. pl.* **о́кон; письмо́,** *gen. pl.* **пи́сем**.

Neuter nouns ending in **-ие**: **свида́ние** 'meeting'

	singular	plural
nominative	**свида́ние**	**свида́ния**
accusative	**свида́ние**	**свида́ния**
genitive	**свида́ния**	**свида́ний**
dative	**свида́нию**	**свида́ниям**
instrumental	**свида́нием**	**свида́ниями**
prepositional	**свида́нии**	**свида́ниях**

Animate nouns

The accusative singular of masculine animate nouns (nouns referring to people and animals) is the same as the genitive singular, i.e. **-а** or **-я**.

Я зна́ю **Ива́на**. I know Ivan.

Вы зна́ете **го́стя**? Do you know the guest?

The accusative plural of animate nouns of *all* genders is the same as the genitive plural.

Я не люблю **писа́телей**. I don't like writers.

Он не лю́бит **же́нщин**. He doesn't like women.

Adjectives, possessives, and pronouns referring to singular masculine animate nouns in the accusative and all plural animate nouns in the accusative will also have the same form as the genitive.

Я зна́ю **ва́шего** го́стя. I know your guest.

Adjectives

Adjectives change form according to the gender, number, and case of the noun they refer to. Most adjectives have 'hard' endings. Example: **кра́сный** 'red'.

	masculine	feminine	neuter	plural
nominative	кра́сный	кра́сная	кра́сное	кра́сные
accusative	кра́сный	кра́сную	кра́сное	кра́сные
genitive	кра́сного	кра́сной	кра́сного	кра́сных
dative	кра́сному	кра́сной	кра́сному	кра́сным
instrumental	кра́сным	кра́сной	кра́сным	кра́сными
prepositional	кра́сном	кра́сной	кра́сном	кра́сных

Э́то **но́вая** гости́ница. It's a new hotel.

Они́ живу́т в **ма́леньком** до́ме. They live in a small house.

1 Some adjectives have the stressed ending **-о́й** in the masculine nominative and accusative singular. Examples: **голубо́й, молодо́й.**

2 Many adjectives are affected by Spelling Rule 1. Examples: **ру́сский, америка́нский.**

A relatively small number of adjectives have 'soft' endings. Example: **си́ний** 'dark blue'.

	masculine	feminine	neuter	plural
nominative	си́ний	си́няя	си́нее	си́ние
accusative	си́ний	си́нюю	си́нее	си́ние
genitive	си́него	си́ней	си́него	си́них
dative	си́нему	си́ней	си́нему	си́ним
instrumental	си́ним	си́ней	си́ним	си́ними
prepositional	си́нем	си́ней	си́нем	си́них

A number of adjectives are affected by both Spelling Rules: masculine nominative singular **хоро́ший**, neuter nominative singular **хоро́шее**, masculine genitive singular **хоро́шего**, nominative plural **хоро́шие**.

Short form adjectives

Short form adjectives have four different forms, agreeing with the subject: masculine, feminine, neuter, or plural.

	masculine	*feminine*	*neuter*	*plural*
busy	за́нят	занята́	за́нято	за́няты
free	свобо́ден	свобо́дна	свобо́дно	свобо́дны

Он **свобо́ден**? Is he free?

Она́ о́чень **занята́**. She's very busy.

Possessives

The possessives **мой** 'my', **твой** 'your (*familiar singular*)', **свой** 'one's own', **наш** 'our', and **ваш** 'your (*formal singular; plural*)' are similar to adjectives in Russian. They change form according to the gender, case, and number of the noun they refer to.

Мой брат и **твоя́** тётя. My brother and your aunt.

На́ше свида́ние сего́дня в три часа́. Our meeting is today at three.

	masculine	*feminine*	*neuter*	*plural*
nominative	мой	моя́	моё	мои́
accusative	мой	мою́	моё	мои́
genitive	моего́	мое́й	моего́	мои́х
dative	моему́	мое́й	моему́	мои́м
instrumental	мои́м	мое́й	мои́м	мои́ми
prepositional	моём	мое́й	моём	мои́х

твой and **свой** have the same endings as **мой**.

	masculine	*feminine*	*neuter*	*plural*
nominative	наш	на́ша	на́ше	на́ши
accusative	наш	на́шу	на́ше	на́ши
genitive	на́шего	на́шей	на́шего	на́ших
dative	на́шему	на́шей	на́шему	на́шим
instrumental	на́шим	на́шей	на́шим	на́шими
prepositional	на́шем	на́шей	на́шем	на́ших

ваш has the same endings as **наш**.

его́ 'his', 'its' (masculine/neuter noun), **её** 'her', 'its' (feminine noun), and **их** 'their' are indeclinable: they do not change form according to the gender, case, or number of the noun they describe.

Это **его́** та́почки. Those are his slippers.

Её брат. Her brother.

свой, the reflexive possessive, refers back to the topic of the sentence, meaning 'one's own', 'my', 'your', 'his', etc.

У меня́ **свой** интере́сы, а у тебя́ – **свой**. I have my interests, you have yours.

Pronouns

	I	you	he	she	it	we	you	they
nominative	я	ты	он	она́	оно́	мы	вы	они́
accusative	меня́	тебя́	(н)его́	(н)её	(н)его́	нас	вас	(н)их
genitive	меня́	тебя́	(н)его́	(н)её	(н)его́	нас	вас	(н)их
dative	мне	тебе́	(н)ему́	(н)ей/(н)ею	(н)ему́	нам	вам	(н)им
instrumental	мной	тобо́й	(н)им	(н)ей	(н)им	на́ми	ва́ми	(н)и́ми
prepositional	мне	тебе́	нём	ней	нём	нас	вас	них

The forms of **он**, **она́**, **оно́**, and **они́** with an initial **н-** are used after prepositions.

У **него́** есть план го́рода. He has a city plan.

Ты скуча́ешь по **нему́**? Do you miss him?

Я не хочу́ говори́ть с **ни́им**. I don't want to speak to them.

Notes

1 'you' forms: **ты** is singular and familiar: it is used when speaking to a person you know well, or to a child. **вы** is plural or polite singular: it is used when speaking to a group of people, or to one person with whom you are on formal terms.

2 **он** 'he'/'it' is used to refer to males and masculine nouns. **она́** 'she'/'it' is used for female persons and feminine nouns. **оно́** 'it' is used for neuter nouns.

3 **они́** 'they' is used to refer to people and nouns of any gender in the plural.

The reflexive pronoun

accusative	себя́
genitive	себя́
dative	себе́
instrumental	собо́й
prepositional	себе́

себя́ means 'oneself', 'myself', 'yourself', and so on, although it is sometimes not translated.

Ты стра́нно **себя́** ведёшь. You're behaving oddly.

Он то́лько ду́мает о **себе́**. He only thinks of himself.

что ('what'), **кто** ('who')

nominative	что	кто
accusative	что	кого́
genitive	чего́	кого́
dative	чему́	кому́
instrumental	чем	кем
prepositional	чём	ком

У **кого́** есть хлеб? Who has the bread?

О **чём** вы ду́маете? What are you thinking about?

этот 'this' and **тот** 'that'

	masculine	feminine	neuter	plural
nominative	**э́тот**	**э́та**	**э́то**	**э́ти**
accusative	**э́тот**	**э́ту**	**э́то**	**э́ти**
genitive	**э́того**	**э́той**	**э́того**	**э́тих**
dative	**э́тому**	**э́той**	**э́тому**	**э́тим**
instrumental	**э́тим**	**э́той**	**э́тим**	**э́тими**
prepositional	**э́том**	**э́той**	**э́том**	**э́тих**

	masculine	feminine	neuter	plural
nominative	**тот**	**та**	**то**	**те**
accusative	**тот**	**ту**	**то**	**те**
genitive	**того́**	**той**	**того́**	**тех**
dative	**тому́**	**той**	**тому́**	**тем**
instrumental	**тем**	**той**	**тем**	**те́ми**
prepositional	**том**	**той**	**том**	**тех**

друг дру́га ('each other')

accusative	**друг дру́га**
genitive	**друг дру́га**
dative	**друг дру́гу**
instrumental	**друг** с **дру́гом**
prepositional	**друг** о **дру́ге**

Они́ хорошо́ зна́ют **друг дру́га**. They know each other well.
Мы помога́ем **друг дру́гу**. We help each other.

Adverbs

Russian adverbs do not change form. Many end in **-о**: **хорошо́** ('well'), **пло́хо** ('badly'), **гро́мко** ('loudly'), **бы́стро** ('quickly').

Он говори́т **бы́стро** и **ти́хо**. He speaks quickly and quietly.
Я чита́ю **ме́дленно** по-ру́сски. I read Russian slowly.
Она́ **гро́мко** говори́т. She speaks loudly.

Negatives

To make a sentence negative, **не** is added before the word which is negated.

Я **не** зна́ю. I don't know.
Ты хо́чешь и́ли **не** хо́чешь? Do you want to, or don't you?
Э́то **не** Ива́н Серге́евич. That isn't Ivan Sergeevich.

'Double negatives'
With the negatives **никогда́** ('never'), **никто́** ('nobody'), **ничего́** ('nothing'), **ника́к** ('in no way'), and **нигде́** ('nowhere'), **не** is also used with the verb.

Я **ничего́ не** зна́ю о футбо́ле. I don't know anything about football.
Никто́ меня́ **не** понима́ет. Nobody understands me.

Verbs

Type Ia verbs (stem ending in a vowel)
рабо́тать – to work (stem: **рабо́та-**)

я **рабо́таю**	I work
ты **рабо́таешь**	you work [*familiar singular*]
он, она́, оно́ **рабо́тает**	he, she, it works
мы **рабо́таем**	we work
вы **рабо́таете**	you work [*polite singular, plural*]
они́ **рабо́тают**	they work

Type Ib verbs (stem ending in a consonant)

ждать – to wait		**е́хать** – to go (by transport)	
(stem: **жд-**)		(stem: **е́д-**)	
я **жду**	I wait	я **е́ду**	I go
ты **ждёшь**	you wait	ты **е́дешь**	you go
он, она́, оно́ **ждёт**	he, she, it waits	он, она́, оно́ **е́дет**	he, she, it goes
мы **ждём**	we wait	мы **е́дем**	we go
вы **ждёте**	you wait	вы **е́дете**	you go
они́ **ждут**	they wait	они́ **е́дут**	they go

If the verb is stressed on the ending, it has **-ё-** instead of **-е-**.

Type II verbs

говори́ть – to speak, talk		**люби́ть** – to love	
(stem: **говор-**)		(stem: **любл-, люб-**)	
я **говорю́**	I speak	я **люблю́**	I love
ты **говори́шь**	you speak	ты **лю́бишь**	you love
он **говори́т**	he speaks	он **лю́бит**	he loves
мы **говори́м**	we speak	мы **лю́бим**	we love
вы **говори́те**	you speak	вы **лю́бите**	you love
они́ **говоря́т**	they speak	они́ **лю́бят**	they love

Some verbs, such as **люби́ть** above, have a slightly different stem from the second person singular onwards.

Reflexive verbs
Reflexive verbs have an additional reflexive ending: **-ся** after a final consonant and **-сь** after a final vowel.

надѐяться Ia – to hope		**волнова́ться** Ia – to worry	
(stem: **надѐ-**)		(stem: **волну́-**)	
я **надѐюсь**	I hope	я **волну́юсь**	I worry
ты **надѐешься**	you hope	ты **волну́ешься**	you worry
он, она́, оно́		он, она́, оно́	
надѐется	he/she/it hopes	**волну́ется**	he/she/it worries
мы **надѐемся**	we hope	мы **волну́емся**	we worry
вы **надѐетесь**	you hope	вы **волну́етесь**	you worry
они́ **надѐются**	they hope	они́ **волну́ются**	they worry

Imperfective and perfective verbs

Most Russian verbs actually exist as not one, but two verbs: an imperfective verb and a perfective verb. These two verbs are used as the basis for different tenses. For example, the present tense can only be formed from the imperfective, whereas adding the normal verb endings to a perfective creates a future tense. Both imperfective and perfective can be used to form past tenses, although with slightly different meanings.

The present

The present tense is formed from imperfective verbs only. Note that the Russian present tense can be translated in one of two ways in English, depending on the context: 'I shop' or 'I am shopping'.

Мы **де́лаем** поку́пки. We are doing the shopping.

Они́ **слу́шают** о́перу. They are listening to an opera.

The perfective future

The perfective future is formed by adding the normal type Ia, Ib, or II endings to a perfective infinitive. This tense is used to refer to a one-off event in the future, or to stress the result or completion of a future action.

За́втра мы **сде́лаем** поку́пки. Tomorrow we will do the shopping.

Они́ **послу́шают** о́перу. They will listen to an opera.

The imperfective future

The imperfective future is formed from the appropriate form of **быть** 'to be' followed by the imperfective infinitive. It is used to refer to repeated events in the future, or to stress the ongoing or habitual nature of a future event.

я **бу́ду лежа́ть**	I will lie / will be lying
ты **бу́дешь лежа́ть**	you will lie / will be lying
он, она́, оно́ **бу́дет лежа́ть**	he, she, it will lie / will be lying
мы **бу́дем лежа́ть**	we will lie / will be lying
вы **бу́дете лежа́ть**	you will lie / will be lying
они́ **бу́дут лежа́ть**	they will lie / will be lying

Я **бу́ду** весь день **лежа́ть** на пля́же. I will lie on the beach all day.

The past tense

The past tense is formed from the imperfective or the perfective infinitive, with the final **-ть** replaced by **-л**, plus a feminine, neuter, or plural ending if required. If the verb is reflexive, the ending **-ся** (after a consonant) or **-сь** (after a vowel) appears at the very end of the form.

	masculine	feminine	neuter	plural
жить	жил	жила́	жи́ло	жи́ли
быть	был	была́	бы́ло	бы́ли
рабо́тать	рабо́тал	рабо́тала	рабо́тало	рабо́тали
роди́ться	роди́лся	родила́сь	родило́сь	родили́сь

The imperfective past

The imperfective past is used to refer to repeated events in the past, or to stress the ongoing or habitual nature of a past event.

Вы всегда́ **жи́ли** (*imperf.*) в Каза́ни? Have you always lived in Kazan?

Мой па́па **рабо́тал** (*imperf.*) на фа́брике. My father worked in a factory.

The perfective past

The perfective past refers to a one-off event in the past, or stresses the result or successful completion of an action.

Я **роди́лся** (*perf.*) в Москве́. I was born in Moscow.

Я **получи́л** (*perf.*) рабо́ту в Каза́ни. I got work in Kazan.

The conditional

The conditional is formed by using the word **бы** with an imperfective or perfective past. **бы** usually appears either as second word in the sentence or immediately after the verb.

Éсли **бы** я **был** свобо́ден, я **бы пое́хал** с ва́ми. I would go with you if I were free.

Я **бы хоте́л** пойти́ с тобо́й. I would like to go with you.

The verb 'to be'

The verb **быть** 'to be' is dropped in the present tense. In writing it is sometimes replaced by a dash.

Я – Ни́на. I am Nina.

Она́ – москви́чка. She is a Muscovite.

The forms of **быть** on their own express the future tense 'I will be', 'you will be', etc.

Я там бу́ду. I will be there.

Что бу́дет за́втра? What's happening tomorrow?

The past tense of **быть** is regular.

Я там был. I was there.

Она́ была́ москви́чка. She was a Muscovite.

Vocabulary glossary

А

а	but, and
а́вгуст	August
авиапо́чта	airmail
авто́бус	bus
автома́т	(vending-)machine
автомоби́ль (m)	car
адвока́т	lawyer
а́дрес	address
америка́нец, америка́нка	American (man, woman)
америка́нский	American
англича́нин, англича́нка	Englishman, Englishwoman
А́нглия	England
англи́йский	English
апельси́н	orange
апре́ль (m)	April
апте́ка	chemist's

Б

ба́бушка	grandmother, old woman
бага́ж	luggage
бале́т	ballet
бана́н	banana
бе́дный	poor
без (+ gen.)	without
беспоря́дки	disturbances
бизнесме́н, бизнесме́нка	businessman, businesswoman
биле́т	ticket
бли́зко	nearby
бли́зко от (+ gen.)	near to
бли́нчик	pancake, fritter
Бо́же мой!	good grief!
бо́лее	more
бо́лен, больна́	ill
болеутоля́ющее	pain-killer
боли́т: у меня́ боли́т/боля́т ...	my ... hurts/hurt
больни́ца	hospital
бо́льше	more, bigger
бо́льше всего́	above all
большо́й	big
босо́й	barefoot
боя́ться II imperf. (бою́сь), побоя́ться II perf.	to be afraid
брат	brother
брать Ib imperf. (беру́), взять Ib perf.	to take
бу́дьте добры́	would you be so kind ...?
букинисти́ческий	second-hand book [adjective]
бу́лочка	bun
буты́лка	bottle
бухга́лтер	accountant
бы́стро	quickly
быть Ib (бу́ду)	to be
бюро́	office

В

в (+ асс.)	in, into, to (movement)
в (+ prep.)	in (location)
ва́жно	important
ваш	your, yours
ведь	you know, you see
век	century
вели́кий	great
венге́рский	Hungarian
верну́ться Ib perf. (верну́сь), возвраща́ться Ia imperf.	to return
ве́рующий	religious
ве́село	happy
весна́	spring
вести́ себя́ Ib imperf. (веду́)	to behave
весь, вся, всё, все	whole, all
ве́чер	evening
вече́рний	evening, night [adjective]
вещь (f)	thing
взять Ib perf. (возьму́), брать Ib imperf.	to take
ви́деть II imperf. (ви́жу, ви́дишь), уви́деть II perf.	to see
визи́тная ка́рточка	(business) card
вино́	wine
ви́шня	black cherry
вку́сный	tasty
вме́сте	together
во вре́мя (+ gen.)	during
води́тель (m)	driver
возвраща́ться Ia imperf. (возвраща́юсь), верну́ться Ib perf.	to return
вокза́л	(main) railway station
волнова́ться Ia imperf. (волну́юсь)	to worry
вообще́ не	not at all
во́семь	eight
во ско́лько?	at what time?
воскресе́нье	Sunday
вот	here is
врач	doctor
вре́мя (n) (gen. вре́мени, nom. pl. времена́)	time

все	everyone
всё	everything
всегда́	always
всего́	altogether, that makes
встре́тьте (imperative)	meet
встре́титься II perf.	to meet (each other)
(встре́чусь, встре́тишься),	
встреча́ться Ia imperf.	
встре́ча	meeting
вто́рник	Tuesday
второ́й	second
второ́е	main course
вход	entrance
входи́ть II imperf.	to go in
(вхожу́, вхо́дишь),	
войти́ Ib perf.	
вчера́шний	yesterday's
вы	you [polite singular, plural]
выбира́ть Ia imperf.	to choose
(выбира́ю),	
вы́брать Ib perf.	
вывози́ть II imperf.	to export
(вывожу́, выво́зишь),	
вы́везти Ib perf.	
вы́зовите врача́ / такси́	call a doctor / a taxi
вы́йти Ib perf. (вы́йду),	to go out, to get off
выходи́ть II imperf.	
вы́писать Ib perf.,	to write out
(вы́пишу),	
выпи́сывать Ia imperf.	
выходи́ть II imperf.	to go out, to get off
(выхожу́, выхо́дишь),	
вы́йти Ib perf.	
вы́ше	taller, higher

Г

где	where
гид	guide
глаз (nom. pl. глаза́)	eye
глубоко́	deeply
глу́пость (f)	foolishness, stupidity
говори́ть II imperf.	to talk, to say
(говорю́),	
сказа́ть Ib perf.	
голова́	head
голубо́й	pale blue
го́лый	naked
гора́здо	much, by far
го́рло	throat
го́род	town, city
горя́чий	hot
господи́н	Mr
гости́ница	hotel
гость (m)	guest
грамма́тика	grammar
гриб	mushroom

гро́мко	loudly
грудь (f)	breast, chest
гру́стно	sad
гру́шевый	pear [adjective]

Д

да	yes; well
да нет	no [emphatic]
да́же	even
дава́й(те) …	let's …
давно́	(for) a long time; a long time ago
далеко́ (от (+ gen.))	far away (from)
далекова́то	quite far
дари́ть II imperf. (дарю́),	to give a present
подари́ть II perf.	
дать perf. (irreg.),	to give
дава́ть Ia imperf. (даю́)	
два (m/n), две (f)	two
дверь (f)	door
де́вушка	girl
де́вять	nine
де́йствовать Ia imperf.	to operate, to be active
(де́йствую)	
дека́брь (m)	December
деклара́ция	declaration
дела́: как дела́?	how's things?
де́лать Ia imperf. (де́лаю)	to do, to make
сде́лать Ia perf.	
де́лать поку́пки	to go shopping
де́лать переса́дку	to change [transport]
день (m) (gen. sing. дня)	day
день рожде́ния	birthday
де́ньги (pl.)	money
де́сять	ten
де́ти (pl.); ребёнок (sing.)	children; child
деше́вле	cheaper
дёшево	cheap
для (+ gen.)	for
до (+ gen.)	as far as, until
до встре́чи	see you!
до свида́ния	goodbye
добра́ться (Ib, perf.)	to get to, to reach
до (+ gen.) (доберу́сь)	
договори́ться II perf.	to arrange
о (+ instr.)	
догова́риваться Ia	
imperf.	
до́брый	good
дое́хать Ib perf. (дое́ду),	to get to, to reach [by
доезжа́ть Ia imperf.	transport]
дойти́ (Ib perf.) до (+ gen.)	to get to [on foot]
(дойду́)	
доходи́ть II imperf.	
дом	house, building
дома́шний	home, home-made
домо́й	home [adverb]

233

дорого́й	dear
доро́же	more expensive
дочь (f)	daughter
друг (nom. pl. друзья́, gen. pl. друзе́й)	friend
друг дру́га	each other
друго́й	other
ду́мать Ia imperf. (ду́маю), поду́мать Ia perf.	to think
дыша́ть II imperf. (дышу́)	to breathe
дя́дя (m)	uncle

Е

его́	his
еда́	food
её	her, hers
е́здить II imperf. (е́зжу)	to go [by transport]
е́сли	if
е́сли ... не	unless
есть	there is
есть imperf. (irreg.), съесть perf.	to eat
е́хать Ib imperf. (е́ду), пое́хать Ib perf.	to go [by transport]
ещё	still, else, further
ещё раз	once again

Ж

жа́рко	hot
ждать Ib imperf. (жду), подожда́ть Ib perf.	to wait
же	used for emphasis
жени́ться II perf./imperf. (женю́сь)	to get married [of a man]
же́нщина	woman
жето́н	token
жить Ib imperf. (живу́)	to live
журна́л	magazine
журнали́ст, журнали́стка	journalist [man, woman]

З

за (+ instr.)	behind (location)
заброни́ровать Ia perf. (заброни́рую), брони́ровать Ia imperf.	to book, to reserve
забыва́ть Ia imperf. (забыва́ю), забы́ть Ib perf.	to forget
за́втра	tomorrow
заказа́ть Ib perf. (закажу́), зака́зывать Ia imperf.	to book, to reserve
зака́нчиваться Ia imperf. (зака́нчиваю), зако́нчиться II perf.	to end
закрыва́ться Ia imperf. (закрыва́юсь), закры́ться Ia perf.	to close
закры́тый	shut
зал	hall
замеча́тельно	it is wonderful; wonderful!
замеча́тельный	wonderful [adjective]
занима́ться Ia imperf. (+ instr.) (занима́юсь), заня́ться Ib perf.	to be occupied (with), to work (on, in)
за́нят, занята́, за́нято, за́няты	busy, occupied
за́падный	western
заплати́ть II perf. (заплачу́, запла́тишь), плати́ть II imperf.	to pay
запо́лнить II perf. (запо́лню), заполня́ть Ia imperf.	to fill in
заче́м	why, what for
звони́ть II imperf. (звоню́), позвони́ть II perf.	to telephone
здесь	here
здоро́вье	health; see на здоро́вье
здра́вствуйте	hello
зима́	winter
знако́м с (+ instr.)	acquainted with
знать Ia imperf. (зна́ю)	to know
зна́чит	so, that means
зна́чить II imperf.	to mean

И

и	and
и ..., и...	both ... and ...
игра́ть Ia imperf. (игра́ю), сыгра́ть Ia perf.	to play
игра́ть в (+ acc.)	to play [a sport]
идти́ Ib imperf. (иду́), пойти́ Ib perf.	to go [on foot]
из (+ gen.)	from, out of
извини́те	excuse me, sorry
измене́ние	change
изменя́ть Ia imperf. (изменя́ю), измени́ть II perf.	to change
изуча́ть Ia imperf. (изуча́ю), изучи́ть II perf.	to learn
и́ли	or
и́менно	namely, exactly
и́мя (n) (gen. sing. и́мени)	(first) name
иногда́	sometimes
институ́т	institute
интере́сно	it is interesting
интере́сный	interesting [adjective]
интересова́ть Ia imperf. (интересу́ю)	to interest

интересова́ться Ia imperf. (интересу́юсь) (+ instr.)	to be interested in
интере́сы	interests
ирла́ндский	Irish
иска́ть Ib imperf. (ищу́), поиска́ть Ib perf.	to look for
иску́сство	art
испо́лниться II perf. (+ dat.)	to reach (an age)
их	their, theirs
ищу́	see иска́ть
ию́ль (m)	July
ию́нь (m)	June

К

к (+ dat.)	to, towards
ка́ждый	every, each
каза́ться Ib imperf. (кажу́сь), показа́ться Ib perf.	to seem
как	how
как жа́лко	what a pity
как же э́то так?	how is that?
как мо́жно скоре́е	as soon as possible
како́й	what sort of, which; what a … !
как-то	somehow
календа́рь (m)	calendar
Кана́да	Canada
кана́дец, кана́дка	Canadian (man, woman)
кана́дский	Canadian [adjective]
ка́рта вин	wine list
ка́сса	ticket-office, box-office, cash-desk
ката́ться (ката́юсь) Ia, imperf. на конька́х	to ice-skate
като́к	skating-rink
кварти́ра	flat, apartment
кино́* (n)	cinema, movies
кни́га	book
когда́	when(ever)
колбаса́	sausage [large Continental type], salami
колле́га (m/f)	colleague
коммуна́льный	communal
ко́мната	room
коне́ц (gen. sing. конца́)	end
коне́чно	of course
конкуре́нт	competitor
конкуре́нция	competition
копе́йка	kopeck [100th part of a rouble]
корми́ть II imperf. (кормлю́, ко́рмишь), накорми́ть II perf.	to feed
кость (f)	bone
котле́та	cutlet, burger, rissole
кото́рый	which; who

ко́фе* (m)	coffee
краса́вица	beauty [a woman]
краси́вый	beautiful
кра́сный	red
крова́ть (f)	bed
кро́ме (+ gen.)	apart from, except
кста́ти	by the way
кто	who
куда́	to where?
культу́ра	culture
купи́ть II perf. (куплю́, ку́пишь), покупа́ть Ia imperf.	to buy
ку́хня	cuisine, kitchen
ку́шать Ia imperf. (ку́шаю), поку́шать Ia perf.	to eat [informal]

Л

ла́дно	all right, very well
ле́гче	easier
лежа́ть II imperf. (лежу́), полежа́ть II perf.	to lie
лека́рство	medicine
ле́то	summer
лече́ние	(medical) treatment
ли	indicating a question
ложи́ться (II imperf.) в крова́ть (ложу́сь), лечь Ib perf.	to go to bed
ло́зунг	slogan
лу́чше	better; rather, instead
люби́ть II imperf. (люблю́, лю́бишь)	to love, to like
люби́мый	favourite
любо́й	any

М

магази́н	shop, store
май	May
ма́ленький	small
ма́ма	mum(my), mom(my)
ма́рка	stamp
март	March
мать (f)	mother
ме́жду (+ instr.)	between
ме́дленно	slowly
ме́ньше	less
ме́сто	place
местожи́тельство	residence
ми́ленький	dear, darling
милиционе́р	policeman
ми́лый	dear, nice
мину́та	minute
мир	world
мно́го	a lot, much
мо́жет быть	maybe

мо́жно	it is possible; it is permitted; one can
мо́жно (+ acc.)	can I speak to … , please?
мой, моя́, моё, мои́	my, mine
молодо́й	young
молоко́	milk
мо́ре	sea
моро́женое	ice-cream
Москва́	Moscow
москви́ч, москви́чка	Muscovite [man, woman]
моско́вский	Moscow [adjective]
мочь Ib imperf. (могу́, мо́жешь), смочь Ib perf.	to be able to
муж	husband
мужско́й	male
мужчи́на (m)	man
музе́й (m)	museum
му́зыка	music
мы	we
мясно́е	meat dishes

Н

на (+ acc.)	on(to), at, to [movement]
сто́лик на трёх/четырёх челове́к	a table for three/four
на (+ prep.)	on, at [location]
на здоро́вье!	enjoy it!
наве́рное	probably
наде́ньте	put on [imperative]
наде́яться Ia imperf. (наде́юсь) на (+ acc.)	to hope (for)
над (+ instr.)	above, over
на́до	it is necessary to; one should
не на́до	one should not; don't
найти́ Ib perf. (найду́), находи́ть II imperf.	to find
накорми́ть II perf. (накормлю́, нако́рмишь), корми́ть II imperf.	to feed
назва́ние	name
нале́во	left
напи́сано	it is written
написа́ть Ib perf. (напишу́), писа́ть Ib imperf.	to write
направле́ние	direction
напра́во	right
наприме́р	for example
напро́тив (+ gen.)	opposite
находи́ться II imperf.	to be located
нача́ло	beginning
нача́льник	manager, boss
нача́ть Ib perf. (начну́), начина́ть Ia imperf.	to begin
начина́ться Ia imperf. (начина́юсь),	to begin

нача́ться Ib perf.	
наш	our
не	not
не́ за что	don't mention it
неда́вно	recently
недалеко́ (от (+ gen.))	not far away, not far (from)
неде́ля	week
недо́рого	it is inexpensive
недорого́й	inexpensive [adjective]
нельзя́ + imperf.	it is not permitted
нельзя́ + perf.	it is impossible
немно́го	a little (bit of)
непо́лный	not complete
непреме́нно	without fail, make sure you …
нет	no; there is not, there are not
нигде́ … не	nowhere
ника́к … не	in no way
никогда́ … не	never
никто́ … не	no one
ничего́ … не	nothing
но	but
но́вый	new
нога́	leg, foot
ноль (m)	zero
но́мер	number, room [in hotel]
норма́льно	OK, all right
ночь (f)	night
ноя́брь (m)	November
нра́виться II imperf. (нра́влюсь, нра́вишься), понра́виться II perf.	to like
ну	well
ну́жно	it is necessary to, one should

О

о, об, обо	about
обеща́ть Ia imperf./perf. (обеща́ю)	to promise
обожа́ть Ia imperf. (обожа́ю)	to adore, to worship
обору́дование	equipment
обы́чно	usually
одева́ться Ia imperf. (одева́юсь), оде́ться Ib perf.	to dress
оди́н, одна́, одно́	one; alone
одна́ко	however
окно́	window
о́коло (+ gen.)	near
октя́брь (m)	October
он	he; it [m noun]
она́	she; it [f noun]
они́	they

оно́	it [n noun]
опя́ть	again
о́сень (f)	autumn
остано́вка	(bus) stop
(gen. pl. остано́вок)	
оста́ться Ib perf. (оста́нусь),	to remain
остава́ться Ia imperf.	
осторо́жно	carefully
от (+ gen.)	from
о́тдых	holiday; rest, relaxation
отдыха́ть Ia imperf.	to rest
(отдыха́ю),	
отдохну́ть Ib perf.	
открыва́ться Ia imperf.	to open
(открыва́юсь),	
откры́ться Ia perf.	
откры́тка	postcard
откры́тый	open
откры́ть Ia perf. (откро́ю)	to open
открыва́ть Ia imperf.	
отку́да	from where?
отлежа́ться II perf.	to rest [in bed]
(отлежу́сь),	
отлёживаться Ia imperf.	
отмеча́ть Ia imperf.	to mark, to celebrate
(отмеча́ю)	
отме́тить II perf.	
о́тпуск	holiday(s)
отходи́ть II imperf.	to leave
(отхожу́, отхо́дишь),	
отойти́ Ib perf.	
о́тчество	patronymic
о́чень	very

П

Пари́ж	Paris
парте́р	stalls
Па́сха	Easter
па́чка	packet, pack(age)
пе́рвый	first
переводи́ть (II imperf.)	to translate
с (+ gen.) ... на (+ acc.) ... from ... into ...	
(перевожу́, перево́дишь),	
перевести́ Ib perf.	
перево́дчик, перево́дчица	interpreter, translator
	[man, woman]
пе́ред (+ instr.)	in front of, before
перее́хать (Ib perf.)	to move to
в (+ acc.) / на (+ acc.)	
(перее́ду),	
переезжа́ть Ia imperf.	
перейти́ на «ты»	to move from вы to ты
пересе́сть Ib perf.	to change [trains, etc.]
(переся́ду),	
переса́живаться Ia imperf.	
переу́лок	lane, narrow street
перехо́д	crossing

пешко́м	on foot
пи́во	beer
писа́тель (m)	writer
писа́ть Ib imperf. (пишу́),	to write
написа́ть Ib perf.	
письмо́	letter
пита́ться Ia imperf.	to have meals, to eat
(пита́юсь),	
пить Ib imperf. (пью),	to drink
вы́пить Ib perf.	
пласти́ческий	plastic [adjective]
плати́ть II imperf. (плачу́,	to pay
пла́тишь),	
заплати́ть II perf.	
плед	rug
пло́хо	badly
пло́щадь (f)	square
пляж	beach
по (+ acc.)	at a certain price
по (+ dat.)	along
побли́зости	near here, nearby
поверну́ть Ib perf.	to turn
(поверну́),	
повора́чивать Ia imperf.	
под (+ instr.)	underneath, under
	[location]
подари́ть II perf. (подарю́),	to give (a present)
дари́ть II imperf.	
пода́рок	present
подеше́вле	a little cheaper
подожда́ть Ib perf.	to wait
(подожду́),	
ждать Ib imperf.	
подписа́ть Ib perf.	to sign
(подпишу́),	
подпи́сывать Ia imperf.	
подходи́ть II imperf. (+ dat.)	to suit
(подхожу́, подхо́дишь),	
подойти́ Ib perf.	
по́езд	train
пое́здка	trip, journey
пое́хали	let's go! we're off!
пожа́луйста	please
поживать: как ты	how are you getting on?
пожива́ешь?	
позва́ть Ib perf. (позову́),	to call
звать Ib imperf.	
позвони́ть II perf.	to telephone
(позвоню́),	
звони́ть II imperf.	
по́здно	late
познако́миться II perf.	to meet
(познако́млюсь,	
познако́мишься),	
знако́миться II imperf.	
позови́те	can I speak to ... ?
пойдём	let's go
пойти́ Ib perf. (пойду́),	to go
идти́ Ib imperf.	

пойти́ на прогу́лку	to go for a walk
пока́	bye!; while
пока́ ... не	until
показа́ть Ib perf. (покажу́),	to show
пока́зывать Ia imperf.	
покупа́ть Ia imperf.	to buy
(покупа́ю),	
купи́ть II perf.	
поку́пка; поку́пки (pl.)	purchase; shopping
поликли́ника	clinic
по́лный	complete, full
полови́на	half
полити́ческий	political
получи́ть II perf. (получу́),	to receive, to get
получа́ть Ia imperf.	
по́мнить II imperf. (по́мню)	to remember
помога́ть Ia imperf.	to help
(+ dat.) (помога́ю),	
помо́чь Ib	
понеде́льник	Monday
понима́ть Ia imperf.	to understand
(понима́ю),	
поня́ть Ib perf.	
поня́тно	I understand, of course
поня́ть Ib perf. (пойму́),	to understand
понима́ть Ia imperf.	
попа́ли: вы не туда́ попа́ли	wrong number
попо́зже	a bit later
попра́виться II perf.	to get better
(поправлю́сь,	
попра́вишься),	
поправля́ться Ia imperf.	
попроси́ть: мо́жно	can I speak to ..., please?
попроси́ть (+ acc.)	[on telephone]
по-ру́сски	in Russian
поря́док: всё в поря́дке	everything's OK
посла́ть Ib perf. (пошлю́),	to send
посыла́ть Ia imperf.	
по́сле (+ gen.)	after
после́дний	last
в после́днее вре́мя	recently
поста́вить II perf.	to put, to place
(поста́влю, поста́вишь),	
ста́вить II imperf.	
пото́м	then, afterwards
потому́ что	because
почём	how much
почему́	why
по́чта	post office
почти́	almost
по́шлина	(customs) duty
поэ́тому	therefore
прав, права́, пра́вы	right, correct
пра́вильно	that's right, correct
пра́здник	(public) holiday, (religious) festival
предпочита́ть Ia imperf.	to prefer
(предпочита́ю),	
предпоче́сть Ib perf.	

представи́тель (m)	representative
предста́вить II perf. (+ acc. + dat.) (предста́влю, предста́вишь), представля́ть Ia imperf.	to introduce someone to someone
предста́виться II perf. (предста́влюсь, предста́вишься), представля́ться Ia imperf.	to introduce oneself
преподава́тель (m)	teacher
при (+ prep.)	by; at; attached to; during the reign of
прибыва́ть (Ia imperf.) в / на (+ acc.) (прибыва́ю), прибы́ть Ib perf.	to arrive (at)
приве́т	hi!
пригласи́ть II perf. (приглашу́, пригла́сишь), приглаша́ть (приглаша́ю) Ia imperf.	to invite
при́городный	suburban
приезжа́ть Ia, imperf. (приезжа́ю), прие́хать Ib perf. (прие́ду)	to come [by transport]
прилёт	arrival [by air]
принести́ Ib perf. (принесу́), приноси́ть II imperf.	to bring
принима́ть Ia imperf. (принима́ю), приня́ть Ib perf.	to take, to accept
при́нтер	printer
приня́ть Ib perf. (приму́), принима́ть Ia imperf.	to take, to accept
провести́ Ib perf. (проведу́), проводи́ть II imperf.	to accompany; to spend, to pass [time]
продово́льственный	food, grocery [adjective]
произошло́	happened
пройти́ (Ib perf.) до (+ gen.) (пройду́), проходи́ть II imperf.	to get to [on foot]; to pass
прости́те	excuse me
про́сто	simply
просту́да	cold, chill
простуди́ться II perf. (простужу́сь, просту́дишься), простужа́ться Ia imperf.	to catch a cold
пря́мо	straight on, straight ahead
прямо́й	direct [adjective]
путеше́ствовать Ia imperf. (путеше́ствую)	to travel
путь (m)	track
пье́са	play
пять	five
пя́тница	Friday

Р

рабо́та	work
рабо́тать Ia *imperf.* (рабо́таю)	to work
рад, ра́да	pleased
ра́дость (f)	joy
раз	time
ра́зве	can it really be …
разгово́р	conversation
раздева́ться Ia *imperf.* (раздева́юсь), разде́ться Ib *perf.*	to undress
ра́зный	different, various
разреши́ть II *perf.* (разрешу́), разреша́ть Ia *imperf.*	to permit, to allow
ра́но	early
рассказа́ть Ib *perf.* (расскажу́), расска́зывать Ia *imperf.*	to tell
регистрату́ра	registration
ре́дкий	rare
ре́дко	rarely
рейс	flight
река́	river
рекомендова́ть Ia *imperf.* (рекоменду́ю), порекомендова́ть Ia *perf.*	to recommend
рестора́н	restaurant
реце́пт	prescription
роди́тели	parents
роди́ться II *perf.* (рожу́сь, роди́шься), рожда́ться Ia *imperf.*	to be born
рожде́ние	birth
Рождество́ Христо́во	Christmas
рома́н	novel
Росси́я	Russia
рубль (m)	rouble
ру́сский, ру́сская	Russian (man, woman)
ру́сский	Russian [adjective]
ру́чка	pen
ры́ба	fish
ры́нок	market

С

с/со (+ gen.)	from
с/со (+ instr.)	with
сади́ться II *imperf.* (сажу́сь, сади́шься), сесть Ib *perf.*	to sit down
сади́ться на (+ acc.)	to get on [public transport]
сам, сама́, само́, са́ми	oneself
са́мый	the most
свари́ть II *perf.* (сварю́), вари́ть II *imperf.*	to boil, to cook
свида́ние	meeting
свобо́ден, свобо́дна, -о, -ы	free
свой, своя́, своё, свои́	one's own
связа́ться Ib *perf.* с (+ instr.) (свяжу́сь), свя́зываться Ia *imperf.*	to contact
сда́ча	change
сде́лать Ia *perf.* (сде́лаю), де́лать Ia *imperf.*	to do, to make
себя́	oneself
сего́дня	today
сейча́с	now
секрета́рь, секрета́рша	secretary [man, woman]
семь	seven
семья́	family
сентя́брь (m)	September
сестра́	sister
сесть Ib *perf.* (ся́ду), сади́ться II *imperf.*	to sit down
сесть на (+ acc.)	to get on [public transport]
сиде́ть II *imperf.* (сижу́, сиди́шь), посиде́ть II *perf.*	to sit
си́ний	dark blue
сказа́ть Ib *perf.* (скажу́), говори́ть II *imperf.*	to talk, to say
скажи́те	tell me
ско́лько	how much
ско́лько раз	how many times
ско́ро	soon
скуча́ть (Ia *imperf.*) по (+ dat.) (скуча́ю)	to miss
ску́чно	bored
сле́дующий	next
сли́шком	too
сло́во	word
сло́жный	complex
слу́шать Ia *imperf.* (слу́шаю), послу́шать Ia *perf.*	to listen
слу́шаю	speaking [on telephone]
смета́на	sour cream
смочь Ib *perf.* (смогу́, смо́жешь), мочь Ib *imperf.*	to be able to
смотре́ть II *imperf.* (смотрю́), посмотре́ть II *perf.*	to look, to watch
снача́ла	(at) first
сно́ва	again
собира́ться Ia *imperf.* (собира́юсь), собра́ться Ib *perf.*	to gather
собра́ние	collection
сове́товать Ia *imperf.* (+ dat.) (сове́тую), посове́товать Ia *perf.*	to advise
сове́тский	Soviet

согла́сен, согла́сна, -ы	agree
сожале́ние: к сожале́нию	unfortunately
сойти́ (Ib *perf.*) с ума́ (сойду́)	to go mad
сотру́дничать (Ia *imperf.*) с (+ *instr.*) (сотру́дничаю)	to collaborate with, to work with
сотру́дничество	cooperation
спаси́бо	thank you
спать II *imperf.* (сплю, спишь), поспа́ть II *perf.*	to sleep
специа́льность (*f*)	profession, trade, speciality
спеши́те	hurry
спина́	back
спи́чки	matches
споко́йной но́чи	good night
спроси́ть II *perf.* (спрошу́, спро́сишь), спра́шивать Ia *imperf.*	to ask
среда́	Wednesday
стадио́н	stadium
стака́н	glass
ста́нция	station [*e.g. of metro*]
стари́к	old man
ста́рость (*f*)	old age
ста́рый	old
стихи́	poetry, poems
сто	100
сто́ить II *imperf.*	to cost
стол	table
столи́ца	capital city
сторона́	side
страна́	country
стра́нно	strangely
студе́нт, студе́нтка	student [*man, woman*]
суббо́та	Saturday
су́мка	bag
счастли́вого пути́	have a good trip
счёт	bill, check
США	USA
сын	son
сюда́	this way, (to) here

Т

табле́тка	tablet, pill
так	so, in this way
тако́й	this sort of
тако́й, как	such as
тало́н	ticket [*for buses, trams*]
там	there
та́почки	slippers
твой, твоя́, твоё, твои́	your, yours
теа́тр	theatre
телеви́зор: по телеви́зору	on the television
телефо́н	telephone
тепло́	it is warm

тёплый	warm [*adjective*]
тётя	aunt
ти́хо	quietly
то	then
тогда́	then, at that time
то́же	also
то́лько	only
тот, та, то, те	that
то́чно	exactly, definitely
трамва́й	tram
тре́тий, тре́тьего (*m/n gen.*)	third
три	three
труд	difficulty
тру́дно	it is difficult
тру́дный	difficult [*adjective*]
туда́	(to) there
тут	here
ты	you [*familiar singular*]
ты́сяча	1,000

У

у (+ *gen.*)	by, at the house of
уви́деть II *perf.* (уви́жу, уви́дишь), ви́деть II *imperf.*	to see
угоди́ть II, *perf.* (+ *dat.*) (угожу́, угоди́шь), угожда́ть Ia *imperf.*	to please
удово́льствие	pleasure
уезжа́ть Ia *imperf.* (уезжа́ю), уе́хать Ib *perf.* (уе́ду)	to leave
уже́	already
узна́ть Ia *perf.* (узна́ю), узнава́ть Ia *imperf.*	to recognize
украи́нец, украи́нка	Ukrainian (man, woman)
у́лица	street
уме́ть Ia *imperf.* (уме́ю), суме́ть Ia *perf.*	to be able to, to know how to
университе́т	university
употребля́ть Ia *imperf.* (употребля́ю), употреби́ть II *perf.*	to use
у́тренний	morning
у́тро	morning

Ф

фа́брика	factory
факс	fax
фами́лия	surname
февра́ль (*m*)	February
фи́рма	firm
форе́ль (*f*)	trout
фрукт	fruit
фунт	pound
футбо́л	football

Х

хлеб	bread
хо́лодно	it is cold
холо́дный	cold [adjective]
хоро́ший	good
хорошо́	OK, well
хоте́ть imperf. (irreg.), захоте́ть perf.	to want
хотя́	although
худо́жник	artist
ху́же	worse

Ц

цветы́ pl. (цвето́к sing.)	flowers
цена́	price
центр	centre
це́рковь (f)	church
цыга́нский	gypsy

Ч

чай	tea
ча́йник	tea-pot
час	hour, one o'clock
ча́стный	private
ча́сто	often
часть (f)	part
ча́шка	cup
челове́к (sing.); лю́ди (pl.)	person; people
чем	than
чемода́н	suitcase
чём	see что
че́рез (+ acc.)	in [with time expressions]; across, after [with spatial expressions]
чере́шня	red cherry
че́стно говоря́	to be honest
четве́рг	Thursday
че́тверть (f)	quarter
четы́ре	four
число́	number, figure, date
чита́ть Ia imperf. (чита́ю), прочита́ть Ia perf.	to read

что

что	what; that [conjunction]
что́бы	in order to
что́-нибудь	anything, something
что́-то	something
чу́вствовать себя́ Ia imperf. (чу́вствую), почу́вствовать Ia perf.	to feel

Ш

шаг	step
ша́пка	cap, hat
шашлы́к	kebab
шесто́й	sixth
шесть	six
шко́ла	school
шоп-ту́р	shopping-tour
шотла́ндец, шотла́ндка	Scot [man, woman]
Шотла́ндия	Scotland
шотла́ндский	Scottish
шо́у	floor-show, cabaret
шу́мный	noisy
щи	cabbage soup

Э

электри́ческий	electric
электри́чка	local (surburban) train
электро́нная по́чта	e-mail
э́то	this is, that is
э́тот, э́та, э́то, э́ти	this

Я

я	I
я́блоко (nom. pl. я́блоки, gen. pl. я́блок)	apple
язы́к	language
яи́чница	fried eggs
янва́рь (m)	January
япо́нский	Japanese

Glossary of grammatical terms

Accusative: The case used for the direct object of a verb and after certain prepositions.

Я ищу́ **гости́ницу**. I am looking for the hotel.
Он идёт в **апте́ку**. He's going to the chemist's.

Adjective: A word used to give information about a noun.

Э́то **но́вая** гости́ница. It's a new hotel.

Adverb: A word used to give information about a verb, an adjective, or another adverb. In Russian, adverbs do not inflect.

Он говори́т **бы́стро** и **ти́хо**. He speaks quickly and quietly.

Agree: To match another word in number (singular or plural), gender (masculine, feminine, or neuter), case, or grammatical person (I, you, etc.)

Case: The grammatically required form of a noun, adjective, pronoun, or possessive. Russian has six cases: nominative, accusative, genitive, dative, instrumental, and prepositional.

Comparative: The form of an adjective or adverb used to express higher or lower degree. See also *Superlative*.

Ру́сский язы́к **трудне́е**, чем англи́йский. Russian is more difficult than English.

Conditional: A verb form used to express what might happen if something else occurred. It is also used to make polite requests or suggestions.

Я **бы хоте́л** пойти́ с тобо́й. I would like to go with you.
Е́сли **бы** я **был** свобо́ден, я **бы поéхал** с ва́ми. I would go with you if I were free.

Dative: The case used to express the indirect object, after certain prepositions, and in some other constructions.

Я позвоню́ **Ива́ну** на рабо́ту. I'll call Ivan at work.
прогу́лка по **го́роду** a stroll around the town

Direct object: The noun, pronoun, or phrase directly affected by the action of the verb.

Я ищу́ **гости́ницу**. I am looking for the hotel.

Ending: A letter or letters added to the stem of the verb to show the subject; also to nouns, adjectives, and some possessives, to show the case, number, and gender.

они́ игра́**ют** they are playing
ру́сск**ие** студе́нт**ы** Russian students

Feminine: One of the three genders in Russian. See *Gender*.

Gender: In Russian, all nouns have a gender, masculine, feminine, or neuter. Gender is reflected in the form of accompanying words such as adjectives, certain possessives, etc.

masculine: вокза́л, хлеб
feminine: ви́за, ма́ма, револю́ция
neuter: сло́во, окно́, пи́во, свида́ние

Genitive: The case used to express possession, to express 'of' in phrases giving quantities, after some prepositions, and in a number of other constructions.

Стака́н **молока́**. A glass of milk.
Э́то для **меня́**? Is that for me?

Imperative: The form of a verb that is used to express orders or instructions, or to suggest that somebody does something.

Да́йте, пожа́луйста, хлеб. Please give me some bread.
Смотри́те! Look!

Imperfective future: The form of a verb used to refer to repeated events in the future, or to stress the ongoing nature of a future event.

Вы **бу́дете жить** в гости́нице. You will be staying in a hotel.

Imperfective past: The form of a verb used to refer to repeated events in the past, or to stress the ongoing nature of a past event.

Вы всегда́ **жи́ли** в Каза́ни? Have you always lived in Kazan?

Indirect object: The noun, pronoun, or phrase indirectly affected by the action of the verb.

Она́ пото́м **нам** ска́жет. She will tell us later.

Infinitive: The basic form of a verb which does not indicate a particular tense or number or person. The infinitive is the form given in the dictionary.

де́лать (*imperf.*), **сде́лать** (*perf.*) to do, to make

Instrumental: The case used to express means of transport, times of the day, 'in' a season, after certain prepositions, and in a number of other constructions.

Мо́жно дое́хать **авто́бусом**, и́ли **по́ездом**. You can go by bus or by train.

Ле́том мы е́здили в Со́чи. In the summer we would go to Sochi.

Intonation: The pattern of sounds made in a sentence as the speaker's voice rises and falls.

Irregular: A word that does not follow one of the set patterns and has its own individual forms.

Masculine: One of the three genders in Russian. See *Gender.*

Modal form: A word used to express possibility or impossibility, necessity, obligation, permission, and so on.

Мне **нельзя́** рабо́тать. I'm not allowed to work.

Neuter: One of the three genders in Russian. See *Gender.*

Nominative: The case used for the grammatical subject of the sentence. In the singular, the dictionary form of pronouns, nouns, and adjectives.

Гости́ница далеко́. The hotel is a long way away.

Noun: A word that identifies a person, thing, place, or concept.

Ива́н Ivan   **гости́ница** hotel

Ordinal numbers: Numbers of the type 'first', 'second', etc.

Object: The noun, pronoun, or phrase affected by the action of the verb. See *Direct object, Indirect object.*

Perfective future: The form of a verb used to refer to a one-off event in the future, or to stress the result or successful completion of a future action.

За́втра мы **сде́лаем** поку́пки. Tomorrow we will go shopping.

Perfective past: The form of a verb used to refer to a one-off event in the past, or to stress the result or successful completion of an action.

Я **получи́л** рабо́ту в Каза́ни. I got work in Kazan.

Person: A category used to distinguish between the 'I'/'we' (first person), 'you' (second person), and 'he'/'she'/'it'/'they' (third person) forms of the verb.

Plural: Denoting more than one. See also *Number*.

Possessive: Words used to show belonging.

моя́ визи́тная ка́рточка my card

Preposition: A word used before a noun or pronoun to relate it to another part of the sentence.

Э́то **для** меня́? Is that for me?

Prepositional: The case used after the prepositions **в**, **на**, **о**, and **при**.

Present tense: The form of a verb used to express something happening or in existence now, or as a habitual occurrence.

Глеб **игра́ет** в футбо́л. Gleb is playing football.

Pronoun: A word used to stand for a noun. Pronouns may refer to things or concepts ('it', 'them'), or people ('she', 'him').

Он говори́т. He is speaking.

Reflexive verb: A verb form containing the reflexive ending **-ся** after a final consonant and **-сь** after a final vowel.

Во ско́лько **открыва́ется** ка́сса? What time does the box-office open?

Regular: Following a common set pattern.

Short form adjective: An adjective having four different forms only, agreeing with the subject: masculine, feminine, neuter, or plural.

Вы **согла́сны**? Do you agree?

Singular: Denoting only one. See also *Number*.

Stem: The part of a word to which endings are added showing person, number, case, and so on.

де́лать 'to do'
я **де́лаю**, ты **де́лаешь**, мы **де́лаем**

Subject: The noun, pronoun, or phrase that performs the action indicated by the verb.

Гость отдыха́ет. The guest is resting.

Superlative: The highest or lowest degree of an adjective. See also *Comparative*.

Она́ **са́мая краси́вая**. She is the most beautiful (woman).

Syllable: A unit of pronunciation which forms either the whole or part of a word.

мой (one syllable) **я/зы́к** (two syllables) **у́/ли/ца** (three syllables)

Tense: The form of a verb which indicates when the action takes place, i.e. in the past, present, or future.

Verb: A word or phrase used to express what is being done or what is happening. It can also be used to express a state.

Фильм **начина́ется** в два часа́. The film starts at 2 o'clock. Она́ **изуча́ла** ру́сский язы́к. She was studying Russian.

Index